D0010599

BLAIRSVILLE SENIOR HIGH SCHOOL
BLAIRSVILLE, PENNA.

DATE DUE

The Third Dimension

Books by Robert E. Spiller

THE AMERICAN IN ENGLAND DURING THE FIRST
HALF CENTURY OF INDEPENDENCE
FENIMORE COOPER, CRITIC OF HIS TIMES
A DESCRIPTIVE BIBLIOGRAPHY OF JAMES
FENIMORE COOPER (CO-AUTHOR)
THE CYCLE OF AMERICAN LITERATURE
EIGHT AMERICAN AUTHORS (CO-AUTHOR)

Edited by Robert E. Spiller

LITERARY HISTORY OF THE UNITED STATES (CO-EDITOR)
THE ROOTS OF NATIONAL CULTURE (CO-EDITOR)
FENIMORE COOPER'S GLEANINGS IN EUROPE (FRANCE AND ENGLAND)
AMERICAN PERSPECTIVES (CO-EDITOR)
CHANGING PATTERNS IN AMERICAN CIVILIZATION
SOCIAL CONTROL IN A FREE SOCIETY
JAMES FENIMORE COOPER, REPRESENTIVE SELECTIONS
THE EARLY LECTURES OF RALPH WALDO EMERSON (CO-EDITOR)

The Third Dimension

STUDIES IN LITERARY HISTORY

Robert E. Spiller

THE MACMILLAN COMPANY, NEW YORK
COLLIER-MACMILLAN LIMITED, LONDON

1965

First Printing

The Macmillan Company, New York
Collier-Macmillan Canada, Ltd., Toronto, Ontario

Library of Congress catalog card number: 65-13122
Printed in the United States of America

ACKNOWLEDGMENT is made to the following for permission to use copyright materials: *College English* VIII (April 1947), 344-352, for "Critical Standards in the American Romantic Movement," copyright © The National Council of Teachers of English 1947; and *College English* XXIV (February 1963), 345-351, for "Is Literary History Obsolete?" copyright © The National Council of Teachers of English 1963. *The Sewanee Review* for "The Task of the Historian of American Literature." *Pennsylvania Literary Review* for "Blueprint for American History." *American Literature* for "The Verdict of Sydney Smith." *The Roots of National Culture* for "The First Frontier," copyright © The Macmillan Company 1933; copyright renewed © Robert E. Spiller 1961. *The New Republic* for "What Became of the Literary Radicals?" Harvard University Press, Cambridge, Mass., for "The Critical Movement of the Twentieth Century" from *American Perspectives: The National Self-Image in the Twentieth Century*, edited by Robert E. Spiller and Eric Larrabee, copyright © The President and Fellows of Harvard College 1961. *English Institute Annual, 1939* for "Science and Literature," copyright © Columbia University Press, New York 1940. Joseph J. Kwiatt and the University of Minnesota Press for parts of "Value and Method in American Studies" which originally appeared in *Studies in American Culture: Dominant Ideas and Images* under the title "American Studies, Past, Present and Future," copyright © University of Minnesota 1960. *The Aims and Methods of Scholarship in Modern Languages and Literatures*, edited by James Thorp, for "The Province of Literary History," copyright © The Modern Language Association of America 1963.

iv

Contents

Preface

The essays in this volume were written at different times during a period of more than three decades when my ideas were oriented to the planning and editing of what became the *Literary History of the United States*. The only justification for collecting them here is that together they may reflect the history not only of one mind but of a movement. With the founding of the journal *American Literature* in 1928, the higher study of the subject in this country may be said to have been accepted.

It was dissatisfaction with the way American literary history had until then been conceived and written, with little or no reference to its roots in the American cultural tradition, that led me to a lifetime of thinking and writing about the problem. My effort has been to profit by the increasing understanding of the literary text which the new criticism has developed and by that of society and culture which has resulted from the work of the behavioral scientists; but to make my own contribution by emphasizing the third dimension, that of time and cause, the perspective of history.

The essays are dated from 1929 to 1963, and most of them were originally delivered to student or professional groups. They are arranged in three parts rather than chronologically. The first is a statement of the problem, both in general and with reference to the literature of the United States; the second deals with specific aspects of American literary history from the earliest days to the present; and the third sums up my views on both the theory of literary history and the present state of scholarship and teaching in American studies at home and abroad. They are here reprinted as themselves historical documents, without any attempt to bring them up to date.

University of Pennsylvania
February, 1964

I

Is Literary History Obsolete?

1961

READ BEFORE THE NATIONAL COUNCIL OF
TEACHERS OF ENGLISH IN PHILADELPHIA,
PENNSYLVANIA, NOVEMBER 25, 1961, AND
PUBLISHED IN *College English* XXIV (1963)
345-351.

THERE WAS A TIME when the literary historian was monarch of all he surveyed. He was the one kind of literary scholar that could claim respectability in the company of scientists and he had a stranglehold on the English curriculum in the university. But times have changed and he is now a very humble companion of the critic, both new and old, in the halls of academe and in the world of art. For some time he has been fighting a retreating action and his fate hangs precariously in the balance.

As a literary historian, I would like to contemplate his sorry fate. But first, I must distinguish the literary historian from the critic in all his forms—analytical, impressionistic, judicial, even historical. He must of course be a critic of sorts in order to be a good historian because he must be able to recognize the data with which he is to deal, and he must be able to evaluate it both intrinsically and extrinsically. But criticism is not his primary function. He is first and last one kind of historian rather than one kind of writer or reader or critic. His special job is to record and interpret the course of past events as related to specific times and places and in terms of cause and effect. Literature is the idiom in which he writes history just as the economic historian tells about what happened when the industrial revolution hit the western world and just when and how it hit England or the

3

United States or is in the process of hitting Russia and China right now. The political historian should be concerned with the wave of revolutions that swept over Europe in the 1830's and with the rise of the Democratic party under Grover Cleveland out of the dark ages of reconstruction Republicanism—and so forth. There are all kinds of history and I happen to be a specialist in the literary history of the United States.

I am assuming that a work of literature is an event like the Fall of the Bastille or the invention of the cotton gin, that it has a life cycle in its time and place like other events as living organisms—Napoleon, the First Continental Congress, the Battle of Gettysburg. Napoleon isn't still Emperor of France, the First Continental Congress is not still in session in Philadelphia, and we are not still fighting the Battle of Gettysburg—or are we? Yet, in another sense, all of these events *are* still alive—in our imaginations, our memories, and our everyday thoughts and actions. Our attitude toward the United Nations is controlled in large part by the inheritance from the First Continental Congress, which is still in the bloodstream of all of us—whatever race or color—and we are a nation because both North and South share in the inconclusive outcome of the Battle of Gettysburg. So we can add to the assumption that each literary work is a historical event with a life of its own, the further assumption that all historical events have a kind of immortality outside of or above their mere existence in the chronological past. Maurice Mandelbaum expresses this dual relationship as an attempt on the part of the historian "to depict the formative influences exercised by a series of events upon the character of one enduring event." [1] This relationship of event to series of events applies equally to a book or a battle.

This statement, however, refers to a series of events which are all of one kind—that is, all books or all battles, but it is obvious that there is some sort of causal relationship between the Fall of the Bastille and *The Tale of Two Cities*, and between the high point in the history of the American whaling industry and *Moby Dick*. In other words, there is a process of crossbreeding between two or more kinds of history. Events in one area of human experience have a habit of growing out of conditions in other areas: for example, slavery as a moral and humanitarian issue is related to the economic rivalry of the North and South in such a way as to cause the political event of Lincoln's election, the literary event of *Uncle Tom's Cabin*, and the military event of the Fall of Fort Sumter. So here is another assumption: literary history can be isolated and recorded in itself, but it cannot be fully understood unless its relationships to other kinds of history are discovered and defined at every point.

Furthermore, every historical event is related to one or more key personalities whose thoughts and actions caused it or who participated in it in some significant way. Battles are always associated with generals like Washington or Wellington or Lee, political events with statesmen like Gladstone or Webster or Bismarck, changes in the history of thought with thinkers like Locke or Darwin or Marx. It is hardly necessary to point out that the Elizabethan drama suggests Shakespeare, the English romantic movement, Wordsworth, the age of French comedy, Molière, and the American renaissance, Emerson and Melville and Whitman.

Let us pause, then, and list some of the basic assumptions that a literary historian must make in order to function as a literary historian. He must assume:

(1) That every work of art, good or bad, major or minor, is an event which is related to other events in its own time and place, and that it cannot be fully understood or appreciated without understanding these relationships.

(2) That every work of art was the product of the experience of at least one man or woman and that the intellectual and emotional state of that person, both in general and specifically at the time of composition, was a prime factor in determining its shape and import.

(3) That each work of art, in its time and place, was a living organism with a life cycle of its own—conception, birth, growth, maturity, death—as well as its own kind of immortality. It was conceived of specific ideas and experiences, produced under certain conditions, read and discussed by its contem-

poraries, and finally relegated to the shelf of classics, or forgotten.

(4) That literary works use as their medium of expression
the language spoken by the people of the time and place of their
composition and that, as language changes, they cannot be fully
understood by a later generation unless the meanings of the
words and phrases to the people who wrote them is taken fully
into account.

(5) That all the works of art produced in a given time and
place have collective as well as individual significance; in short,
that literary movements, schools, -isms, trends, and forms are
historical realities in themselves and in relation to other similar
realities. They are therefore related in some sort of causal con-
tinuum on their own level as art and they are related to each
other in the context of the total culture of which they are parts.

(6) That, as any given work of art is a product of the entire
imaginative experience of its creator and must involve his sensory,
emotional, and intellectual perceptions and controls, so art as an
aspect of culture must involve the whole imaginative experience
of the people in the time and place of which the culture is composed.

(7) That some works of art are "good" and some not so good,
and that their importance in *literary* history *per se* depends on
some kind of judgment in these terms; even though, like Tom
Paine's *Common Sense* or the Communist Manifesto, they may
be literature of a sort but have their historical importance outside
the realm of literary history and in terms of other than literary
value judgments.

And finally, (8) That history of any kind is important because
the dimension of the past is an essential part of the living present—to say nothing of the future—and that literary history,
although not to be confused with literary criticism or with other
kinds of history, is a noble and essential pursuit of any culture
that is to survive.

In my enthusiasm, I may have overstated the case for literary
history, but I suspect there are few who would not agree with
me, at least in part and in principle. How can we account, then,

for the sharp reaction against it in recent years as a subject for study and research in school and college? A few years ago the study of literature was pushing into the high school "core curriculum" beside history and the social studies, books about literature were chiefly biographies and "facts and backgrounds" manuals, the college major in English was composed chiefly of survey and period courses, and the doctorate in literature was awarded for a contribution, however small, to the sum of historical knowledge about authors and their works.

Today, the critical reading of a work of art has taken over the center of the educational stage. I'm not altogether sure just what is happening in the schools, but I note in the colleges an increasing emphasis on class and collateral reading of separate works rather than of anthologies and narrative texts in literary history. The small handful of "new" critics who, ten years ago, were outside or on the fringes of academic respectability now occupy key chairs in the best universities; dissertations and learned articles are offered in the elaborate analysis of the symbolism or rhetoric of specific works—the analyses, especially in the cases of lyric poems or short stories, often running to many times the length of the original work. Examinations in literature—at least from the level of the college entrance to that of the doctors' finals—are often wholly composed of interpretations of quoted passages of prose and poetry with careful suppression of any hints of authorship, time or place of composition, or context of any kind. This is called "practical criticism." Aesthetic or rhetorical or linguistic analysis has taken over the basic textbooks and the required courses to the near exclusion of the survey or background course so generally and emphatically that any suggestion of a historical reference is considered distracting, superficial, even at times (it would almost seem) immoral. Publishers are issuing paperbacks by the carload containing a brief story accompanied by an anthology of critical analyses and interpretations; collections of "Discussions of Literature," books on "Understanding" poetry, fiction, or drama; heavily edited texts, usually with slight or no biographical or historical introductions, and anthologies, arranged in terms of graded difficulty of reading rather than the chronological or other developmental relationship of the contents, are flooding the textbook market at all levels. When Professor Morton White gave the title, "The Age of Analysis" to his paperback anthology of twentieth-century philosophy, he was not thinking specifically of literature and its teaching in the schools and colleges, but he surely put his finger on the pulse of the modern temper in our world of literary study as well as in that of his own universe of philosophy. We are analysts all.

I do not wish to imply that I think this trend to be necessarily bad and that I would like to see a return to the degree of historical emphasis in literary study under which I was trained. If I weren't by age alone committed to being a *laudator temporis acti,* I might well acclaim the new trend. But today I will try to be content with merely observing what that trend is, to the best of my ability, examining its causes, and speculating on its results: in short, treating it as a literary historian should—as itself a historical event.

First, then, the immediate problem. Why has analysis taken over from history in the academic study of literature? A simple answer can be found in the realization, a few years ago, that Johnny can't read—Johnny in this case being Professor X, Ph.D., of the English Department of the University of Y. I remember one such professor who gave a course in Shakespeare. At the end of the sixth lecture, a student came to his desk and said, "Professor, your lectures are perfectly fascinating, but— when are we going to discuss the plays?" Research in literature had become what Professor Lowes of Harvard once called, "Learning more and more about less and less." I remember a standard biography of a major author which opens with a long and detailed chapter, based on contemporary documents, to determine the exact lodging house to which the poet's mother was taken in her last illness. And I have myself been lured by James Fenimore Cooper into an article on a finance controversy in the French Chamber of Deputies because Lafayette asked Cooper to supply him with some statistical information on comparative American finance, and into a guidebook study of tourist routes in Switzerland in 1837 because Cooper was then taking his family *en calèche* through the Alps. I also remember my own Professor Schelling warning a class that his predecessors had been reapers and harvesters in the field of Elizabethan scholarship, that his generation was that of the gleaners, and obviously his class was left to do the work of crows. The tendency of historical scholarship was dangerously centrifugal, and it was possible to lecture eloquently on an author without reading a word of his own writings. I know because I have been tempted.

But I hardly need say that these are examples of the pitfalls of historical scholarship and should not be taken as evidence that all external data is irrelevant to literary study. Surely important differences between *The Merchant of Venice* and *The Tempest* are attributable to their first productions respectively in the Globe Theatre and in Whitehall Banqueting Hall; visits even to modern London, Rochester, and Canterbury immeasurably enrich the reading of Dickens; the study of abnormal psychology and religious mysticism help with the symbolism of Blake; and a knowledge of the religious and political controversies of the English Civil War illuminates *Paradise Lost*. Good and genuinely relevant historical scholarship has its place—and an important one—in the study of literature. But it is of no use if we fail to reread Shakespeare, Dickens, Blake, and Milton and apply our new information to the creative act of understanding the text itself. And this is what the "new" criticism has done. It has sent us back to the text and taught us again to read.

But unfortunately the movement has gone too far. In a successful effort to lean over backwards it has cracked its skull on the concrete pavement of historical fact. We do not have to *eliminate* historical data just because we have previously overemphasized it. Common sense calls for balance between the two functions; they cannot get along without each other. Until I studied the French finance controversy, I could not understand why Cooper and Lafayette were such close friends, and when I learned what issues in the revolutionary war of ideas in the 1830's they had in common, I could help to shift the emphasis of Cooper scholarship from romance to social criticism and, with this new prism, open up a generation of new interpretation of the major novels as serious and adult studies of life's problems. It took a long time for this new light to take effect, but Marcel Clavel, James Gross, Marius Bewley, Thomas Philbrick and many others are doing the job of synthesizing historical findings with analytical and judicial criticism, while James Beard continues the work of supplying further historical data.

I would like to leave the question of the decline of historical scholarship on this optimistic note if I could, but I am afraid that the issue lies deeper than this superficial answer can reach. The more basic reasons for the reactions against it lie far below the level of mere exasperation at bad or inadequate reading of texts, and the solution lies in a far more drastic intellectual revolution than a mere swinging of the pendulum of emphasis back to a commonsense median. I wish it were as simple as that.

There is evidence on every hand that students of literature are not alone in their swing from historical and developmental scholarship to analysis.

The nineteenth century has been accurately called by Henry D. Aiken "The Age of Ideology," an age in which the philosopher's central concern turned from the quest for "theoretical knowledge of the most pervasive traits of being" to "one which seeks to establish the basic commitments involved in being a man, being a person, being rational, or being civilized" [2] Morton White has countered by describing the twentieth century as "The Age of Analysis," [3] an age in which new theories of science once more provide a usable system for rational analysis of man's being. The universes of Newton and Einstein are alike in being reducible to intellectual and mathematical systems that can be objectively and rationally studied; that of Darwin is one of chaos and flux available first to the senses and the emotions. The popular philosophy of life of Western European and American man in the nineteenth century was based on the concept of a fluent, developing, organic universe of which he was a living if somewhat perplexed part; that of the same man in the twentieth century is based on the concept of a static and relative universe of mathematical components. The organic metaphor of the poets and philosophers has given way to the equation, and the idea of a progressive continuity of causes and effects to the mechanical balance and interrelation of knowns and unknowns.

History, as the romantic philosophers of the nineteenth century defined it, is interested in the birth, growth, maturity, decline, decay, and rebirth of living and constantly changing cultural elements. Literature has always described experience as organic in such images as the ages of man, the wings of the dove, the whale, the river of life, the tree, the womb, the tiger prowling in the wilderness of night, the albatross, the innocence of childhood, and the dark wisdom of experience; but in ages of reason like the eighteenth century and today, the images of literature are derived more from fixed forms, as an ideal order of monuments (as against the evolution of a literary type), a rhetoric of motives (as against conflict and crisis in motivation), and such images as the wheel, the shut gate, the bridge, a game of chess, orbited mice, and the blue guitar. The first group are all organic and dynamic, the second mechanistic and static.

Have we come to believe that life does not change and that values lie in the mechanical relationship of its parts to each other and in the sum of its parts to the whole? I hesitate to say so, but I am pretty sure that the organic and evolutionary view of life which underlay the philosophy of history from Herder to Dilthey—approximately a century—has given way to a belief in pattern, interrelationship, and structural form, which, because it is concerned primarily with static components, does not lend itself to history as history was studied and written throughout the period of the Romantic Movement—from the late eigtheenth to the early twentieth century. And literary history, which came into its own for the first time during this period, is now threatened because a static view of life breaks down the connecting causal links which relate one work of art to another and to other elements in an evolving culture. For there was no literary history in the modern sense prior to Vico's *Scienza Nuova* (1725) and the idea of creative culture as an evolving process which formed the basis of Herder's *Outlines of the Philosophy of History of Mankind* (1803). Literary evo-

lution became a tenable concept in the thought of Schlegel,
Hegel, Comte, Cousin, and Taine, and was taken up by Coleridge
and Emerson, but literary history as a national, cultural, and
linguistic process did not fully mature until almost the end of
the nineteenth century in such men as Frazer, Brandes, Tyler,
Saintsbury, and others of the great day of historical philology
and cultural history which most of us can remember because we
took part in it.

A reaction against the organic and evolutionary aspects of
cultural study was inevitable sooner or later, and, as a member
of the elder generation, I suppose I have the right—perhaps even
the obligation—to view such events with alarm. As I walk
about the corridors of my university after classes have been
dismissed, I see blackboard after blackboard covered with mathematical equations, but I cannot tell by the evidence whether the
last class was in physics, mathematics, philosophy, literature,
language, anthropology, economics, or even history. For most of
the best historians I know now are either antiquarians or sociologists, depending on whether they prefer to analyse past or present
cultures. This is an age of the equation metaphor; that of the
organic metaphor is past.

What, then, can those of us do who, whatever virtues we
recognize in the new ways of thinking, still believe that we
should hold on to literary and all other kinds of history as
expressions of evolving cultures?

First of all, we need not surrender; from our vantage point
as historians we can realize that the Age of Analysis is, after all,
an age like any other, with a beginning, middle, and probably an
end—someday, even if not in our own lifetime. There have
been ages of analysis before this—the Augustan Age was one,
as was that of medieval scholasticism and that of neoclassicism.
But life *does* change, and it moves through time in cyclic revolutions. No pattern is completely described before it has shifted
its kaleidoscopic components into another configuration. The
pendulum swings, the hands of the clock go round. Even such
mechanical images as these describe how life grows, matures,
dies, and is born. We can be patient. This present age of analysis

is a needed corrective to the disintegrating influences of an age which was too much concerned with the sweeping forces of evolution, emotion, progress, dreams, and decay. Something had to be done about the Hegels, the Nietzsches, the Marxes, the Spencers, and the Spenglers. Change had become cosmic, and poor bewildered man had nothing left to cling to. If, like the spider, he began to imitate permanence by rebuilding his fine symmetrical web, we can hardly blame him. He must relearn, with Keats, to "mingle Grecian grandeur with the wasting of Old Time."

But, practically speaking, what can or should the teacher and student of literature do if he still believes in the importance of historical perspective and causal relationships to three-dimensional truth? I'd like to conclude with a few rules-of-thumb for curriculum planning and classroom behavior.

(1) Emphasize the literary text and read carefully—yes—but fight to the death against anonymous and unidentified texts in classroom and examination. Common sense demands that the aspirin and arsenic bottles be labeled before therapy is undertaken.

(2) Use your historical knowledge from the inside out rather than from the outside in. You can start with Hamlet's play within a play and move out to the conditions of dramatic production on the Elizabethan stage and in the Court; or read Milton's sonnet on his blindness and *then* point out that the blindness was real. Don't wallow in Poe's abnormal psychic inhibitions and addictions for their own sakes but only as aids to the study of imagination vs. hallucination. Move from Cooper's Leather-Stocking to the significance of the wilderness frontier and of the democratic theory, and from Emerson's *Nature* to the meaning and historical incidence of the Transcendental movement. In short, start with the work of art as the analytical critics demand, but move outward to the context. Myth and symbol provide an easy transition.

(3) Forget about the intentional and affective fallacies that Wimsett and Beardsley have made so ominous, and avoid rather what might be called the ontological fallacy, the idea that a

work of art can exist outside of any context. A poem cannot *be* unless it has had an author who intended it, consciously or not, and an audience to read or hear it, either actual or theoretical. Literature is a form of communication, whether the melodies are heard or are the sweeter ones of the imagination.

(4) Remember that American literature is the expression of the civilization of the United States, English literature is the voice of the British people, and Greek literature speaks for Athens; but also remember that a good tragedy is a fine drama and a bad one is melodrama whenever or wherever or by whomsoever it was written. The two ways of considering literature are supplementary, not mutually exclusive.

(5) And finally, see to it that every major student of literature who comes your way has an opportunity to study literary history as a branch of *history* and as an indispensable link between his study of literature and his appreciation of the stored wealth of human experience since the beginning of recorded time. Man cannot long be content with a present in which the only reality is in being. Only by an appreciation of the past can he set his experience in the dimension of time and regain his faith in the reality of becoming. There is a long journey ahead, as there is one behind.

NOTES

[1] Maurice Mandelbaum, *The Problem of Historical Knowledge* (New York: Liveright Publishing Co., 1938), p. 8.

[2] (New York: Mentor, 1956), p. ix.

[3] (New York: Mentor, 1955.)

The Task of the Historian
of American Literature

1935

READ BEFORE THE AMERICAN LITERATURE
GROUP OF THE MODERN LANGUAGE ASSOCIA-
TION OF AMERICA AND PUBLISHED IN THE
Sewanee Review, XLIII (1935), 70–79.

EVER SINCE Professor Pattee issued his classic "Call for a Literary Historian" in *The American Mercury* for June, 1924, there has been a feverish activity on the part of students of our literary past. So detailed and miscellaneous has been the character of their findings and so sweeping their generalizations that the time may perhaps have come for something approaching an inventory of accomplishment and a new charting of the course toward a goal which has not yet been reached.

In order to isolate the problem fairly and clearly, it is necessary to distinguish literary history from its inevitable and close associates, literary criticism and the history of civilization as a whole. Literary history conceives of literature as one aspect of organic evolution, limited by time and space for the purpose of study, and determined by forces and factors both within and without the individual and collective experience of the writers who lived in that time and place. Its primary concern is with relations rather than with absolute values, but it is dependent on criticism for appraisal of these values, and on other forms of history for the analysis of its causes. The result is that the literary historian is often a critic or a social or economic historian as

well, and it is right that he should be. No student can confine
himself wholly to one idiom of thought or to one field of investigation because, in the final analysis, no human knowledge
can be isolated; but it is important that he recognize his peculiar
province and devote his major attention to it, relying, when he
can, on the work of others for related knowledge.

The province of the literary historian is therefore limited to
the forms and movements in literature in time and place and in
the literary developments of individual writers. His fields of
study are further restricted by race, nation, and period. The race
with which we have to deal in American literary history is a
composite of the Aryan races of Europe, with some admixture of
the Indian, the Negro, the Mongol, and other strains. It was
primarily Anglo-Saxon in its origins, but no longer is even thus
far limited. The nation with which we have to deal is one which
came into existence only a century and a half ago, but which
has since gained a strong sense of organic and cultural unity.
Our period is primarily the later eighteenth century, all of
the nineteenth, and a part of the twentieth. We must depend
upon the ethnologist and the anthropologist for the detailed examination of the racial factors in our study, upon the historian
of economic, political, and social forces for the examination of
other than literary factors in our national unity, and upon
historians of other forms of culture for related studies of the
aesthetic life of our people.

The work of our early literary historians was deficient in
correlative knowledge. When Samuel Knapp first attempted a
chronological treatment of our literature in 1829, he was handicapped by a complete ignorance of background understanding
of American civilization. The result was that he related American
literature to English civilization and literature because it happened to be written for the most part in the English language.
In so far as he succeeded in an examination of the work of our
early writers in terms of its native causes, his comment was miscellaneous and unsynthesized. His successors, Griswold, Richardson, Allibone, Duyckinck, Stedman, and Tyler, attained to a
greater degree of synthesis in terms of organic evolution, but

for the most part they merely pushed his unrelated analyses
further and confined themselves to fact-finding. The fundamental fallacy that American is merely a department of English
literary history persisted almost to our own day. We were not
freed from this handicap until social historians like Merriman,
Turner, and Fox, philosophical historians like Riley and
Schneider, and economic historians like Beard made a fresh
study of our civilization in these related terms. When the illog-
ical and now almost obsolete *Cambridge History of American
Literature* appeared in 1917, the work of the new historians
was still in its comparative infancy, and that ambitious task,
still laboring under the fallacious principles of the old order, was
only partially enlightened by anticipatory flashes of insight into
the new.

It was obvious that the American literary historian had a gigantic task ahead of him, a task which he has undertaken with
great zest, but which is still far from completion. He must turn
for the moment from his primary concern, the study of the evolution of our literature in its own terms, to a study of the bearing
which the new findings and opinions of workers in related fields
have upon his problem. The epoch-making work of this transition period is, of course, Parrington's *Main Currents in American
Thought*, a survey which I believe was originally undertaken as
a literary history, but which developed into an examination primarily of the Jeffersonian theory of democracy, in its application to our agrarian and industrial development, and in its
expression in our writings. This is not literary history, but it was
a prerequisite to the new literary history, and only a literary
historian could have done it successfully.

The fact-finders and the interpreters of the new order had
already set to work, the former more successfully than the
latter. Rusk's *Literature of the Middle Western Frontier* anticipated Parrington by two years, and Jones' *America and French
Culture* came in the same year as the *Main Currents*. Literally
thousands of similar studies of more narrowly limited problems
were undertaken, many of which have since been published.
Gradually we are accumulating the materials for the interpreta-

tion of our literary history in these new terms, but an appalling
amount of work still needs to be done. This work is not strictly
literary history, but it must be done by students of literature.
The transition period in our scholarship is not yet at an end.
Attempts at synthesis like Lucy Lockwood Hazard's *The Frontier in American Literature* and the school histories which have
appeared in the last few years fail of conviction because they
are too much handicapped by the old idiom of thought or because they rush ill-advisedly to conclusions which are confused
and unsound. Foerster's *The Reinterpretation of American Literature* has charted the course by essay and bibliography; Boynton's
The Rediscovery of the Frontier approaches a realization of the
ideal; and Constance Rourke's *American Humor* is more comprehensive and significant than its limiting title would imply.

II

The problems for the student of American literature's relationship to American civilization are two. First, he must relate our
writings to our national origins and development in philosophical, economic, social, political, and cultural terms; and second,
he must study in greater detail the influence which the traditional cultures of Europe have exerted upon the American
literary mind.

The studies of the Puritan, and of the frontier in the middle
nineteenth century, are nearing a satisfactory degree of completion; but those of the earliest frontier, the settlement of the
original colonies, are still unrelated to literary history. The racial
and religious factors in our origins, to which James Truslow
Adams gives so much attention in his *Epic of America*, the
Quaker and other elements on the Middle Atlantic seaboard, the
civilization of the Indians, both Northern and Southern, and of
the Spanish and French settlers, are only a few of the problems
which concern the earliest period in our history and which have
not yet been related in a satisfactory manner to literary history,
although much work has recently been done upon them by
other kinds of historians. In the period of the awakening literary
consciousness immediately before and after the Revolutionary

War, there is need of a similar study of the life of the Atlantic seaboard cities and of the factors in American life which produced, between 1820 and 1840, an aggressive sense of cultural autonomy, with its resultant literary experiments. Our study of the period before the Civil War has been too strictly limited to New England, and too little attention has been paid to the sense of national insecurity which caused the collapse of the Federalist party, and to the religious liberalism which gave rise not only to Unitarianism, to the extension of the Evangelical movement in the South, and to other forms of "heresy" outside the Congregational fold. We have failed also to understand fully that the first steps in the middle western frontier movement were undermining the supports of Concord and Cambridge security long before Hawthorne, Melville, and Emerson began to write. Even the later stages of the frontier need further analysis in literary terms before we can see the Gilded Age as something other than an enemy to culture; the social revolt from the evils of unlimited immigration, of industrialism, and of the agrarian movement of the late nineteenth century is similarly misunderstood in its bearing upon our literature; and the social and economic factors immediately before and after the last war have connections with our contemporary writings which are only appreciated in the vaguest terms. There is much still to be done before American literary history can be related closely and accurately to the kaleidoscope of American civilization, and before our historians can discover more exact terms than "Convention, Revolt, and General Chaos" to describe the recent past.

The other aspect of the same problem, the cultural links with Europe, has received slightly more attention, but here, likewise, there is room for further study. Faust's *The German Element in the United States,* Jones' *America and French Culture,* Ward's *The Dutch and Swedes on the Delaware* and other similar works indicate but do not develop fully the influences of these racial strains on our literature; and the parts played by the Spanish in our early history, or by the Irish, Italian, Polish, Norwegian, Bohemian, and other later immigrant groups, are only partially understood. The writings of travelers to and from America have been examined for themselves, but their bearing upon our literature deserves further comment. The influence of imported books, too, is being gradually appreciated. The catalogues of the Library Company of Philadelphia and other such organizations, as well as of the early booksellers, need closer study as a contribution toward an understanding of the relationship of eigthteenth-century English literature to our first literary experiments, and the appreciation of the significance of an Oriental library in Concord as a determining factor in the thought of Emerson and Thoreau is only one of many such factors which are now beginning to be appreciated. Cairns opened an entirely new field in his studies of the British criticisms of American writings, but we lack such comprehensive reviews of French, German, Italian, and other foreign periodicals, and even the work of Cairns is little more than a survey of possibilities. Foreign influences on American periodicals have come in for similar survey treatments in recent times, but even here there is room for more detailed study than has yet been made, although many such projects are in progress now, as the articles in such periodicals as *American Literature* and doctoral theses bear witness.

III

Much of this form of study is now concentrating its efforts upon the growth of the literary minds of our major writers. Franklin, Thoreau, Howells, and many others have given us firsthand evidence of the direct influence of their travels and reading upon their work, but for the undoubted influence of Balzac and Scott on Cooper, and other such problems in the literary growth of men who were not diary-minded, we must set ourselves to much analytical study of internal evidence and much hypothesis. Here, too, there is work to be done before the gaps in the background of our literary history are filled.

There are two sides to the problem of the relation of such background studies to the study of literary history. Not only did the peculiar Anglo-Dutch aristocratic heritage of New York society shape the lives and thought of the Knickerbocker group, but it becomes the subject of Irving's *Knickerbocker's History*, Paulding's *A Dutchman's Fireside*, Cooper's *Home as Found* and *Satanstoe*, and Halleck's *Fanny*. The Mississippi is not only an economic factor in Mark Twain's biography, but it is an epic theme in *Huck Finn* and *Life on the Mississippi*. The decline of New England acted as a check on the aesthetic maturity of Hawthorne and Melville and as a theme for novels from *The House of the Seven Gables* to *Deep Haven*. We must understand all of these elements in our civilization, both as causal factors in the lives of American authors and as materials of American literature. Until we appreciate their significance from both points of view, the preparation of our materials and our concepts for the writing of the new American literary history will not be completed.

Except that there are now many workers to undertake these tasks, it is a pity that there is still so much to be done. Ours is perhaps the only field of endeavor today in which there is no danger of unemployment. But these background analyses have their bad side, in that they divert attention from the problems more properly the prerogative of the American literary historian. In cases where other historians like Riley, Faust, Beard, and Turner have done much to clear the ground and to establish facts and factors, we may concentrate on our task of applying their discoveries to literary history, but where they have not, we must swerve temporarily from our main course. In the few cases in which even the application has been made with a reasonable degree of thoroughness, we may proceed to our special task of charting literary history in terms of forms and movements, thereby shifting our emphasis from the grounds of the philosophical, social, political, and economic historian over toward that of the literary critic, and finding our rightful places as literary historians.

Perhaps the most significant single contribution to this aspect of our thought was the clear definition of a romantic movement in our literature by Foerster in his anthologies and in his study of our naturalists and critics. His pioneer work has been carried on

by Clark and others to a point at which we can now distinguish
a native romantic movement as clearly as we can that of a similar
movement in England, Germany, or France. Now that we
recognize the Concord and Cambridge renaissance of 1835–1855
as an autonomous literary movement, motivated by aspirations
and experimentations common to romanticism in all times and
places, and determined in ideas and forms by the circumstances
of the American background, we may adjust our values so that
Melville can take his place above Alcott; Thoreau may be appreciated as something more than a rough diamond; Hawthorne
may be accepted for the artist that he was rather than as a mere
by-product of Puritan repressions; and the imitative and occasional work of Longfellow and Lowell may be distinguished
from that which reveals flashes of true poetic insight.

Once this pole of the movement is established, we discover that
Cooper, Irving, Bryant, and the other Knickerbockers are explicitly related to the New England group, not because they were
transcendentalists in embryo, which of course they were not,
but because they were romanticists of a more elementary and
imitative kind than their Northern successors. The significance
of local groups is lessened as an understanding of the organic
growth of the movement establishes broader, and more specifically literary, relationships between the work of writers in the
different seaboard cities. Similarly, Poe ceases to be a sport,
unaccountable in terms of his background, and makes his very
significant contribution to our story by bringing the Gothic
element, already apparent in the work of Brockden Brown, to
the level of aesthetic maturity; and Freneau appears less important as "the poet of the Revolution," taking his place as the
first American romantic poet of genius.

But we still continue merrily to divide our history by wars and
presidential campaigns, and we fail to draw these flashes of true
aesthetic insight into a unified whole. As we move backward
and forward from the pole which we have established in the
Concord group, our thought becomes more and more cloudy and
confused. The significance of the Knickerbocker group in its
relationship to the movement is only beginning to be recognized,

and that of the Philadelphia and Princeton groups, Brown, Hopkinson, Freneau, Brackenridge, Godfrey, and Royall Tyler, is scarcely noted. The importance of the Revolutionary War as a political phenomenon hovers over this early period as an undisputed tyrant. Writers of literary history must make their obeisance to it and are commanded to treat their subjects, not as groups of men with sincere literary aspirations, but as agents for the expression of patriotic or unpatriotic ideas. The result is that we have failed to attempt an analysis of the types of imitative romanticism which gave shape to the period as an epoch in American literary history. The Gothic, the historical, and the sentimental interests were all present, and were all closely related to parallel interests in Europe. And we have also failed to distinguish imitative neoclassicism from imitative romanticism. English literary history of a century was telescoped in America to a quarter of that time.

Neither have the types of imitative romanticism been distinguished from the native factors which made the later romanticism more truly American. The patriotism of the period is important to us here, not because it won a war and gave us a constitution, but because it gave Americans a sense of cultural autonomy —or rather, a sense of the need for one, which in effect is the same thing. The dozen or more essays on the need for a national literature which preceded Emerson's *American Scholar* and which expressed practically all of the leading ideas in that classic essay, have never been brought together and given a place in our national literary history as one of the primary causes of the romantic movement.

Similarly, the independence of mind and the demand for a liberty of conscience which dates back to Roger Williams, Thomas Morton, and William Penn, which developed in the conviction of John Wise and in the inner struggles of Jonathan Edwards, and which matured in the deism of Franklin and Paine, continue to be regarded as aspects of religious and political rather than of literary history. This movement, too, has a direct bearing on later romanticism in America by developing the speculative habit of mind, but even our most radical of contemporary his-

torians, Ludwig Lewisohn, proceeds on the theory that Calvinism
has been merely a destructive force in our literary development
until the very recent past. Transcendentalism, a by-product of
Calvinism, is more important to literature than to philosophy because it gave us Emerson and Whitman.

A third factor in the growth of the movement, the interest in
science and nature, is closely related to the other two and was
early apparent in the natural history essay and in the choice of
native scenes for poetry and novels. The Bartrams, Crèvecoeur,
Wilson, and Audubon are slighted in even our most recent histories.

Again, the imitative neoclassicism that appeared in America
simultaneously with the earlier evidences of romanticism has
been recognized in the Hartford Wits, but even here perhaps
the emphasis has been too strong on its political and religious
rather than on its literary bearings, and its significance has not
been tied in closely enough with its aesthetic companion and
opposite, imitative romanticism.

IV

These are only a few of the problems in the determination of
forms and movements in early American literature, and I have
been able to do no more than hint at their scope. I might attempt a similar analysis of the problems of realism and the
romance of local color, not only in their social relationships to
sectionalism and the back-trailer movement, but, following in
the lead of Pattee, Garland, and others, I might point out the
many half-solved problems which are attendant upon the definition of a realistic movement in the American novel after about
1870 and a naturalistic movement in American poetry and the
novel of the recent past. This would follow the reappraisal of
Whitman and Mark Twain in their relationships to both movements, and would open the question of the proper place in our
literary history of James, Adams, Dreiser, and many others. Even
Upton Sinclair must have an aesthetic as well as a sociological
significance if he is to occupy the place in our literary history

which the emotional power of *The Jungle* seems to demand for him.

I think, however, that I have indicated enough specific problems to establish my thesis that the new race of American literary historians, who must be philosophers and economists as well as critics, have still much work ahead. They must perfect our knowledge of correlated backgrounds where they lack the aid of historians in other fields; they must concentrate on the problem of the specific applications of this knowledge to literary history proper; and then, turning to their rightful province, they must continue from the bare start that has been made in the definitions of the romantic and realistic movements to a complete charting of our literary history in similar terms. Further, they must do for American poetry, the essay, and the novel what has been done by Quinn for the American drama and, to a lesser extent, by Pattee and others, for the American short story. Until we have complete and detailed histories of the development of these five literary forms in America, no satisfactory history of our literature can be written.

It is evident that our first task as research investigators is not, at the present time, the writing of this new history, but the conservation and classification of the sources from which it is to be written, and the continued and intensive fact-finding in limited fields and on specific problems, upon which we have all been engaged. We must be patient.

Blueprint for American Literary History

1941

READ AT THE CENTENNIAL CELEBRATION OF
FORDHAM UNIVERSITY, NEW YORK, IT
SERVED AS AN INFORMAL "WORKING PAPER"
DURING THE EARLY STAGES OF PLANNING
THE *Literary History of the United
States*. [PUBLISHED BY THE STUDENTS OF
THE UNIVERSITY OF PENNSYLVANIA IN THE
PENNSYLVANIA LITERARY REVIEW, VIII
(1957), 3–10.]

IN UNDERTAKING TO SKETCH a working plan for a new literary history of the United States I must ask you to climb first to such a peak of perspective as we may be capable of attaining and from there chart our territory in rough outline. Four facts seem clear: (1) American literature, before the nineteenth century, was written in the service of ends other than art, and the greatest minds were essentially unliterary; (2) the nineteenth century produced perhaps a dozen literary figures of major stature, most of them either born in, or closely associated with, the thirteen original colonies; (3) at the same time there was much writing, associated principally with westward expansion, which was primarily unliterary in purpose and effect; and (4) the twentieth century has produced a large group of vigorous and profound writers whose dominating motives are literary and who live in all parts of our present territory.

It is comparatively easy to distinguish a real literary movement

26

in the new nation of 1783, whether we call it "romantic" or not. It was felt within the first decade of independence and gradually gathered form and momentum, culminating during the middle years of the century. Among its greatest writers were Poe, Hawthorne, Thoreau, Melville, Emerson, and Whitman. Before them came Cooper, Irving, and Bryant, Freneau, Brown, and Brackenridge; with them appeared Whittier, Boker, Simms, Longfellow, and Lowell; following them came Mark Twain, Lanier, Dickinson, Howells, and James. Behind all of these original and creative writers were a host of lesser men and women who partook of their thoughts and feelings but reflected, perhaps in some cases even better than they, the current temper of the American people. The first major problem for the new historian of our literature is a close study of this group, its product and its background.

The most striking fact about it is the restricted geographical horizon of most of the central figures. The America that they knew was focused in Boston, New York, Philadelphia, and the southern seaboard cities; the area of their knowledge extended from Maine to Georgia and penetrated only sporadically into the Alleghenies and the woods and plains beyond. Cooper's wilderness was in upstate New York, Thoreau traveled far "in Concord," Poe and Irving ranged the coastal cities, Emerson and Whitman went west only after their literary molds were cast, Melville roamed the South Seas but knew nothing of his own hinterland, Simms and Lanier knew their south, and even toward the end of the century Howells and Mark Twain struggled to fit themselves into the frame of eastern culture. Many of these writers and their lesser contemporaries, Irving, Halleck, Leland, Taylor, James, Howells, knew Europe far better than they knew the Mississippi and Missouri, or even the Ohio valleys. The historian is confronted therefore at the start with perhaps his basic truth: the United States behind our nineteenth century literature was not, geographically, the country for which we use that name today. How can he chart logically the history of American literature when there have been, geographically speaking, not one but at least two nations producing that literature?

I shall not take the time to review in detail the social, religious, economic, intellectual, and other contrasts between these two nations. Suffice it to note that the earlier nation was agrarian, the latter predominately industrial; the former dominated by strong religious and moral conviction, the latter largely materialistic and agnostic. In other respects the contrast is equally striking, once the two poles of development are indicated.

I have deliberately overemphasized this contrast in order to stress my main point, that no single history of American literature can ever be written without confusion and contradiction in dealing with the transition period from 1870 to 1910, and, as a result, of all other periods. Neither the decline of the main surge of romanticism nor the rise of realism can be explained satisfactorily as a continuous literary chronicle. Nor can our contemporary writers be explained and understood solely against the background of the major writers of the mid-nineteenth century. We need two histories of our literature, the one the literature of the new nation, the other that of the whole nation. We cannot chart our literary history in a single curve, rising and falling in terms of romantic vs. neoclassical or other reactionary movements; we must have two such curves, the one reaching its apex in the middle years of the nineteenth century, the other at or near its highest point today. The two cross and, to a degree, merge somewhere between 1870 and 1890.

The chief value of a pattern such as this is that it provides a new instrument for the measurement of old and well-considered facts. The method of setting up a hypothesis is well known to scientific inquiry and may be borrowed without apology by the literary historian. In fact, it has already been used effectively by Lovejoy, Lowes, Matthiessen, and others. The hypothesis need not stand forever the test of ultimate and absolute truth; suffice it that it be founded on established facts and be reasonably sound for the area of knowledge that it attempts to describe.

With this tool we can proceed to a classification and arrangement of the literary great of the nineteenth century. Central in the picture is Emerson, with his moral conviction, his transcendental idealism, his Yankee common sense. Around him, the

Concord group converges as moons about a central sun, with Thoreau a somewhat recalcitrant reflection, Hawthorne a brooding shadow. These men were obviously reacting to the same impulses in terms of divergent temperaments. Into a wider circle are drawn Melville with his demonic transcendentalism and Whitman with his cosmic consciousness of the destiny of humanity in general and of the American poet in particular. A few miles away, the same romantic and moral idealism found gentler voices in Bryant, Lowell, Longfellow, Whittier, and innumerable lesser writers. Even Poe, with his shout of "Eureka" upon the discovery of a mathematically unified universe of reason and imagination, obviously shares in the some movement.

We cannot here consider the connections between this group and the romantic movement elsewhere, particularly in Germany, England, and France; nor are its intellectual sources in Neo-Platonism, Puritanism and Asiatic mysticism our immediate concern. Such problems have been well considered and a vast deal of fact and opinion collected for their review by the historian. For the present also we cannot trace the emergence of this group from its economic, political, theological and social milieu. Emerson—Channing—Edwards—Mather: such sequences are not difficult to discover, reaching back into the past. The whole surge of the Reformation moves these waters.

But in writers less stirred by moral earnestness there is an impulse almost as strong stemming from what Mr. Santayana has called the Revolution, the second the three "R's," and a third from the Renaissance with its love of life and its humanistic rationalism. Perhaps we should have four, not three of these "R's," for Rationalism is a force in itself and it took firmer hold in America than did the aesthetic impulses of the awakening. In the middle states and in the South these other surges were more deeply felt. Irving's love of life and his restless search for beauty were not all sentimental, were in very small part moral. Cooper was a stern moralist in his restrained and more thoughtful moods, but the glorious vigor of the open air of woods, sea, mind, and heart was often too strong for him and carried him out on the long chase when he planned a dignified commentary on his times.

Freneau, Brown, Simms, Kennedy, Poe himself, felt these other forces more strongly than they did that of transcendental ethics.

The mention of Poe suggests the need of rather special study of the literary awakening of the South before the Civil War, for Poe was at heart a Southerner, however much he lived and worked in New York and Philadelphia. His primary impulse to write was born in Richmond, as the evidence of his kinship to Chivers, Timrod, Hayne, and Lanier in poetry alone would testify. The South has not yet fully defined the course of its own romantic movement, differing from, though sharing with, that of New England and the Middle States, particularly the latter. But its background was more purely Renaissance than that of its neighbors, and a movement was born in the 'thirties which reached a culmination even more abortive than that of the North on the eve of the Civil War and on the threshold of westward expansion. The literary history of the South in this period needs new definition.

The historian has many such problems to think through, but the outline of his story is established in so far as the literature of the new nation is concerned. What we used to call "The First National Period" is in fact a romantic movement with a beginning, middle, and end, with a cycle that required almost a century to run, and with a background in the individualistic agrarian eastern seaboard states.

When we turn to the later writers who participated in this movement, however, we discover a sense of disquietude, different and less confident moods, new themes, less common and solid ground. Lanier, Mark Twain, Whitman himself questioned their own souls and the world in which they lived in a language that Emerson or Lowell could only partially understand. Basically of the same movement, they mark its decline, and the opening out of the channeled stream into wide and sometimes marshy land. This is the negative aspect of their work; of the positive, more in a few moments. For the decline of enthusiasm and conviction, the concern with shallower strata of the soul, is distinguished more clearly in the later Lowell, Longfellow, and Boker, in Holmes and Ticknor, and with unmistakable certainty

in Stedman, Aldrich, and Sill. The impulses which formed our
first literary movement had expended their most vital forces.

The old analogy of the pendulum occurs immediately when
the literary historian notes the declining years of a romantic
movement. Literature, in the traditional view, becomes classic
or neoclassic by a normal process of reaction. But a pendulum,
to function efficiently, must continue to be hung in the same
clock. In American mid-century, the clock itself was altered.
Evidences of a neoclassical movement may perhaps be noted
in the appearance of criticism and in the standardization of verse
and fiction in the third quarter of the century, but it lacked
conviction. Too much was happening. The West opened with
the rush of floodgates, the Civil War challenged and altered the
economy of half the nation. A new period of national expansion
was in full swing, and expansion fosters romanticism rather than
its contrary in literature.

It is at this point that the true nature of the creative impulses
of men like Mark Twain and Walt Whitman becomes apparent. Their geographical horizons were wider than those of
their contemporaries, even though some of them, like Whitman,
saw the farther ranges largely in their imagination. They were
beginning to write the new American literature, the literature
of the whole nation. Mark Twain's *Roughing It* is contemporary
in spirit with Irving's *Knickerbocker* rather than with Longfellow's *Christus* or Lowell's *My Study Windows*, which appeared
almost at the same time. But Mark Twain was of a different
literary history. To place him, the historian must create a new
orientation. Much of the confusion, apology, and debate which
clusters about his name is a result of trying to relate his work to
the end of one rather than to the beginning of another romantic
movement, an effort which he himself attempted to his cost.
But he is not the only victim of this false perspective. "The
Gilded Age" followed "The Golden Day" in Mumford's and
in Brooks' early work, and it became the custom to apologize for
the materialism and confusion of the modern period rather than
to search for its central meaning. The powerful, though perhaps
dark, currents of contemporary literature are not adequately

described by the phrase, "convention, revolt, and general chaos."
More accurate is the phrase, "the *rise* of realism," used by Parrington, Wann, and others, because in it there is a sense of the
upward direction of new forces. It was a rise, as well as a decline,
but it involved far more than realism. The descriptive terms for
this new literature of the whole nation are as yet to be devised,
but the literary history of the period must first be charted.

Our historian-critic-architect would doubtless draw a deep
breath before plunging into the turgid waters of contemporary
American literature were his hypothesis not there to goad him
off the safe shores of the past. We must anticipate him in that
plunge. We must look with the same candid and appraising eye
at O'Neill, Robinson, Thomas Wolfe, Steinbeck, Jeffers, Eliot,
Dreiser, and a host of others, that we have attempted to focus
on the great writers of our infant literature. Among these writers
somewhere we should find the culminating forces of our literary
past as a nation reaching from sea to sea and from the Canadian
to the Mexican border. There may be greater writers to come,
and we may be wrong in our relative judgments of those cur-
rently writing. Whether the second curve of our literary
history has reached its apex or not, we need not finally proclaim.
All we need to discover is a living and mature literature in the
past quarter century of our history.

We have become so habituated to the notion that modern
writers are sordid defeatists singing the swan song of a dying
civilization, or obscure escapists counting their fingers in the
solitude of their ivory towers, that any contrary opinion has little hope of a cordial reception. We are so inured to the idea that
literature to be great must have a positive and optimistic message
that a basically pessimistic literary movement can seem to us
only an end of all good things, a running thin of the vital juices
of living, the death of art. But how much of the great art of the
past has had a positive and optimistic message? In English literature, we rate Chaucer, Shakespeare, Milton, Donne, Dryden,
Pope, Johnson, Coleridge, Arnold, and Hardy above Sidney,
Isaac Watts, Tennyson, Henley, and Kipling. The Greek tragedies, the Roman satires, the plays of Racine and Molière, Goethe

and Schiller—which of these finds good, wholesome answers to the human problems which they discuss? Surely the greatness of a literary work lies in its ability to ask rather than to answer significant questions significantly. It moves in a moral sphere, but it does not moralize.

Amos Wilder [1] called attention to the fact that this is exactly what our contemporary poets are doing and have been doing for some time. The questions were frail and conventional in the lyrics of Hovey and Aldrich, Mifflin and Lizette Reese. They probe more deeply and with more passionate earnestness in Moody, Robinson, and Frost. They burn to the bottom with white heat in Jeffers, Sandburg, Eliot, and Hart Crane. The same trend may be noted in the fiction from Taylor and Stowe, to Harte, James, and Howells, to Stephen Crane and Frank Norris, to Dreiser and Upton Sinclair, to Lewis, Hemingway, Steinbeck, Faulkner, Caldwell, and, most passionate if most confused of all, to Thomas Wolfe, who seems in some strange profound way to be crying across the years to Melville, that still sated but unsatisfied soul. [2]

Increasing intensity has similarly marked our drama and our essay, and parallel with it there has been a critical movement which has nicely mixed fury and dismay with ruthless analysis and uncompromising judgment. Counting backward from Mac-Leish, Krutch, Wilson, Chamberlin, Ransom, and a host of others to Eliot, Bourne, Brooks, Mumford, Mencken and More, to Macy, Brownell, Trent, Woodberry, and Scudder, the procession is formidable, with intensity, penetration and significance almost certainly on the increase. The diversity of schools in this critical movement, and the internecine war among them, is but further evidence of its vitality. Is it possible to deny the searching power of much of American literature today, or—strange but indispensable companion to power if it is to become great—its understanding and mastery of effective form? "Where to? What next?" "Is it the wind that drives all men like dead ghosts fleeing?" "For whom tolls the bell?" These are basic and unanswerable questions, asked in such a way that answers are imperative.

If time allowed, I should like to discuss the continuously deepening stream of regional fiction from Eggleston and Jewett to Cather and Glasgow and on to Rachel Field, Paul Green and a host of others, the revival of that hardy perennial, the novel of early American history, the experiments in epic and narrative forms of Bénet, Van Doren and LaFarge, and the range and depth of modern biography. The theatre, assaulted by Broadway on the one hand and Hollywood on the other, has retreated to the country and produced both comedies and tragedies of a sincerity and a force that speak of anything but a dying art. We cannot pause to argue what is good and what inferior in all this excited literary outpouring, but we can at least recognize its volume and its vitality, leaving the sorting and sifting to later critics of greater perspective. We can also ask pertinent questions about its nature, and, as literary historians, about its causes and its ancestry.

I have already hinted, without calling names or too dogmatically defining "isms," that it seems to me a result of the great vitality of a nation, first in the process of expanding horizons, and then of self-discovery when its new boundaries are tentatively described. Our present geographical area has been held to its limits for fifty years or more by the Pacific Ocean and by its northern and southern neighbors, as the Allegheny Mountains and the Indians checked the frontier movement in an earlier day and caused an epoch of cultural self-development. To understand this process, we must follow the history of our United States backward, not only to the explorers and the signers, but to Daniel Boone, Kit Carson, Jay Gould, Edison, and other empire builders. This is a separate though closely related study to to that of Colonial and Revolutionary thought and expression. Yet it would be absurd to assume that the same ideas and experiences went into both streams of national development. Only by separating our two literary histories can they be accurately studied. Bret Harte, Mark Twain, Howells, Garland, and all their successors are as little a part of the literary history of the thirteen original colonies as are Freneau, Brown, Irving, Cooper, and Bryant a part of the literary history of the British nation.

Our early literary historians were bound or perverted in their study of American literature by the assumption of the close kinship of our early writers to their English predecessors and contemporaries. Our modern American literary historians are equally bound and misled by the assumption that American development was single rather than dual. Any self-respecting anthology of writings of the latter nineteenth century is forced by chronology to make Huckleberry Finn and Christopher Newman uneasy bedfellows. They would be more comfortable in different hotels.

I realize that I have raised as many problems as I hoped to have laid by slicing our literary history into two with one diagonal sweep of the knife. The whole hypothesis can easily be dismissed by pointing out that the frontier movement, with its consequences, was a continuous process from the days of Columbus to at least the driving of the gold spike into the Union Pacific tracks in 1869. Even were we to admit that it moved with uneven speed, there were not, one might argue, two such major pauses of definable length as I have assumed. The territory of the orginal colonies extended to the Mississippi, and James Hall was writing in a similar vein and at the same time as Cooper and Simms. Furthermore, the last Puritan among us has not yet died untimely, nor has Jefferson ceased to prowl, a ghost, even on the Pacific slope. There is more continuity in our literary history than this hypothesis will allow.

My answer is that my theory of our literary history has use, even though it be but a half-truth, and that it is needed as a corrective to false assumptions and undigested facts. American literature came to be studied seriously and effectively only after its bond with English literature was severed and the novels and poems and plays that appeared on our shores were seen primarily as native growths, taking their richest nourishment from the soil and air of their native land. Similarly, we will never understand our literary present and its antecedents until modern, industrial, cosmopolitan America is distinguished from and related to the land of Franklin, Jefferson, Emerson, and Longfellow in new perspective. The new nation is dead except as a precious heritage, the whole nation demands the resourceful inquiry of the scholar into its literary past.

NOTES

[1] *Spiritual Aspects of the New Poetry* (New York, 1940).

[2] Hindsight would, of course, suggest some changes in the names listed in this and the next paragraph were the essay written today.

❧ II ❧

The Verdict of Sydney Smith

1929

WRITTEN IN ENGLAND IN 1928 AND PUB-
LISHED AS THE FIRST ARTICLE OF THE FIRST
ISSUE OF THE JOURNAL, *American Litera-
ture*, 1 (1929), 3–13.

OF THE MANY Englishmen who expressed themselves upon the subject of adolescent America and American literature, no one out of public life had greater influence than the Reverend Sydney Smith, Canon of St. Paul's Cathedral and founder of the *Edinburgh Review*. The reasons for this power are not far to seek. His plea that he was always the friend of the American cause is alternately supported and denied many times by his statements in print; he knew and entertained more American visitors than did any other English man of letters of the time, with the possible exceptions of Sir Walter Scott and Samuel Rogers, and he was admired and enjoyed by his contemporaries in England as well as in America for his deep human sympathies, his keen wit, and his liberal opinions. Yet it was this man who characterized Daniel Webster as "a steam-engine in trousers"—who asked, with reference to Mrs. Trollope's *Refugees in America*, "And why should not the Americans be ridiculed if they are ridiculous?"—who characterized the United States as "the native home of the needy villain";—and whose other verbal crimes against his American cousins are too numerous to mention.

Sydney Smith's incidental opinions on this subject are scattered through his letters and through those books of anecdotes about him that were collected by his English and American admirers soon after his death in 1845. His more important criticisms are

39

to be found in two places: in the pages of the *Edinburgh Review*, to which he contributed three articles containing extensive analyses of America as a nation and as a people, and in the *Morning Chronicle*, where he published in 1843 his three letters regarding the threatened repudiation of state debts during the American financial depression of that period.

The articles in the *Edinburgh* come first in point of time and should therefore be considered first.

In his first article,[1] a review of four of the earlier books of travel in America by Englishmen, Smith reveals a predisposition in favor of American theories of government and liberal institutions. This is prompted chiefly by negative motives. He was, throughout his life, a consistent Whig, believing in a more liberal government than England enjoyed prior to 1830. In reading these books on America, he was impressed by the value of the principles underlying the American state, and he was prompted to sympathize with his authors in their praise of the dignified simplicity of the "Ex-Kings," Adams and Jefferson.

He early gives evidence, however, of two motives which biased his views at this time, instinctive fear of the growing power of America and ignorance of the *facts* of her life. His review opens with the statement that these books "will probably decide the fate, and direct the footsteps, of many human beings, seeking a better lot than the Old World can afford them." The charge which Irving, Cooper, and others laid against such books—that they were in reality anti-emigration propaganda—seems, therefore, to have been well founded. At all events the charge is implicitly admitted by Sydney Smith, perhaps because of an instinctive jealousy, which was prompted by the comparisons not favorable to the Old World which are implied by the mere fact of emigration to the New.

He proceeds to enumerate the points in which America has improved upon her parent: government is cheap and salaries are low—"their Mr. Crokers are inexpressibly reasonable,—somewhere about the price of an English doorkeeper, or bearer of a mace." American experience has proved that universal suffrage is practical and is not necessarily followed by tumult and revolution. The Americans have demonstrated that the services of the tailor and the barber are not essential to justice. "A Judge administers justice without a calorific wig and particoloured gown, in a coat and pantaloons. He is obeyed, however: and life and property are not badly protected in the United States." England could well take note of these points; but here the catalogue of virtues ends, and with it the liberality and much of the humor of Smith's views.

Two brief paragraphs follow which amply illustrate the second of the reviewer's liabilities in a discussion of America, his ignorance of facts:

There are no very prominent men at present [1818] in America; at least none whose fame is strong enough for exportation. . . .

Literature the Americans have none—no native literature, we mean. It is all imported. They had a Franklin indeed; and may afford to live for half a century on his fame. There is, or was, a Mr. Dwight, who wrote some poems; and his baptismal name was Timothy. There is also a small account of Virginia by Jefferson, and an epic by Joel Barlow—and some pieces of pleasantry by Mr. Irving. But why should the Americans write books, when a six weeks' passage brings them, in their own tongue, our sense, science and genius, in bales and hogsheads? Prairies, steam-boats, grist-mills, are their natural objects for centuries to come. Then, when they have got to the Pacific Ocean—epic poems, plays, pleasures of memory, and all the elegant gratifications of an ancient people who have tamed the wild earth, and set down to amuse themselves.—This is the natural march of human affairs.

The lurking antipathies which are sensed throughout these lines become more apparent in the concluding treatment of slavery. After quoting some of the atrocities committed under the American laws on this subject—as described by his authors— Smith concludes: "Let the world judge which is the most liable to censure—we who, in the midst of our rottenness, have torn off the manacles of slaves all over the world,—or they who, with their idle purity, and useless perfection, have remained mute and careless, while groans echoed and whips clank'd round the very walls of their spotless Congress." Exemplary oratory this, and prompted by the righteous indignation of a man who, by his actions, long proved himself a friend of suffering humanity—but not without prejudice.

The often repeated prophecy of American disunion is to be found here also: "The Americans are a very sensible, reflecting people, and have conducted their affairs extremely well, but it is scarcely possible to conceive that such an empire should very long remain undivided, or that the dwellers on the Columbia should have common interest with the navigators of the Hudson and the Delaware."

Part of the superficiality of this first criticism of America by Sydney Smith may well be attributed to the haste in reading which journalistic reviewing seems to cultivate if not demand. In a letter to Earl Grey, November 30, 1818, he recommends these books, all four of which, he says, may, with ease, be read through between breakfast and dinner. He then reiterates his belief that a nation which expands so rapidly cannot remain unified, as well as most of the other points of his review.[2]

Smith's second article[3] on "Jonathan" appeared a year later and contains that classic paragraph under the sting of which the Americans writhed for so long. It is a review of a rather unassuming book, a statistical analysis of the United States, which, in the reviewer's opinion, "will form a pretty complete picture of America, and teach us how to appreciate that country, either as a powerful enemy or a profitable friend."

With the exception of a warning against the inflammatory eloquence of David Porter and Stephen Decatur, the bulk of the review is devoted to a summary of the statistical information in the book—an article of a "dry and discouraging nature," says Smith.[4] The concluding paragraph alone contains acid.

Thus far, [says the reviewer] we are the friends and admirers of Jonathan: But he must not grow vain and ambitious; or allow himself to be dazzled by that galaxy of epithets by which his orators and newspaper scribblers endeavour to persuade their supporters that they are the greatest, the most refined, the most enlightened, and the most moral people upon earth. The effect of this is unspeakably ludicrous on this side of the Atlantic—and, even on the other,

we should imagine, must be rather humiliating to the reasonable
part of the population. The Americans are a brave, industrious, and
acute people; but they have hitherto given no indications of genius,
and made no approaches to the heroic, either in their morality or
character. They are but a recent offset indeed from England; and
should make it their chief boast, for many generations to come,
that they are sprung from the same race with Bacon and Shakespeare
and Newton. . . . In the four quarters of the globe, who reads an
American book? Or goes to an American play? Or looks at an
American picture or statue? What does the world yet owe to American physicians or surgeons? What new substances have their chem-
ists discovered? Or what old ones have they analyzed? What new
constellations have been discovered by the telescopes of Americans?
What have they done in the mathematics? Who drinks out of
American glasses? Or eats from American plates? or wears American coats or gowns? or sleeps in American blankets?—Finally, under
which of the old tyrannical governments of Europe is every sixth
man a Slave, whom his fellow-creatures may buy and sell and
torture?

When these questions are fairly and favourably answered, their
laudatory epithets may be allowed: But, till that can be done, we
would seriously advise them to keep clear of superlatives.

The American nation and its press were, of course, furious
at this indictment—much more nearly true at the time of its
utterance than it was a few years later. A quarter century of
debate is summed up by E. A. Duyckinck, one of Smith's most
sympathetic American critics: "This is the famous passage which
has been the peg to hang many wearisome dissertations upon.
Not needed to excite rapid American invention, it has become
simply an historical landmark, from which to date extensive national achievements. Its questions in politics, art, science, literature, are an index to American triumphs." [5]

The third article,[6] in striking contrast to the other two, is
sane and tolerant, revealing a man of the broad human sympathies
which we are taught to associate with the name of the Canon
of St. Paul's. When enumerated, the points here made are almost
identical with those of the first article, but their spirit is quite
the antithesis of that manifest earlier.

It is very natural that we Scotch [with a sly wink at his native-born colleagues], who live in a little shabby scraggy corner of a remote island, with a climate which cannot ripen an apple, should be jealous of the aggressive pleasantry of more favoured people; but that Americans, who have done so much for themselves, and received so much from nature, should be flung into such convulsions by English Reviews and Magazines, is really a sad specimen of Columbian juvenility. . . . We really thought at one time they would have fitted out an armament against the *Edinburgh* and *Quarterly Reviews,* and burnt down Mr. Murray's and Mr. Constable's shops, as we did the American Capitol.

This surprise at the popular indignation which swept over the American press like a prairie fire after the Smith catechism of 1820 is the only weapon of offense here directed across the sea. The rest are aimed at home evil in contrast to American good, "because we think the example of America will in many instances tend to open the eyes of Englishmen to their true interests." The points in which England could improve herself from the example are: by a national economy that would permit low salaries to public officials without impairment of their service; by a religious toleration which, far from excluding a Catholic lord from the presence of the king, actually makes a Jew (M. M. Noah) the High Sheriff of New York ("In this particular," declares Smith, "the Americans are at the head of all the nations of the world"); by an interstate liberality of trade and commerce impossible in the Old World because of feudal traditions; and finally, by a high development of public education, based on a division of the country into local educational districts. "These facts," concludes Smith, "quite put into the background everything which has been done in the Old World for the improvement of the lower orders, and confer deservedly upon the Americans the character of a wise, a reflecting, and a virtuous people."

The remainder of the article is devoted to a discussion of the crudities and peculiarities of daily life in America, all of which, with the exception of his pet aversion, spitting, he seems now to see in a just and sane light as the natural, and, in many cases, creditable, results of pioneer conditions.

In his conclusion he reverts once more to the subject of slavery, but he treats it as America herself came to treat it, all too late, after the Civil War.

America seems [he says] on the whole, to be a country possessing vast advantages, and little inconveniences; they have a cheap government, and bad roads; they pay no tithes, and have stage coaches without springs. . . . In all this the balance is prodigiously in their favour: but then comes the great disgrace and danger of America— the existence of slavery, which, if not timously corrected, will one day entail (and ought to entail) a bloody servile war upon the Americans—which will separate America into slave states and states disclaiming slavery, and which remains at present as the foulest blot in the moral character of that people. . . . No one can admire the simple wisdom and manly firmness of the Americans more than we do, or more despise the pitiful propensity which exists among Government runners to vent their small spite at their character; but, on the subject of slavery, the conduct of America is, and has been, most reprehensible.

It is interesting to note evidence that, in spite of his professed admiration of America, Smith was not wholly trusted on this subject by his editor and warm friend, Francis Jeffrey. It was apparently with reference to the first of these reviews that Jeffrey wrote to him in 1818. The letter, unfortunately, does not seem to have been preserved, but Smith's answer reveals its meaning: "I entirely agree with you respecting the Americans, and believe that I am to the full as much a Philo-yankeeist as you are. I doubt if there ever was an instance in a new people conducting their affairs with so much wisdom, or if there ever was such an extensive scene of human happiness and prosperity. However, you could not know that such were my opinions, or if you did, you might imagine I should sacrifice them to effect: and in either case your caution was proper." [7]

A second warning came after experience had taught that Smith's wit was not wholly harmless when consigned to paper.

An even more revealing letter was addressed to the editor of the *Edinburgh* on March 17, 1822:

I had written three parts in four of the review I promised you of Miss Wright's book on America, and could have put it in your hands ten days since; but your letter restricts me so on the subject of raillery, that I find it impossible to comply with your conditions. There are many passages in my review which would make the Americans very angry, and—which is more to my immediate purpose—make you very loath to publish it, and therefore, to avoid putting you in the awkward predicament of printing what you disapprove, or disapproving me, I withdraw my pretensions. I admire the Americans, and in treating of America, should praise her great institutions, and laugh at her little defects. The reasons for your extreme prudery I do not understand, nor is it necessary I should do so. I am satisfied that you are a good pilot of our literary vessel, and give you credit when I do not perceive your motives.[8]

No review of this book was published.

Sydney Smith's last writing on the subject of America—in fact, his last public utterance in print—was in a controversy which can only excite mixed praise and blame for both sides. It seems that the Canon had invested some money in bonds of the State of Pennsylvania, the interest upon which—some £50— failed to appear in 1843.[9] Not only was the dividend passed in this one instance, but there was general talk of repudiation of the public debt in Pennsylvania, and in other states as well. The quick temper and the sharp wit of Smith were at once provoked, both in the interest of his own claim, and of the moral issue involved in the question. He addressed an open petition to Congress, which was printed in the *Morning Chronicle* and soon became a chief topic of debate in the press and among the people of both countries.

That Smith, in this denunciation of the "infamy" of the State of Pennsylvania, and therefore of the nation which tolerated such state action, was entirely sincere is beyond doubt. His original petition is heavy with righteous indignation, and what wit it contains might better be termed wrath.

The fraud [he declares] is committed in the profound peace of Pennsylvania, by the richest State in the Union, after the wise investment of the borrowed money in roads and canals, of which the repudiators are every day reaping the advantage. It is an act of bad faith which (all its circumstances considered) has no parallel, and no excuse. [The chief evil resulting, he feels, is] that immense power which the bad faith of America has given to aristocratical opinions, and to the enemies of free institutions, in the Old World, . . . for the United States are now working out the greatest of all political problems, and upon that confederacy the eyes of thinking men are intensely fixed, to see how far the mass of mankind can be trusted with the management of their own affairs, and the establishment of their own happiness.[10]

One cannot help feeling that the sharpest sting, to Sydney Smith, lay in the injury which he believed the State of Pennsylvania had done to those theories of popular government and that confidence in the basic good of humanity which lay at the foundation of his own political creed. His protest rings with something of the "*et tu Brute*" note, and his vehemence is colored by his personal disillusionment.

His heavy mood did not last for long, however. It will not be necessary to go here into the details of the controversy which raged in the American press. "My bomb," he writes to Mrs. Grote, in December, 1843,[11] "has fallen very successfully in America, and the list of killed and wounded is extensive. I have several quires of paper sent me every day, calling me monster, thief, atheist, deist, etc. Duff Green sent me three pounds of cheese [to repay the debt in part], and a Captain Monigan a large barrel of American apples."

So great was the reaction that the author of the petition felt obliged to take up the question again in the pages of the *Morning Chronicle* (November 3, 1843). "After some weeks' reflection," he states, "I see no reason to alter my opinions, or to retract my expressions." But his tone is undeniably lighter, and his protestations of admiration for the "honest America" of the past are vehement. Statements are now supported by sta-

tistical data which show that the attack had come from no idle
cleric, ignorant of the affairs of the material world. Finally, wit
triumphs and the old Sydney Smith is apparent: "I never meet
a Pennsylvanian at a London dinner without feeling a disposition
to seize and divide him;—to allot his beaver to one sufferer and
his coat to another—to appropriate his pocket-handkerchief to
the orphan, and to comfort the widow with his silver watch,
Broadway rings, and the London guide, which he always carries
in his pockets. . . . This new and vain people can never forgive
us for having preceded them 300 years in civilization. They are
prepared to enter into the most bloody wars in England, not
on account of Oregon, or boundaries, or right of search, but
because our clothes and carriages are better made, and because
Bond Street beats Broadway." But this cannot be done without
credit, and the letter concludes with a moving exhortation to
the "drab-coloured men of Pennsylvania" to start up from that
trance of dishonesty in which they are plunged, for there is but
a moment left before they and the whole United States will
become "the common-sewer of Europe, and the native home
of the needy villain."

His last public letter on the subject (November 22, 1843),
an answer, again in the *Morning Chronicle*, to that same Duff
Green of the cheese, is somewhat milder and shows a weariness
of the subject.

Hate America! [he exclaims] I have loved and honoured America
all my life; and in the *Edinburgh Review*, and at all opportunities
which my trumpery sphere of action has afforded, I have never
ceased to praise and defend the United States; and to every American to whom I have had the good fortune to be introduced, I have
proffered all the hospitality in my power. But I cannot shut my
eyes to enormous dishonesty. . . .

And now [he concludes] having eased my soul of its indignation
and sold my stock at 40 per cent. discount, I sulkily retire from the
subject, with a fixed intention of lending no more money to free
and enlightened republics, but of employing my money henceforth
in buying-up Abyssinian bonds, and purchasing into the Turkish
Fours, or the Tunis Three-and-a-half per Cent. funds.

What can now be made of such bombast, irony, logic, and fact? It is a curious mixture. No wonder his contemporaries were amazed and aroused. One of his most loyal American friends, George Ticknor, addressed a long letter in defense of his claim to the Boston *Semi-Weekly Advertiser* when the initial petition to Congress was made public, "the only article savouring of politics that I remember to have written since I was twenty-one years old." [12] But when the second letter appeared, his feeling changed. "How foolish, then, is Sydney Smith in his last letter," he writes to Charles Lyell, on November 30, 1843, "to treat us all as pickpockets. He does his cause a great mischief by it. . . . Nobody in this country can be glad of what he has written, unless it be the few who wish to build up their political fortunes by repudiation. He is on *their* side." [13] In England the controversy provoked feeling, as well as some amusement, like that of the following jingle:

> The reverend joker of St. Paul's
>   Don't relish much their plunder,
> And often at their knavish tricks
>   Has hurled his witty thunder.
> But Jonathan by nature wears
>   A hide of toughest leather,
> Which braves the sharpest-pointed darts
>   And *canons* put together.[14]

Sydney Smith's personal attitude at this time may in part be discovered by the frequent references to the subject in his letters to the Countess Grey and others:

I receive every day from America letters and pamphlets without end. I verily believe the United States are cracking. A nation cannot exist in such a state of morals. . . . I hope you were amused with my attack upon the Americans. They really deserved it. It is a monstrous and increasing villany. . . . I shall not be unobservant of what is said in the American papers, and, if need be, address a few more last words to Jonathan. . . . The question is, will they [his letters] make them angry or honest,—or both? I did not however mean to say what would make them pay, but to show them that their conduct had been shameful in not paying before, and should leave upon them this feeling, whether they ultimately paid or not.[15]

The concluding episode to the story was the arrival in New York on the "Great Western" of a nobody who called himself "Sydney Smith," and who was mistaken for the Canon. "What was to be done?" writes Smith's American friend, J. M. Wainwright, on July 15, 1844.[16] "Should he be tarred and feathered, or lynched? Quite the contrary. He was to be *fêted*, rejoiced in, and even Pennsylvania was to meet him with cordial salutations. A hundred dinners were arranged at the moment, and the guests selected." The letter concludes with a cordial invitation to give solace for the disappointment by a visit to America, enclosing an invitation also from the Bishop of New Jersey. "I hear Morpeth is going to America," Smith had written to Lady Grey a few years before, "a resolution which I think very wise, and which I should decidedly carry into execution myself, if I were not going to Heaven." [17] With this characteristically cryptic statement, let us leave the matter.

In a survey of the opinions of any man on a single subject throughout his life, any generalizations are dangerous. But the opinion of Sydney Smith on America and its literature did not, it would seem, materially change. It deepened with increasing knowledge, and it was embittered by personal disappointment, but in several respects it was reasonably consistent. It was prompted by a deep-rooted belief in liberal political and social institutions, with the logical corollary to such conviction, an instinctive sympathy for that nation which professed and practiced such principles. It was hampered by imperfect knowledge and by unwarranted prejudices, derived from unreliable sources, such as the accounts of English travelers in America. And it was colored profoundly, in its expression, by the quick turns of thought, the exaggerations, the emotional rises and falls, and such other misleading qualities as are native to a man of keen sensibilities and sharp mentality, rather than of sober judgment and measured statement. It is hard, even at this distance of time, to view Sydney Smith's criticism of America dispassionately, but it is perhaps safe to believe him an often misguided but frequently penetrating critic and friend.

NOTES

[1] A review of narratives of travel in the United States and Canada by Lieutenant Francis Hall (London, 1818), John Palmer (London, 1818), Henry B. Fearon (London, 1818), and John Bradbury (London, 1817). *Edinburgh Review*, XXXI, 132–150 (December, 1818).

[2] Lady Holland, *Memoir of Sydney Smith* (London, 1855), II, 166–167.

[3] A review of Adam Seybert's *Statistical Annals of the United States of America* (Philadelphia, 1818). *Edinburgh Review*, XXXIII, 69–80 (January, 1820).

[4] Letter (n.d.) to Edward Davenport. *Memoir*, II, 209–210.

[5] E. A. Duyckinck, *Wit and Wisdom of the Rev. Sydney Smith* (New York, 1858), p. 188n.

[6] A review of three more travels in the United States and Canada, by John M. Duncan (Glasgow, 1823), Adam Hodgson (London, 1824), and "An English Gentleman" (London, 1824). *Edinburgh Review*, XL, 427–442 (July, 1824).

[7] Letter to Francis Jeffrey, Esq., November 23, 1818. *Memoir*, II, 166.

[8] *Memoir*, II, 224.

[9] Payment on the Pennsylvania bonds was resumed in 1845.

[10] *Letters on American Debts* (2nd ed.; London, 1844), 7–10.

[11] *Memoir*, II, 508.

[12] Letter to John Keynon, June 29, 1843, in *Life, Letters and Journals of George Ticknor* (London, 1876), II, 214.

[13] *Ibid.*, II, 215–216.

[14] An English "New Song to an Old Tune" ("Yankee Doodle"), quoted in Duyckinck's *Wit and Wisdom*, 70–71.

[15] *Memoirs*, II, 505 ff.

[16] *Ibid.*, I, 303.

[17] *Ibid.*, II, 449.

The First Frontier

1933

PART OF THE INTRODUCTION TO *The Roots of National Culture* (NEW YORK: THE MACMILLAN COMPANY, 1933). AN ATTEMPT TO BUILD A THEORY OF AMERICAN LITERARY HISTORY BY COMBINING THE "TURNER THESIS" WITH AN ORGANIC CONCEPT OF LITERARY GROWTH DERIVED LARGELY FROM EMERSON, COLERIDGE, AND MY EARLY TEACHERS AND GUIDES, F. E. SCHELLING, C. G. CHILD, AND OTHERS.

AMERICAN LITERATURE was as cosmopolitan in its origins as it has been in its mature developments. Most of its distinguishing characteristics may be traced by one channel or another to European tradition. Our national culture, with the exception of the Indian, Negro, and Mongol strains in it, is a product of the migrations of the Western European peoples. The substratum of folksong, legend, and dance, which is present in all literatures, occurs in that of the United States chiefly among the Indians, and, in a transplanted form, among the Negroes, and the pioneers. Our literature of conscious art is largely derivative, or is a product of the impact of older cultures on a new environment.

The importance of the frontier movement in the later periods of American literature has received deserved emphasis, but the larger meaning of that movement as a phase in the westward progress of European civilization does not always receive the attention it deserves. In this larger view, the settlement of the eastern seaboard is the first chapter in the history of the American frontier, the explorers are the earliest pioneers, and the explorations of the interior by the French and Spanish are footnotes to that chapter. The first mature literary culture in America, the romantic movement which culminated in the writings of Emerson and his contemporaries, grew in the soil of the thirteen original colonies. There is some doubt as to whether the literature of the continental nation, as it was heralded by Walt Whitman, has even yet reached its maturity.

The first stage of literary culture in any primitive environment is the initial impact of the old upon the new. The pioneer blazes his trail and the settler follows with his ax. If these men write, their eyes look westward and they record first impressions and primitive emotional responses. They write narratives of discovery and settlement, and songs and ballads of the trail and camp.

The second stage of literary growth on the frontier results from the effort of men to make homes for themselves in the new environment. With group settlements of a more or less permanent nature, men begin to exchange their ideas and impressions among themselves. They discuss political, social, and religious problems. The local newssheet prints stories and verse copied from journals the pioneer has brought with him from his former home, and each community soon produces its own storytellers and its own bards. Eyes have already begun to look back to the land of origin, and there is a curious and crude mingling of the old with the new. The back-trail movement is already suggested, and with it, conscious literary production begins. The crude materials of the new environment are roughhewn into the traditional forms.

The third stage in the progress toward culture is a sudden revulsion from the crudities of the new environment. The settler has become homesick for his racial past and he goes back to the eastern sources of wisdom and beauty in order to improve his condition. Physically he remains the man of the frontier; mentally he has become the complete back-trailer. Whether he be Brockden Brown with his eyes on England, or William Dean Howells with his eyes on Boston, his mind and heart are those of the back-trailer.

The final stage is that in which civilization strikes root in new soil and sends out its own branches. The materials of the new environment are no longer rough-hewn into old forms. Life has matured, and its expression is complete—both old and new at once, and in harmony. The new environment is understood for itself and finds its own expression in accord with tradition.

If we apply this process to American literary history, we find all four stages represented in the period that we are here studying. The explorers and settlers of the eastern seaboard mark the first stage with their narratives of adventure. The process of settlement continued in these terms until the wall of the Appalachian Mountains and the resentful Indians together arrested the pioneer and brought about a permanent settlement along the coast from Boston to Charleston. Without too arbitrary an insistence upon dates, we may fix this period as extending from 1492 to about 1700. The second stage extends from 1700 to about 1760. During this time the settlers were developing their communities, establishing their first schools, printing their first newspapers, magazines, and books, debating their political, social, and religious ideals, collecting their libraries by importation from Europe, and in general adjusting their desire for a civilized life to an environment which was not yet ready to supply all the amenities of civilization. The third stage extends from 1760 to the close of the century and beyond. The Revolutionary War was the result and not the cause of adolescent pride in awakening powers and knowledge. The desire for independence is the first sign of manhood. In literary history, the characteristic production of this period is not so much the controversial writing of patriots and tories as a sudden torrent of novels, verse, plays, and essays in imitation of English and continental classics and best sellers. The back-trailer movement was the determining factor in spite of a strong and growing spirit of nationalism. In the terms of literary criticism, this was predominantly a period of convention, because even romantic writings were imitative and therefore in the spirit of convention. The final stage is marked by the beginning of an American romantic movement in the work of Channing, Bryant, Cooper, Irving, and their contemporaries.

These men were divided in their cultural loyalties between a growing comprehension of the meaning of the American environment and a romantic interest in European culture. Put Cooper's *The Pioneers* beside his *The Bravo* and the conflict in their minds is vividly illustrated. The essay in exhortation for a national literature was invariably written by a man who respected and feared Europe while he loved and overrated America.

American literature reached its first maturity in the Concord and Cambridge groups, and in the work of Poe, Melville, Whittier, Boker, and Simms, between 1820 and 1850. The evolutionary development was thus allowed to complete its cycle on the Atlantic seaboard at the same time that the process was being repeated in the first of its four stages, but this time against the background of the whole nation, with pioneers like Daniel Boone and Davy Crockett.

The only native literature with which the white settlers came into direct contact was that of the Indians. These races, originally nomadic, had developed a settled habit of life by the end of the fifteenth century, when the mistake of calling them "Indians" was first made by the searchers for a western trade route to the source of spices. In the Southwest and in Mexico they had built up a civilization which was comparable in its level of culture to many of those of Europe and Asia. The tribes of the Atlantic seacoast had developed a less complex civilization, but they had nevertheless a sense of tribal unity, of political, economic, and social organization and at least an oral literature of their own. Indians figure in the works of Freneau, Paulding, Cooper, and even Longfellow, not so much for what they were as for what the white man believed them to be. Only recently has their culture been at all understood for itself and absorbed into our literary tradition.

The Indian provides the first element in the cosmopolitan origins of our literature; the explorers and early settlers, the second. America was discovered and settled first by Spaniards; the French were as active as the English during the seventeenth century; and the Dutch, the Swedes, and almost all the other races of Europe made their contributions to the westward migration which established the white man on our shores. Even today a cursory study of the Atlantic seaboard will reveal cultural survivals of the Spaniards in Florida, of the Dutch in New York, of the Germans in Pennsylvania, and of the French in southeastern Canada. The Mississppi Valley has not entirely forgotten its French origins; and the Southwest and far West are still proud of their Spanish traditions. To forget Columbus, Coronado, Champlain, and their fellows is to ignore vital factors in the story of America's cultural origins. But like that of the Indians, the part which these early adventurers contributed to the ground work of our literary history has only recently been recognized as our heritage in the writings of Willa Cather, Archibald MacLeish, and Mary Austin, and of the historians, archaeologists, and anthropologists.

Our principal attention must therefore still be directed to the small band of English settlers on the Atlantic seaboard. The dogged perseverance of the Puritans and the serene confidence of the Quakers in the face of appalling obstacles leaves the modern mind aghast. Less unified perhaps, but nonetheless enduring were the motives for settlement in the South. The Catholic cavaliers of Maryland and the Virginia gentlemen shaped the destinies of these colonies in the early days, but the middle-class pioneer and small farmer did the actual work of clearing the forests and of laying the foundations for an agricultural society in the South as they did in the North. The progress of these English tradesmen and farmers from the bare conquest of a wilderness to a state stable enough for the luxuries of culture was slow. The Spaniards, the French, and the Elizabethan seamen gaily transplanted their cultures and went home again, leaving them to decay and to survive only in memory and in written record. The English middle class were less concerned with the amenities; they laid the foundations of a new state in religious, economic, and social adjustment to a primitive environment, and, with their German and Scots-Irish neighbors, left the development of culture to their descendants of later generations.

With such origins, the Colonial mind could hardly be unified. Its predominant characteristic is diversity rather than una-
nimity of opinion on questions of first importance to man on this
earth. No men could be more at odds in their readings of life
than were John Smith and John Winthrop, Cotton Mather and
William Byrd. Puritanism was only one, even though probably
the most enduring, of many elements in seventeenth and eighteenth century thought in America. Even within Puritanism itself
the strict Calvinism of the Massachusetts Bay Colony is offset
by a liberalism among the Plymouth colonists, which historians
have traced back to John Wyclif and his Lollard priests of
Chaucerian England. Except for the Quaker influence in Pennsylvania, the dominant trait of the middle and southern colonists
was a practical interest in the problems of this world, which led
them to science, agriculture, the law, society, and politics. It was
the blending of this secular practicality and rationality with the
disciplined idealism of New England that laid the philosophical
foundations for the political thinking of the revolutionary period.

The four colonies which did most to determine colonial
thought were Massachusetts, Virginia, Pennsylvania, and New
York. The other nine were either offshoots of these four, or were
strongly influenced by them. New York and Virginia were basically cavalier and aristocratic; Pennsylvania and Massachusetts,
middle class and democratic. The Church of England had its
greatest following in the first pair, the dissenting sects in the second. New York was distinguished from Virginia in that its social
organization was created by the Dutch patroons, whereas that in
the South was modeled on an English pattern. Pennsylvania's
differences from Massachusetts were not social. Penn, himself
a landed proprietor at home, attracted to his following the same
classes of tradesmen and farmers that came over in the *Mayflower*
and the *Arbella*. Difference in religious beliefs, however, shaped
their social attitudes and made the resultant colonies very different in character.

Virginia and Massachusetts have retained their distinctive
characters even to the present; and at least one cause of the Civil

War seems to have been the clash between their sectional interests and ideals. Paulding recognized this situation as early as 1812
when he likened the "Southland" to the ticklish eyes, and the
"Down East" to the ticklish nose, of the nation. But by his time
the New York proprietors had lost their influence because of
their tory sympathies, and the "Middlelands" could be characterized as "steady, sober-minded farmers." The "Far West" was to
him a vague region of little character at all. The colonial writers
of Massachusetts and of Virginia each strongly reflect their respective backgrounds of religious, social, and economic ideals.
New York and Pennsylvania writers reveal backgrounds almost
as narrowly determined in the early days, but by the end of the
eighteenth century the sharper lines in their thought had been
softened; and it was they who first attempted an orderly expression of their lives in literary and other art forms. The so-called
"Philadelphia" and "Knickerbocker" groups were the first to
take literature seriously and for its own sake.

The story of the New England church-state is told in the rise
and fall of the Mather dynasty through four generations. The
dogmatism of Richard Mather and John Cotton, the founders
of the family, is mild when compared to that of their grandson
and namesake, Cotton Mather. They and their contemporaries,
however, accepted fully the doctrine that the Puritans were a
second chosen people and that Massachusetts was a new Canaan.
Life in this world was shaped in terms of rewards and punish-
ments in the next, meted out by a God who was just in the old
Judaic sense, and whose praise was sung by poets from Michael
Wigglesworth to Robert Frost. From the Mayflower Compact
to the Half-Way Covenant of 1662, the progress of American
Puritanism is marked by an increasing determination on the part
of a few strong-willed leaders to establish a Holy Commonwealth
in fact as well as in theory. The wars with the Indians without
and Satan within were holy wars that culminated in the witchcraft trials at the end of the century, an example of religious
fanaticism that can only be explained by a zeal born of despera-
tion and fear. The greatest of the Captains of the Lord was Increase Mather, of the second generation. His was a war with

heresy which had become organized in the defiance of the Brattle Street Group and the Stoddardeans during the final decade of the century; but with the revocation of the Massachusetts charter in 1692 the temporal authority of the church came to an end. The zeal of its leaders was vainly intensified in Cotton Mather, of the third generation, who lived his best years during this period of loss of power. His history and defense of the movement, the *Magnalia,* has aptly been termed by Schneider to have been, "even at the time of its publication in 1702, little more than a ponderous monument erected over a dead cause." Increase Mather died in 1723, Cotton in 1728. Samuel Mather, of the fourth generation, carried on the war with his *Apology for the Liberties of the Churches in New England* (1738), but temporal power was gone.

The fall of the church-state in New England may be interpreted, in political terms, as the failure of an oligarchic dictatorship to master a people of independent spirit. But the deeper causes of its failure lie buried in the creed upon which it was founded. The desire for liberty of conscience which brought the Pilgrims to America was the seed of that critical independence of mind which flowered in the rationalism of Franklin and Paine, and not in the determinism of the Mathers. The Puritans were better organized in the early days than were their antagonists, but the latter were nonetheless vocal and persistent, and the end of the Colonial period is marked by their complete triumph.

The first step in the destruction of Puritan authority came from within the Massachusetts Bay Colony itself in the Arminian and Antinomian heresies, in the persons of the early radicals, and in the political liberalism that grew out of the attacks on church government. Thomas Hooker was a mild liberal, but Roger Williams, the most influential of these early radicals, attacked both the dogma and the organization of the church-state. In the "Bloudy Tenent" controversy with John Cotton, he assailed the root of that dogma, the doctrine of "persecution for cause of conscience." But Williams was primarily a political and social rather than a religious thinker. The enduring significance of his revolt lies rather in his substitution of the social compact for the divine right theory of the state, whereby he laid the foundations for Jeffersonian democracy. Like Williams, John Wise began his revolt on theological grounds, but his real interest was in the institutional rather than the doctrinal problems of the church, and his thought led to similar conclusions. In the revolt of these two men, and in the broad tolerance of William Penn, may readily be discovered the roots of the political idealism which brought about the Revolutionary War and determined the character of our government.

A more philosophical form of reasoning, the analytical study of science and natural phenomena, disturbed the Calvinistic integrity of the two ablest defenders of the faith, Cotton Mather and Jonathan Edwards, the former in his age and the latter in his youth. More serious, however, was the call to reason as opposed to authoritarian dogma which was early heard outside the fold of the elect. Robert Calef made a direct attack upon the witchcraft fanaticism of the Mathers, but his mind was not sufficiently orderly to produce a positive philosophy as a substitute for that which he scorned. It was Benjamin Franklin and his friends in the Middle and Southern colonies who first accomplished a satisfactory transition from dogma to reason.

Although the term "philosopher" was perhaps applied more frequently to Franklin, both at home and abroad, than to any other American of his day, he was not a metaphysician in the strict sense. His was a natural philosophy, the product of an objective curiosity about nature and a belief in man. Although his earlier essays contain a clear statement of a deistic creed, he was more utilitarian than contemplative in his habit of mind. He was a pragmatist a century before the term was invented, and he formulated a creed and a philosophy in order to use rather than to enjoy them. Having established an objective nature, he proceeded to devote his attention to its scientific analysis, an impulse which Mather and Edwards had felt before him, but without the same philosophical justification. After convincing himself of the free will of man by arguing its contrary, he turned the moral zeal of his ancestors toward teaching him how to live happily and profitably in this world rather than to prepare for the next. His belief in a benevolent God of limited powers allowed him to take that personage for granted in his interesting and active daily life; while his spirit of inquiry stimulated an intense activity in the sciences of botany, medicine, and electricity, particularly in Philadelphia in the work of men like John Bartram and Benjamin Rush, during the years immediately before and after the war.

The deism of Tom Paine, in his *Age of Reason* (1793–95), was of a more metaphysical nature than was that of Franklin. During his sojourn in America, Paine thought more about politics than religion or philosophy, but his *Age of Reason* is so logical a climax to his earlier radicalism that it must be claimed for American literature if the political pamphlets on the Revolutionary War are included. Entirely unoriginal as it was, this tract carried the thought of French and English rationalists to the banks of the Ohio and the mountains of Kentucky.

Similar in its inquiring spirit and its emphasis on common sense was the philosophy which found congenial soil at Princeton after the advent of President Witherspoon in 1768. It must be remembered that Brackenridge, Freneau, and Madison were among the students who came under this influence, just as Godfrey and Hopkinson came under a similar influence at the infant University of Pennsylvania; and the seething political activity of these undergraduates bears testimony to the absence of other-worldliness in their intellectual life. Calvinism had little power in the states of Pennsylvania and New Jersey when the minds of Franklin, Mason, Jefferson, Adams, Hamilton, and their fellows were transmuting these "commonsense" philosophies into the system of government and the social organization which gave first form to the national character.

The philosophical idealism that early developed, both within and without the fold of Calvinism, has even more place in American literary history than have these more materialistic schools of thought because, in its late development in the minds of Emerson and the Concord transcendentalists, it became one of the most vital factors in the romantic movement in this country. Its influence had already been clearly felt in New England before Bishop Berkeley came to Newport, Rhode Island, in 1729 and discussed with his American friends the theory that matter does not exist. His threat to the dogmatic and authoritarian position of the New England Calvinists lay rather in the incentive he gave to free and speculative thought than in any fundamental heresy in his system. But there was no holy war; the danger was too far-reaching to be immediately alarming. Berkeley made few American friends or disciples except Samuel Johnson, tutor at Yale and later president of King's College (Columbia). Franklin revealed his sympathy with the movement by assuming the expense of printing the latter's *Elementa Philosophica*, which was used as a text at both Columbia and the College in Philadelphia.

As an undergraduate at Yale, Jonathan Edwards expressed, in his paper *Of Being*, an idealism almost identical with that of Berkeley, but investigation has failed to prove that there was any direct influence of the English philosopher upon him. Rather, we may attribute the early liberalism, which later hardened into a dogmatic Calvinism, to his reading of Locke and other rationalist philosophers in college. His youthful experiences during a personal religious awakening led him to a mysticism not unlike that of Woolman and the Quakers. The "sense of divine things" of which he writes in his personal narrative brought to him a humility that was intense and immediate. There was no intermediary authority, either of Bible or minister, between his own soul and the spirit of beauty that was his God. The Judaism of the Mathers broke down before the intensity of this personal experience, and the last of the great Puritan divines prostrated his spirit before the "fresh Visitations of Heavenly Love," of which the Quaker Woolman wrote with such singleness of heart. That early evangelical revival at Northampton, which has been termed the "Great Awakening," was the result, when Edwards himself became the authority that administered justice, and the spirit of the Mathers returned. But his mysticism never entirely left him, and it prepared the way, a century later, for the intensely personal religion of William Ellery Channing and the Unitarians, and later for the revolt of Emerson, that archrebel among rebels, who finally declared that self-reliance rather than reliance upon book and dogma was the only key to salvation.

During the century between Edwards and Channing there was

little development of idealism as a metaphysical system. The issues which led up to the Revolutionary War, and the problems of reconstruction, turned men's minds from abstractions to more materialistic habits of thought. There was, however, one countermovement, in spirit akin to Edwards' most extreme mysticism. Between 1738 and 1769, George Whitefield, one of the most enthusiastic and compelling followers of Wesley, made seven trips to America in order to preach the Evangelical revival. An enemy to common sense and dogma alike, Whitefield made many converts to the faith which comes from emotional conviction. The movement took firmest root in the South, but its influence was felt throughout the colonies, and at least a slight connection may be traced between it and the more intellectual liberalism of Channing.

Channing's attack on Calvinism was direct and vigorous. Slight in body, but silver-tongued, his persuasive eloquence carried the younger elements in New England with him when, in his Baltimore sermon of 1819, he gave the Unitarian revolt its first clear definition. Abroad, his name was linked with those of Irving and Cooper in the first group of writers in that national literature for which he pleaded so earnestly. As a literary critic, his work was limited to a few reviews in the *Christian Examiner*, and it all was colored by his religious convictions. But his thought gave courage to the fearful and provided a metaphysical reason for independence, a valuable supplement to the political independence derived from the commonsense rationalism of Franklin.

The political events that caused the Revolutionary War focused all of Colonial thought on an immediate and practical issue. It was not difficult to lead the various types of individualism developed by Roger Williams, Jonathan Edwards, and Benjamin Franklin up to Tom Paine's succinct conclusion: " 'Tis repugnant to reason, to the universal order of things; to all examples from former ages, to suppose, that this continent can long remain subject to any external power." He cut the issue clearly: "Should the colonies remain a part of the British Empire, or should they not?" His answer was that they should not, and this he called common sense; but not all his intelligent compatriots saw the problem in so white a light. John Dickinson, temperamentally a conservative, was whipped into the rebel position by what he believed to be unjust taxation. Franklin made up his mind slowly and gave his love of conciliation full play. Jefferson, the wisest political philosopher in the rebel camp, reasoned himself to a firm conviction in democracy and wrote arguments similar to Paine's into the Declaration of Independence. Samuel Adams and Patrick Henry were born agitators, and rebellion came easily to them. But lawyers and statesmen like Alexander Hamilton, John Adams, and James Wilson reached a similar point of view less hastily; for not all political radicals favored a break with England, not all conservatives were tories. The revolutionary issue was less one of reasoned political philosophy than an indignation against tyranny in a specific case. Rebels were not all Democrats, nor were all tories Federalists, when the later issue, the best form for the new government to take, shaped itself into a clash between liberal and conservative thinkers.

The Loyalists fell into such extreme disfavor after the break with England that their writings have received less emphasis than they deserve. Samuel Seabury, the first American bishop of the Protestant Episcopal Church, was a man of cultivated mind and the author of a number of vigorous sermons and political tracts. William Smith, the first Provost of the College in Philadelphia, was a thorough liberal in his thought on religion, education, and politics, but his oath of personal allegiance to the King made it impossible for him, as it was for Seabury, to endorse absolute separation. Jonathan Boucher, also an Anglican clergyman, gave perhaps the most vigorous expression to toryism in sober prose, as did Jonathan Odell in satire and Joseph Galloway in pamphlets almost as vigorous as Paine's. Nor were the Loyalists without their verse apologists, as the ballads of the Revolutionary War will bear witness.

The poetry of the so-called "Hartford Wits" reveals clearly the distinction which must be made between the revolutionary and the national issues. Conservative as Dwight was in theology, he joined with Trumbull, Barlow, and their lesser associates in patriotic zeal and the spirit of rebellion. But Barlow alone of the group was a Democrat in the post-Revolutionary days. His later poems and pamphlets are as radical as his earlier, and his visit to France made him follow Paine's thought in most matters of importance to government and religion.

The literary groups of New Jersey and Pennsylvania were similarly divided upon the two issues. Francis Hopkinson was a Loyalist up to the eve of the war, devoted his poetry to the cause of revolution, and served the Federalists with his prose satire after the peace. Philip Freneau was, however, a rebel and later a Jeffersonian Democrat, as was his college mate, Brackenridge.

Although there were many shades of opinion on the national issue between Democracy and Federalism, the extreme spokesmen of the two groups were respectively Thomas Jefferson and Alexander Hamilton. John Adams was a Federalist of milder stamp than Hamilton, and James Madison joined with the latter in the series of papers which took its name from that of the party in whose support it was published.

Jeffersonian Democracy in its purest form rests upon faith in the integrity, idealism, and capacity for self-government of the average man. It was suggested in the thought of Williams, Wise, Penn, and other early radicals, but it came to America, in 1775, in an almost unpolluted stream from the French encyclopaedists. This political philosophy in its application to the immediate situation in America found perhaps its briefest statement in the Declaration of Independence. Hamilton's *Federalist* essays served a similar purpose for the opposing belief that man is selfish and ignorant, and that he requires a strong and arbitrary government to regulate his actions. The war between these two political philosophies shaped the early and influenced all the later years of our national life. Their effect upon our literature was indirect, as most of our early literary men were not active in politics after the turn of the century, but Cooper, Irving, Bryant, and many others were strongly influenced by their political sympathies.

By the middle of the eighteenth century, therefore, the men of our first frontier had marked out the geographical and mental boundaries of a new civilization and had laid foundations in political, social, economic, religious and philosophical thought upon which we as a nation have been building ever since. The time was ripe for the later generations to turn to the amenities of a more settled and cultured life.

New Wine in Old Bottles

1957

READ IN THE WINTERTHUR LECTURE SERIES OF THE UNIVERSITY OF DELAWARE, FEBRUARY 20, 1957. MOST OF THE QUOTATIONS FROM EARLY AMERICAN LITERATURE WILL BE FOUND IN *The Roots of National Culture*. THIS ESSAY WAS NOT PUBLISHED, BUT THE SAME IDEA WAS ADAPTED FOR A SERIES DELIVERED IN THE UNITED STATES INFORMATION SERVICE LIBRARY IN LONDON IN OCTOBER, 1958, AND PUBLISHED IN *The Great Experiment*, EDITED BY CARL BODE (LONDON: HEINEMANN, 1961).

PRIOR TO ABOUT 1770, published American writing took the forms chiefly of speeches, sermons, and tracts on political and religious topics. Much of this writing was literary in the sense that it observed the rules of rhetoric and composition, but its primary purposes were occasional and utilitarian. No novels were written and no plays professionally produced—perhaps partly because there were no regular publishers or theatres—and the scores of minor poets and essayists allowed their work to remain in manuscript or seek the anonymity of local newspapers and broadsides. Poets like Edward Taylor, who had to wait more than two centuries to be "discovered," were apparently far more numerous even than poets like that Tenth Muse, Anne Bradstreet, whose gentle and imitative verses were spirited away and issued in London, much to her chagrin. Although the researches of Ralph Rusk, Harold Jantz, and others have indicated that there is—or, at least, was—far more of this kind of production than we now realize, I think it can safely be said that the idea of literature before 1770 was pretty well limited to belles lettres, for which there was little time in so busy a land as the western Atlantic colonies. Franklin was the exception when he wrote and published vigorous prose satires in the manner of Swift, but on American themes. To the inhabitants of the New World, the written word had a more serious mission in life than to entertain in idleness, and such "literature" as there was was English.

The year 1770 has no special significance in American political or literary history. Perhaps no less eventful year could be found in all that eventful era; it was what the farmers call a "weather-breeder," a calm day before a storm. On September 12th of that year, the twenty-year-old John Trumbull delivered an oration at the public commencement of Yale College on the "Prospect of the Future Glory of America"; and, exactly a year later, Philip Freneau and H. H. Brackenridge read their graduation poem on the same subject at Princeton. Looking back over the past century and a half, these young men could see only the steady growth of the infant colonies in peace and prosperity; looking ahead to the infinite and unexplored possibility of the future, they felt they could promise that

Paradise anew
Shall flourish, by no second Adam lost.

The decade which followed had little resemblance to Eden before even a fortunate fall. It was one of storm and stress, in which the diverse colonies were to be welded into a single nation and the poems and essays of these same young men were to desert the Augustinian calm of Addison and Pope for rougher and more polemical kinds of satire and invective in prose and verse. There was little published during that decade other than volumes of sermons and political pamphlets, except for a scattering of experimentation in the magazines in the satirical manners of Butler, Swift, and Johnson. If there was a belles lettristic movement under way, it was pretty much submerged in the tempestuous currents of the times.

With the Treaty of Paris in 1783, two quite contradictory

tendencies became apparent almost at once. In what I am tempted to call for the purposes of this discussion "the literature of use," the note of protest against political injustice gave way to that of vigorous nationalism, while in "the literature of art" there was a sudden and unannounced crop of poems, plays, novels, and essays, modeled mainly on the then current modes of London and the Continent but expressing American ideas and scenes. Noah Webster issued his challenge on behalf of an American grammar and dictionary adequate to express distinctively American conditions and institutions, Jedidiah Morse compiled his American geography, and Jefferson's *Notes on Virginia* and *The Federalist* papers defined the two basic philosophies of American government. At the same time, Freneau, Trumbull, and Barlow published their most characteristic poems; Hopkinson, Dennie, and Brown produced American versions of the Addisonian essay; and Thomas Wignall produced Royall Tyler's *The Contrast* in the John Street Theatre in New York. Except for the novel, which was a latecomer in English literature too, the United States could, by 1790, be said to have the beginnings of a "polite" literature of its own. A perceptible line had been drawn between utilitarian writing and belles lettres, and the latter was becoming a recognizable product of the new nation.

The final decade of the eighteenth century saw these trends carried forward and their promises confirmed. The young poets, dramatists, and essayists seemed to establish their positions, while the novels of Rowson, Brackenridge, and Brown, and the nature essays of Bartram and Crèvecœur began the literary exploitation of the American way of life and the American scene. It is one of the unsolved mysteries of our literary history, therefore, that the end of the century witnessed also the virtual end of this movement. By 1810, this entire generation of writers had died, left the country, or turned to more practical pursuits like law, politics, and journalism. All of them had virtually ceased the publication of poetry, essay, fiction, and drama, and all the magazines to which they had contributed had folded. A quarter of a century passed before the new generation of writers—of which Cooper, Irving, Bryant, and Halleck were the leading figures—again established the movement which Freneau, Brown, Brackenridge, and Tyler had abandoned at what was apparently the moment of its first success.

This much we can therefore say at the beginning of our study: Whatever literary movement had already started at the time of the Revolution received a shot in the arm from the nationalistic spirit of the war period and its aftermath. With peace and increased national challenge, it developed steadily until the end of the century, when it seems to have stopped abruptly, not to be reactivated until a whole new literary generation had taken over. Irving's *Sketch Book*, Cooper's *The Spy*, and Bryant's first collection of poems appeared almost simultaneously in 1820 and 1821.

II

There are two questions which confront the literary historian who must try to explain these facts: first, what was the nature of this literary movement and in what ways was it distinctively American? and second, why did it stop just when it seemed to have established itself?

A closer look at this handful of writers and at the conditions under which they worked may supply a few clues to the answer to these questions. They were young men of pretty much the same generation, and most of them were drawn together and inspired to creative writing while they were students or tutors at one or another of the recently founded colonial colleges. The earliest group seems to have been that at the College in Philadelphia under its first Provost William Smith; another—the so-called "Hartford Wits"—were all associated in one way or another with Yale College; a third with the newly founded Nassau Hall, or Princeton, then under the presidency of John Witherspoon. All of these groups were inspired by a desire to reform the curriculum by the introduction of work in contemporary English literature rather than by uniformly radical social, political, or theological ideas. In fact, Timothy Dwight, a leading member of the Connecticut group, was later to become one of the last defenders of the strictest Puritan theology. On

the other hand, Dwight's college friend Joel Barlow later became famous—or infamous—for his Jacobin radicalism and
agnosticism.

This common interest in contemporary literature was also
reflected in the founding of circulating libraries and of informal
literary clubs for the reading and writing of verse and prose
in most of the seaboard towns, an interest that was further
fostered by the increase of bookstores which served as meeting
places for these discussions as well as agencies for the publication of experimental magazines and newspapers and the loaning
as well as the selling of the latest imported books. Booksellers
like Mathew Carey in Philadelphia, John Wiley in New York,
and later James T. Fields in Boston and John Russell in Charleston have played a more important role in American literary
history than we sometimes realize. But even before 1800, there
was scarcely a town of reasonable size in any of the colonies
which could not boast its bookseller who also provided a library
and social center for a literary group. The fact that these groups
were so local and that there was comparatively little interchange
among them may be one reason for the intensity and also for
the short duration of the movement.

The versatile lawyer, musician, and writer Francis Hopkinson,
the painter Benjamin West, and the playwright Thomas Godfrey were all members of the little pioneering group which, although not all students at the College, came under the influence
of Provost William Smith during the late 'fifties and 'sixties
and were encouraged by him to read contemporary literature
and to try their own hands at poems, paintings, music, and
plays. Philip Freneau and Hugh Henry Brackenridge shared
the excitement of revolutionary ferment with James Madison
at Princeton, where all three were members of the Class of
1771; and John Trumbull, Joel Barlow, Timothy Dwight and
others of the group of Connecticut Wits were variously associated with Yale, Dwight being its president from 1795 to 1817.
Stimulated by these associations, these young men and others
like them started to keep notebooks of their own poems and
essays, to read original work to one another, and to start, with

the help of their bookseller friends, local magazines, and newspapers. All went well until the responsibilities of life caught up with them and they found that at best literature would serve as an avocation. Some of the diehards complained and persisted, and for them Robert Slender, Esq., Freneau's cobbler-essayist who signed his Letters "O.S.M." or "One of the Swinish Multitude," supplied a wry analysis of the lot of his fellow American authors. You should, he advises, beware of patrons, who were "first invented by slaves and have been continued by fools and sycophants." You should also avoid doctors of law and divinity and other wearers of "square black caps," for a scholar and an original author are "as different from each other as a fresh and salt water sailor." Do not, he advises, depend upon advance subscriptions, but be content to live in poverty in a garret, preserving your pride, or, if this course fails, "retire to some uninhabited island or desert, and there, at your leisure, end your life with decency." But in a more realistic mood, he admits amazement that we should have any authors at all in a land two hundred years ago peopled only by savages and since then continually under a republican form of government, and he advises his fellows for the present to graft their "authorship upon some other calling . . . in the same manner as the helpless ivy takes hold of the vigorous oak."

One of the obstacles that Robert Slender did not mention was the absence of any copyright before 1790 for American authors and the total lack of protection for many years after that against his uncopyrighted British contemporaries. Most of the contents of American magazines and almost all of the books printed by American booksellers in these years were by British authors, because there was less work and less risk in republishing imports than in helping unknown Americans. The passage of a national copyright act in 1790 tended to stimulate rather than curb this uneven competition because the American act protected only writers of American citizenship whereas the British common law practice protected rights by prior publication in England. It was not until James Fenimore Cooper learned how to turn this situation to the advantage of the American author by publishing his novels first in England that his compatriots could establish themselves professionally in the literary market.

Circumstantial as well as other factors therefore tended to force the young American author of the later eighteenth century to imitate the latest imports from England even though his ideas and impulses might be wholly American. Because it was easier for him to find a place in a newspaper or magazine than to publish a book, his first efforts were likely to be in the established literary forms of the familiar essay, the prose satire, and the short poem, usually lyric or satiric. But with the hard facts of life in the New World confronting him and with the issues of political revolt from England pressing, he was likely first to choose prose and to avoid literary embellishment. Benjamin Franklin tells us that he early learned to write by imitating Addison, but he must also have known Swift and Defoe, for his later political satires, like "The Sale of the Hessians," follow closely the form of "The Shortest Way with Dissenters" and "A Modest Proposal." Most other American political writers, however, did not attempt so subtle a device as satire. Tom Paine, James Otis, Joseph Galloway and others threw themselves into the War of the Pamphlets and wrote straightforward political argument.

III

In no other department did American writers of these days draw the line so sharply between such utilitarian aims as these and what the eighteenth century delighted in calling "belles lettres," or literature for its own sake, as in the periodical essay. An honorable ancestry that went back to the *Spectator*, the *Tatler*, Johnson's *Rambler*, and Fielding's *Champion*, this highly conventionalized literary mode was copied avidly in the American periodicals. The Philadelphia group of Provost Smith contributed to his *American Magazine or Monthly Chronicle for the British Colonies* (1757-1758) essays by "Timothy Timbertoes," the "Antigallican," "Miss Barbara Shallow," and "The Prowler," while Smith himself dispensed religious and moral advice under the penname of "The Hermit." But the withdrawal of several of the "society of Gentlemen" responsible for these contributions brought the magazine to an end after only a year, and those which succeeded it under the editorship of Tom Paine, H. H. Brackenridge, and other political stalwarts were too much engrossed in the issues of the day to indulge in anything lighter than the "essays moral, religious, and literary" which were later collected into solemn volumes by Noah Webster, the lexicographer, Dr. Benjamin Rush, and Brackenridge himself, who had hoped, in the *United States Magazine* (1779), to prove to the British officers that "liberty is of so noble and energetic a quality, as even from the bosom of a war to call forth the powers of human genius, in every course of literary fame and improvement."

This was also much the tone of the periodical essays which sprang up like mushrooms after the peace. Brockden Brown's "The Rhapsodist" in the *Columbian Magazine* (1789) and "The Man at Home" in the *Weekly Magazine* (1788) chatted solemnly on such topics as the values of meditation, financial solvency, and learning the niceties of English, together with much speculation on yellow fever and other maladies. The poet Freneau, who has already been quoted in the person of his Robert Slender, dedicated his works "to the Freeman, the Lovers of Liberty, the Asserters, Maintainers, and Supporters of Independence throughout the United States," and, like a latterday columnist, strove to "make democracy live." These essays are lively and full of concrete instances, but in a more mellow mood Freneau also celebrated nature's nobleman and the delights of solitude in "The Philosopher of the Forest."

Various other discoveries by the "Neighbor" (*Massachusetts Spy*), the "Gleaner" of Mrs. Judith Murray, and Noah Webster's the "Prompter" prepared the way for that prince of American Addisonians, Joseph Dennie, who, as "The Lay Preacher" in the *Farmer's Museum* (1795) and later in the Philadelphia *Port-Folio*, inveighed against Wine, Slothfulness, Immodesty in Dress and Ornament, Demagogues, and Democrats. Dennie's essays would probably have killed the genre of its own weight had it not been revived in 1808 by Irving, Paulding, and their Knickerbocker pals to "instruct the young,

reform the old, correct the town, and castigate the age" in
Salmagundi (1807–1808). With this new and livelier generation, the periodical essay came of age as an expression of the
American genius. The solemn moralizing of the earlier American Spectators, born of British urban manners rather than native
American puritanism, had surrendered to Yankee wit and au-
dacity. The form was the same, but the contents had spilled
over.

IV

In poetry, there was even less invention in form, even more
straining of ideas to burst their belles lettristic barriers. Francis
Hopkinson, author of perhaps the liveliest of the early essays on
"White-Washing," or the disease that afflicts the female of the
species each spring and causes her to put the male out on the lawn
with the furniture while she performs her annual cleaning, was
also the author of some of the liveliest early verse. Together with
pseudo-Elizabethan songs and eighteenth-century rhymed satires,
he produced perhaps the most famous of Revolutionary ballads,
"A Pretty Story," a little over a decade after Bishop Percy's
Reliques had revived the ballad form in English poetry. This
witty satire on the British occupancy of Philadelphia tells how
Washington's troops, higher up on the Delaware, launched pos-
sibly the first attack with floating mines in military history.

> Gallants attend and hear a friend,
>   Trill forth harmonious ditty,
> Strange things I'll tell which late befel
>   In Philadelphia city.

Hopkinson had a grace and a flexibility in all that he wrote,
which is not so evident in the verse of John Trumbull, Timothy
Dwight, Joel Barlow, and the Connecticut Wits in general.
These earnest young men illustrate perhaps better than any other
American writers of the day the paradox of trying to express
ideas of liberty and revolt in the stiff neoclassical and quasi-
romantic forms of Butler, Pope, Goldsmith, Cowper, and Gray
and to describe the unruly American scene in meters suited to

the placid English countryside. The much admired and imitated *Hudibras* provided the mock-heroic tetrameter line for Trumbull's poetry as well as for many other verses of this group. Rabelais and Cervantes lie in the shadows behind Butler's attack on the Puritans in England, but in the American versions, Rabelais is missing and Cervantes has lost much of his gaiety and absurdity. Trumbull is out to explore hypocrisy in his attack on Yale undergraduates, *The Progress of Dulness* (1772–1773), who

> With sleepy eyes and count'nance heavy,
> With much excuse of *non paravi*,
> Much absence, *tardes*, and *egresses*

finally

> Stalks abroad with conscious stride,
> In all the airs of pedant pride,
> With passport sign'd for wit and knowledge,
> And current underseal of college.

But his satiric ire reaches its full force in his exposé of the Tory squire hung to the Liberty Pole in *M'Fingal* (1775). The *ad hoc* court assembled at the pole waited "in silent awe" while the clerk proclaimed the "dread decree"

> That Squire M'Fingal having grown
> The vilest Tory in the town,
> And now in full examination
> Convicted by his own confession,
> Finding no tokens of repentence,
> This Court proceed to render sentence

that, like Whittier's Skipper Ireson, he be tarred and feathered and carried in a cart.

There is grim humor, if humor at all, in this tirade on liberty, for the events and issues under review were too immediate and too serious for the light touch of satire, but the mock-heroic tone is maintained, and one can smile—even though somewhat grimly—at the predicament of the Squire who could no longer

> prove his claim to human nature,
> As a two-legg'd, unfeather'd creature.

It is not for their major works that the Connecticut versi-
fiers are chiefly remembered. Trumbull wrote nothing more
ambitious than *M'Fingal,* became a staunch Federalist and practiced law for fifty years, and died, after three years of Andrew
Jackson, in 1831. Timothy Dwight, a fellow wit and tutor at
Yale, wrote, in addition to sermons and tracts, two religious
poems, *The Conquest of Canaan* (1785) and *The Triumph of
Infidelity* (1788), conservative in politics and theology and neoclassical in form, but he is remembered for his pastoral meditation, *Greenfield Hill* (1794). Joel Barlow stormed the gates of
immortality with his massive American epic, *The Columbiad*
(1787, 1807), but lives rather as the author of a whimsical and
homesick mock-epic on his beloved *Hasty Pudding* (1796), a
meditation in a French café on the homely joys of yellow corn
meal mush.

Both Dwight and Barlow were inspired in part by Goldsmith's *Deserted Village*—Barlow by the idea that a humble poem
may urge an important reform in the habits of men and Dwight
more directly in an effort to prove that Connecticut could boast
rural charms to equal or excel the best of England's.

Barlow opens with an exhortation:

> Ye Alps audacious, thro' the heavens that rise
> To cramp the day and hide me from the skies,
> Ye Gallic flags, that o'er their heights unfurl'd,
> Bear death to kings, and freedom to the world,
> I sing not you. . . .
> I sing . . . the charms I feel
> My morning incense, and my evening meal,
> The sweets of Hasty-Pudding.

Pope's *Iliad* is here in spirit and form, though the subject be
the common man rather than the hero. Democracy, with tongue
in cheek, is writing her own poetry, as she does again in Dwight's

> Fair Verna! loveliest village of the West;
> Of every joy, and every charm, possess'd. . . .

Yes, let the proud despise, the rich deride,
These humble joys, to Competence allied:
To me, the bloom, all fragrant to my heart,
Nor ask the pomp of wealth, nor gloss of art.

Despite the obvious echo of Goldsmith's

Sweet Auburn! loveliest village of the plain

Greenfield Hill is based more immediately on Denham's *Cooper's Hill*, even though its mixtures of Spenserian stanzas, heroic couplets, and blank verse form a loosely knit poem on rural scenes and rural joys, with the various parts reminiscent of Goldsmith, Beattie, Thomson, Pope, and Gray respectively.

Patriotism rather than political radicalism and appreciation of natural beauties rather than of formal gardens were not explosive enough materials to carry these poets much if at all beyond the limits of such neoclassical nature poets as Thomson and Pope. There is no touch of the village intimacy of Crabbe, the Gothic melancholy of Gray and the other "graveyard" poets, or the immediate simplicity and awareness of Wordsworth—or even of Cowper or Burns. On the other hand, their New Jersey contemporary Philip Freneau seems to have been aware from the start of all these other currents in the romanticism to come. In fact, he even anticipated Coleridge and Shelley in some of their most characteristic ideas and themes. Why this is so is hard to say, because Freneau was an adventurer rather than a scholar and he wrote mainly about what he himself had seen and experienced.

Yet a degree of scholarship to which I myself do not pretend could probably do a pretty good job on the sources of Freneau's poetry and ideas. His biographer, Lewis Leary, has collected enough evidence to make a good case for the influence of his studies, of his personal reading, and of his friendships while an undergraduate at Nassau Hall. But Leary also makes the point that he was first of all a man of emotion, with a consuming ambition to be a poet, rather than a philosopher or politician. Probably he was fortunate to have arrived at Princeton when the Scottish Presbyterian minister John Witherspoon was presi-

dent, for Witherspoon *was* a philosopher—specifically of the
empirical school of the Scottish rationalists rather than of that
of the Berkeleyan idealists—as well as a firm believer in the liberty of the individual both as citizen and as college undergraduate. He imbued the students with the spirit of independence in
political matters and of inquiry in their studies. Freneau's reading moved from an early enthusiasm for Pope, Dryden, and
Thomson directly back to Milton and Shakespeare, to Horace
and Virgil, and to Sappho and Homer. From Horace, he seems
first to have learned how to be a poet, for his own copy of the
Odes is full of marginalia analyzing and classifying the meters
and forms of each poem, and noting literary sources. Later he
translated from Ovid, Seneca, Juvenal, and other Augustan poets
as well as from the satires of Horace. Similar marginalia show
a critical study of the art of Pope with as much attention to the
thought as to the verse. Yet, unlike almost all of his American
contemporaries, this vivid and eager young man seems to have
absorbed all these influences and made them his own. In his
free and joyous song to "The Power of Fancy," written when he
was only sixteen, he concludes:

> Fancy, to thy power I owe
> Half my happiness below; . . .
> Come, O come—perceiv'd by none,
> You and I will walk alone.

In such spirit he surely read also the best of the contemporary
poetry, criticizing, absorbing, and making use of what he could
for the training of his own Muse. With a poet of derivative mind,
source study is both rewarding and depressing; with a live and
discriminating original genius like Freneau, it is tantalizing and
misleading.

Freneau's first editor, F. L. Pattee, saw his patriotic zeal as
his main theme and called him the "Poet of the Revolution."
As far as it went the description was fit. Not only did he write
with his classmate Brackenridge the best tribute so far to "The
Rising Glory of America," as his graduation ode, but he continued to celebrate the signing of the Declaration of Independ-

ence and the victories of American arms on land and sea
—particularly the latter—throughout the period of conflict.
Turning then from ecstatic praise to searing scorn, he attacked
Cornwallis, the British prison and hospital ships, and the British
government with satire that was barbed by tense emotion as
well as wit. Compare his satirical verse during this period with
that of Trumbull or Hopkinson, or even Pope or Johnson, and
the romantic temperament is brilliantly apparent, even though
working through neoclassical forms.

A later editor, H. H. Clark, has justly pointed out that
Freneau's patriotism was not an end in itself. Behind it lay a
love of nature that was both specific to her manifest forms—as
in the poems to the wild honeysuckle and to a katydid—and
deeply imbued with the naturalistic view of her ultimate power.
For Freneau, as poet rather than as philosopher, early absorbed
and wholly adopted the eighteenth-century religion of nature
which had then so nearly supplanted both traditional Christianity
and the idealism of Berkeley and Edwards. Intensely and passion-
ately religious by temperament, he had no God other than that
supplied by the Deists:

> Religion, such as nature taught,
>   With all divine perfection suits;
> Had all mankind this system sought
>   Sophists would cease their vain disputes,
> And from this source would nations know
>   All that can make their heaven below

These lines, written at the end of his poetic career (1815), state
the same faith which gives philosophical importance to that early
Gothic orgy, "The House of Night" (1779), in which, among
horrors that would make Poe cringe, this earlier poet kills off
Death himself in order to prove that individual forms of nature
may perish, but life in nature is itself eternal:

> Hills sink to plains, and man returns to dust,
> That dust supports a reptile or a flower;
> Each changeful atom by some other nurs'd
> Takes some new form, to perish in an hour.

If further proof were needed that Freneau is the exception that
proves the rule, the romantic who broke through all the neoclassical barriers except the final one of form—that was left
finally to Whitman to do almost a century later—a study of his
wholly derivative poem on "The American Village" with
Dwight's *Greenfield Hill*—where the sources are the same but
the results quite different—would fully reveal the problems faced
by the American poet in this transitional period. Freneau alone
in his day seems to have had the power to accept and to declare
effectively the New World challenge in Old World forms. He
defies rather than imitates Goldsmith, who, he thinks,

> mourns his village with a patriot sigh
> And in that village sees Britannia die,

while he, the American poet, with eyes to the future, can

> Describe the village rising on the green
> Its harmless people born to small command,
> Lost in the bosom of this Western land

and then turn where

> New scenes invite me, and not more I rove
> To tell of shepherds, or the vernal grove.

Without changing his mode of expression, the poet has turned
from memory to hope as he faces the West and the future.
Freneau uses the old meters and forms of eighteenth-century
British poetry, but his verses seem to bristle and sparkle as he
uses them, so dynamic is the feeling he imparts to his message.

V

In the drama, the problem of the artist in America is revealed
even more obviously. The first play by an American to be
produced in America by a professional company was Thomas
Godfrey's roaring and soaring melodrama *The Prince of Parthia*.
It need not detain us here; but the first comedy—now on an
American theme—to be written by an American and produced
by a professional company, Royall Tyler's *The Contrast* (1787),
is not a bad play by any standards. The situation of the patriotic

American writer in the 1780's, determined to write an American work but finding only British or continental forms in which to clothe his plans, is nowhere more sharply presented than in this still engaging domestic comedy.

A native of Boston and a graduate of Harvard, Tyler was only thirty years of age when, as a major in the Army he was sent to New York on a mission to Governor Clinton in March of 1787. While there, he haunted the John Street Theatre and saw, among other plays, Sheridan's *School for Scandal*, the new type of sentimental comedy which, in its mingling of satire on hypocrisy with the defense of moral integrity, had supplanted the brittle amorality of the Restoration farce on the stages of Covent Garden and Drury Lane. The contrast between the wiles of Joseph and the somewhat irresponsible honesty of Charles Surface was not too hard to translate into that between the sophistication of the Old World and the blunt integrity of the New. The theme was ready-made for an international comedy in which Brother Jonathan had only to be made a bit more rigorous in his morality in order to expose his worth in contrast to the hypocrisy of the British. Colonel Manly, who was everything that the name implies, was but the honest Charles Surface reformed of his waywardness, but his servant (or "waiter," as he preferred to be called), the forthright Yankee Jonathan, was a new creation. The fop Dimple and his scheming servant Jessamy could be left much as such characters were found in the plays of Goldsmith and Sheridan, changing what in the original was a *class* differentiation into a difference in national character. The prologue could then exclaim:

> Exult, each patriot heart!—this night is shown
> A piece, which we may fairly call our own; ...
> Our Author pictures not from foreign climes
> The fashions or the follies of the times;
> But has confin'd the subject of his work
> To the gay scenes—the circles of New-York.

Nowhere else in all this early literature does so blatant and so naïve a bit of chauvinism occur, but it is perhaps warranted. The play is convincingly American. The character of Manly is a perfect mixture of Puritan rectitude with utilitarian foresight. His final speech is straight from Ben Franklin's catalogue of virtues:

And I have learned today that probity, virtue, and honour, though they should not have received the polish of Europe, will secure to an honest American the good graces of his fair country-women, and I hope, the applause of the Public.

Jonathan, the first of a long line of stage Yankees, is the humble reflection of his rather stuffy master, the prototype of the accepted image of the common man, to recur and recur again in our history as Hosea Biglow, Artemus Ward, Will Rogers, and even Calvin Coolidge. Royall Tyler had made a discovery: he had created the essential American by putting what he had learned from his back-country New England neighbors into a comic form imported from the London stage and transferred, with only the merest twist of emphasis, to the gay circles of New York.

Other American playwrights followed the same pattern, putting the Benedict Arnold and the Pocahontas stories into the forms of melodramas and historical tragedies like Dunlap's *André* and Barker's *The Indian Princess*, and playing variations on the contrast of international manners in such plays as the same author's *Tears and Smiles* and Mrs. Mowatt's *Fashion*. Because the British stage was in its turn largely controlled by the modes and forms of French and German farce and high drama of the day, original American plays had even less freedom of medium than had poetry or fiction. About all that could be done by aspiring and patriotic dramatists was to fit New World figures like the country bumpkin or the Indian or woodsman into the already established continental stage types and to give to old stories a new twist or two in order that they might seem slightly more native.

VI

The novel, on the other hand, was far more flexible than the drama, partly because it was still so new a literary form. The first

English novel of character, Samuel Richardson's *Pamela* (1740), was republished by Benjamin Franklin in Philadelphia four years later, the first novel of any kind to appear in America. British fiction developed rapidly during the next half century, and, when Americans began to imitate these popular imports, they merely stretched and adapted the existing English modes and forms to New World experiences, scenes, and ideas without much more than superficial changes in structure and style. In general, three types of English fiction can be distinguished during the closing years of the eighteenth century: (1) the sentimental novel of intrigue and assaulted virtue, deriving from Richardson but developed mainly by the Blue-Stocking ladies; (2) a modernization of the picaresque or rogue story from Cervantes and Lesage to fit the English youth in a series of adventures as pictured by Fielding and Smollett; and (3) the novel of Gothic horror and crime as exemplified by Walpole's *The Castle of Otranto*, Mrs. Radcliffe's *The Mysteries of Udolpho*, and, somewhat modified by social propaganda, Godwin's *Adventures of Caleb Williams*. All of these types are found in the sheaf of American novels that appeared in the last decade of the century.

The first American novel was in the first of these modes. *The Power of Sympathy* (1789), a weak imitation of the epistolary form of Richardson by a minor essayist, William Hill Brown, tells the two stories of a threatened incestuous marriage and a seduction, with one death from shock and two from suicide, thereby exposing the "Dangerous Consequences of Seduction." The current stereotype was merely removed to the western shore where human nature, in this one respect at least, seemed unreformed. Among other American novels of the same type were Hannah Foster's *The Coquette* (1797) and the more famous *Charlotte Temple* (1791) by Susanna Haswell Rowson, the latter of which was perhaps outsold among all-time American best sellers by only *Uncle Tom's Cabin* and *Gone with the Wind*. One need only turn to one of the most moving seduction scenes in all literature to realize why it was so popular. The poor schoolgirl Charlotte, connived against by her French teacher and the villainous Belcour, was an easy prey to the generous, liberal, good-looking Army officer Montraville whose unthinking passion had been perverted by his evil friend:

"I cannot go," said she: "cease, dear Montraville, to persuade. I must not: religion, duty forbid."

"Cruel Charlotte," said he, "if you disappoint my ardent hopes, by all that is sacred, this hand shall put a period to my existence. I cannot—will not live without you."

"Alas! my torn heart!" said Charlotte, "how shall I act?"

"Let me direct you," said Montraville, lifting her into the chaise.

"Oh! my dear forsaken parents," cried Charlotte.

The chaise drove off. She shrieked, and fainted into the arms of her betrayer.

Is there a stony reader's heart that is not moved by this touching scene? That Charlotte, after the conventional death from poverty in New York where she has followed her happily married betrayer, was supposedly buried in American soil does not Americanize either the plot or the style of this international story by a lady who lived and wrote in both London and Boston.

H. H. Brackenridge does a somewhat better transplanting job in his burlesque of a burlesque, *Modern Chivalry* (1792–1815). The quixotic Captain Farrago is but Brother Jonathan on horseback—or rather, nag-back, and his squire Teague O'Regan, the irresponsible servant who accompanies him on his journeys. It is Teague's unquenchable curiosity that gives the author his chance to expose American customs and institutions to good-natured ridicule: a local election, a college class in Greek (or was it Creek Indian?), a learned society meeting, or a congressional debate. Things apparently have not been much reformed, however, by this good-natured spoofing, for Brackenridge's report reads almost as though it were taken from a recent issue of the *Congressional Record*. Mr. Cogan, Mr. Bogan, and Mr. Hogan engage in a heated argument as to whether or not a certain bill, the subject of which is not given, is "of a dangerous tendency" because, if it is passed "the cows will have fewer calves, and the sheep less wool; . . . our watches go too slow; corns grow upon our toes; . . . snow will be found in the heat of harvest, and dog days in winter. The rivers will revert; and the shadows fall to the east in the morning. . . ." "Was it not such a bill as this," concludes the eloquent Mr. Cogan, "that changed the old stile; that made the eclipse in the time of Julius Caesar; that produced an earthquake, and sunk Port Royal?" The other gentlemen arise to correct these historical references, after which the bill is carried by a majority of twenty-five.

It is in the third genre, the pseudo-Gothic tale of crime and horror, that America produced its most original novelist of the period and, with Freneau, the nearest thing to a professional man of letters that the times developed. Charles Brockden Brown was somewhat younger than most of the writers I have discussed, but his precocious genius, coupled with his romantic frailty of person, brings him into our abortive literary movement at its peak and at its end, 1799–1800. Author of four novels published within two years, as well as of lesser tales and uncounted essays and poems, Brown comes as close as anyone to providing us with our clue to the mystery of the rise and sudden fall of America's first real literary movement. Violent and original in his temperament, free and experimental in his choice of characters, themes, and scenes that he knew in and about Philadelphia, he turned to Godwin's *Adventures of Caleb Williams* for the model of both his social and moral philosophy and his literary form. Essentially a study in class conflict and a plea for the underprivileged, Godwin's novel is also a psychological examination of the criminal mind, and a horror plot of intrigue and murder. It is not "Gothic" in that its scene is the contemporary English countryside rather than medieval castles, cliffs, and dungeons, but it mixes the morbid elements of the Gothic mode with new elements of psychological and social perversion.

The introversive Brown was attracted to the social philosophy of his British model as well as to his analysis of the mechanics and the motivation of crime. Freedom, feminism, and moral integrity give his tales their excuse and their meaning for both author and reader. In the "Advertisement" to his first and best novel, *Wieland* (1798), he states his purpose as "neither selfish nor temporary" but aimed "at the illustration of some important

branches of the moral constitution of man." "The incidents related are extraordinary and rare," he continues, but "the power
which the principal person [the younger Wieland] is said to
possess can scarcely be denied to be real." A study of colossal
delusion, provoked by use of the art of ventriloquism, and
driven to violent action by a complex of circumstances rather
than by evil design, the novel puts all possible strain on the
credulity of the reader, but still has the power of suspense and
of vivid descriptive and narrative writing. The scene, on the
banks of the Schuylkill at the mouth of the Wissahickon, is
convincingly described in its then unspoiled beauty, and the
characters, although types, are at the same time individuated and
strongly defined and developed. That some of the threads of the
plot are lost and never wholly unraveled and that some of the
action is not convincingly motivated need not trouble us now,
for Brown pioneered where Poe, Hawthorne, and Henry James
followed in the use of the pseudo-sciences for cause of his action and in the use of morbid psychology to establish a false and
terrifying point of view for his narrative

The whole of *Wieland*, like "The Fall of the House of Usher"
or "The Turn of the Screw," is seen through the mind of a
narrator who is strained to psychopathic distortions by fear and
melancholy. Brown was creating a genre which was to become
characteristically American in its violence and in its psychological
curiosity. That he used the Indians, the caves, and the wooded
stream valleys of his native Pennsylvania for his scenes and people, and that he explained his apparently supernatural actions
by ventriloquism, disease, spontaneous combustion, sleepwalking,
and other phenomena of the popular sciences are further reasons
to give him a place at the head of an American tradition in fiction
that is even more persistent than that of Cooper with his history,
his Indians, and his ships.

Brockden Brown, of course, published his own novels with
various booksellers and probably sold few of them—certainly
not enough to provide him with a living. Having abandoned the
law, he—like Freneau—turned to journalism, but died early.

With him, the dawn of an American literature proved false once again.

It might be possible to explain his failure, as well as those of the other young American writers I have discussed, by the mere inadequacy of the book and printing trades, but even though this is undoubtedly a factor, as well as the absence of international copyright protection, it is not explanation enough. The real reason will, I think, be found in the more general cultural factors of the time and place—far less easy to isolate and define than are the circumstances of printing, circulation, and readership.

VII

The main reason which I would like to propose, both for the rise of this literary movement and for its decline, is linked to the timing of the transfer of the culture of Western Europe—particularly of Britain—to this then unsettled and primitive continent. When political independence was finally assured in 1783, it was only natural that the American people would feel the need and lack the means of producing a literature that would declare and illustrate their cultural independence as well. This state of mind was not articulated until the 1830's, when Cooper, Channing, Emerson, and many lesser commentators wrote essays in defense of nationalism and in defiance of imitative traditionalism, but it was obviously felt—largely in an inarticulate form—by Freneau, Tyler, Brown, and the other members of this earlier group. American literary enthusiasm was bursting at the seams; its clothing in imported types and modes was too light and too formal.

Perhaps the mere alien quality of the available means of literary expression is sufficient to explain the situation, but I look to a kind of cultural lag as the basic cause. The American experience was romantic in a profound and disturbing sense. Not only was the New World scene far more awesome and terrifying in its mysteries and grandeur than anything in England or even on the Continent, but the ideals of independence for which the Americans fought were the realization of the most romantic dreams that Europeans had ever had about the nature and destiny of man. At the same time, the *literatures* of England and Europe had got off to only a very feeble start and were still more concerned with their own medieval past than with the themes of nationalism, individualism, and idealism which were to occupy them during the nineteenth century. Eighteenth-century Old World writers were still limited and directed by the literary forms and conventions of the neoclassical movement, even though they had admitted the validity of many of the new romantic ideas, particularly those which dealt with the past rather than with the present or the future. American writers were suddenly endowed with a great wealth of new and vital material, all of which concerned the present and the future. *Without* what both Cooper in his day and Van Wyck Brooks a century later called "a usable past" or a past of any known kind other than that which they shared with the Old World and which had little relevance to the New, and *with* an oversupply of new experience and ideas, they were faced with two clear alternatives: either they had to disregard their cultural heritage and merely speak out about the matters which immediately concerned them in the best and simplest prose that they could master, or they had to twist, adjust, and adapt their new experiences to the established and available forms of a neoclassical convention which English and European writers were soon also to find too restricting. The American Revolution, which was a part of the general revolt of Western European man against the old regimes and the remnants of feudalism as well as a specific revolt against George III, had come to us early—well ahead of its counterpart in France and its echoes in England and elsewhere in Europe. On the other hand, the freedom of literary expression allowed by romanticism was delayed in America, which needed it most, until it had almost run its full course in Germany, France, and England. The explosive ideas of the people and the untamed powers of nature in the new land were forced into the stiff molds and modes of an urban, sophisticated, and imported literature. The foot did not fit the shoe.

Critical Standards

in the

American Romantic Movement

1947

READ BEFORE THE ROMANTICISM GROUP OF
THE MODERN LANGUAGE ASSOCIATION OF
AMERICA IN DECEMBER, 1946, AND PUB-
LISHED IN *College English*, VIII (1947),
344–352.

THE SEARCH for the critical standards which guided the romantic movement in the United States is an even more difficult task than a similar search for the contemporaneous standards in European literatures. Not only must one take into account the criteria of romanticism throughout the Western world, but one must also recognize the differences between Europe and America.

In its broader historical terms, the romantic movement in Western European literatures may be regarded as the literary expression of the revolutionary political, social, religious, and other ideas which attempted to overthrow traditional patterns of society and thought during the latter part of the eighteenth and the early part of the nineteenth centuries. In this sense, the very existence of the United States as a nation was a product of romanticism. In its specifically literary sense, the movement was a revolution against neoclassical standards and forms of expression and became itself a more or less stable body of ideas and attitudes which spread from literature to literature.

The distinguishing features of the movement in America are

not, however, at first apparent. Regarded as a body of developing ideas in a historical period, with specific reference to literature, romanticism in America seems at casual glance to parallel closely the movement in European literatures. When I first wrote this essay, I showed it to a friend, who pointed out that, in his opinion, there was in America a first phase of pseudo-classicism; then an intermediate stage of pouring new ideas into old molds; and then, around 1840, the full blossoming of the truly romantic movement. He further pointed out that in both Europe and America there was a close relationship between the political and the aesthetic problems and that in America as in Europe political liberalism was parallel to aesthetic liberalism.

This line of reasoning is historically sound as far as it goes and may even be documented by the evidence which I shall here present in an attempt to shift the focus of the problem and to gain a slightly different perspective. Romanticism was a movement which followed a fairly consistent pattern of development throughout occidental literatures and in which America, as an offshoot of Western Europe, participated fully. A stimulating paper could be written on this parallelism. Historical sequences would be subordinated to organic forces, and it would be discovered that the same factors were operative in all cases.

But it is precisely because such correlations are so easy to establish that this argument blocks a full understanding of American romanticism as an indigenous movement. In this paper, therefore, I shall concern myself mainly with those factors which distinguish American romanticism from its European analogues and perhaps overstate my case in order to make my point more clear. We can assume the parallels; let us see whether there are differences. I shall attempt to show that there was no regular progress in America from an indigenous pseudo-classicism to a mature and native romanticism and that the correlation of political and aesthetic factors in Europe and America is therefore imperfect and misleading.

II

Our starting point is a recognition of one fundamental difference between Europe and America. Europe in the eighteenth century was an old and familiar land with rooted traditions and cultures; America was a new land without indigenous traditions and cultures other than those of the Indians, which were at first totally rejected and have only recently been faintly recognized and absorbed into our cultural stream. For the European immigrant in early America, even to the third or fourth generation of settlers, the cultures of Europe were still the dominant and shaping inheritance. The life that he knew and the land that he wished to describe and interpret were alien to the modes of thought and the forms of writing to which he was habituated. In no country of Europe was the gulf between the materials to be expressed and the available forms of expression so vast. To be sure, shifting populations and the creation of new nations gave rise to somewhat parallel circumstances in European literary history between 1760 and 1860, but for the most part they were incidental and sporadic. In America, the discrepancy between material and form is the central and overwhelmingly significant factor at this stage of our literary history.

There did not occur, therefore, in America a first phase of pseudo-classicism in the sense in which one occurred in Europe. During the seventeenth and eighteenth centuries, when pseudo-classicism reigned, the colonies of the eastern seaboard were still more or less distinct entities, each with closer cultural ties to the country of its origin than to any other colony in this hemisphere. Neoclassicism appeared sporadically in American literature toward the end of the eighteenth century, but it never took hold and never became a part of our indigenous literary history. The whole concept of romanticism as a revolt against neoclassicism is invalid for our literature because we had no common literary criteria, no schools, and no traditions of our own at the time when the revolt was taking place in Europe. There was no neoclassical movement as such in American literature because there were virtually no literary traditions.

Similarly, our romantic movement in its earlier phases was either completely lacking in literary self-consciousness or was overwhelmingly imitative. There was no unified romantic movement because there was no indigenous neoclassicism for it to revolt against. Prior to the occurrence of the movement, there was an English, a French, a German, an Italian, a Spanish, a Russian literature, whether the peoples concerned had achieved political autonomy or not. Each of these consisted of a tradition of expression coming from a people who spoke more or less a common language, had lived for some generations in a single locale, had suffered the same political and religious viscissitudes, and had a common sense of cultural heritage. The romantic movement in Europe was therefore an alteration—in some cases a reversal—of existing cultural patterns.

In America there was no such common cultural heritage except as it was imported. Political independence from England established the need rather than the actuality of cultural unity. Without the background of a rooted cultural tradition, a literary movement of any kind, in the usual sense in which historians use the term, was impossible. The significant dichotomy in American literary history is therefore that between imitative romanticism (including an addendum of imitative pseudo-classicism) and an organic and emotional romanticism of slow but indigenous growth and closely related to the American adventure. This dichotomy can be followed through the nineteenth century and down even to our own day. It established the conservative and the liberal traditions in our literary history.

It is somewhat misleading, therefore, to proceed by the customary methods in our examination of the evidences of romanticism in American literature in the century from 1760 to 1860. Because American literature was, during that period, undergoing a basically formative process, the generally accepted symptoms of romanticism might be found, but they would not have the same meaning that they had in the established literatures of older countries. The problem of tracing the indigenous romantic movement in American literature cannot be divorced from the problem of describing the beginnings of our national literature. These two problems are not identical, but they are closely interrelated.

The errors to which a historian might be subjected were he to ignore this fact are easily illustrated. Take, for example, three generally accepted identification tags of romanticism at this period: medievalism, awareness of primitive nature, and experimentation in form. In European literatures, medievalism represented the desire for escape from the stereotyped uses of classical material to the material of a Christian and as yet unexploited culture. The new anthropomorphic view of nature was in part a reaction against the artificial code of nature-appreciation which had become stereotyped on neoclassical models in the seventeenth and eighteenth centuries. Experimentation in form was an effort to discover new ways of saying old things.

All three of these trends are found in American literature of the period, but the motivation behind each of them is different from that behind European authors, sometimes, indeed, quite the reverse. Classicism and medievalism were equally meaningless against an American background; neither had any roots in this hemisphere. The shift from the use of one of these traditional cultures to that of the other was merely the change from the imitation of one kind of material to that of another, both imported. In both cases, the compelling motivation was imitation rather than increased freedom, and the resultant American writing in the medieval mode should not be called romanticism in an organic sense of the word. Medievalism in Freneau or Brown has not the same significance as has medievalism in Keats or Scott.

Similarly, motives for the expression of the grand and rugged in nature were different, though the results were similar. Europeans were reacting against conventions, whereas Americans were striving to make articulate their feelings about the untamed world at their doorstep. And, while in Europe experimentation in form was an effort to discover new ways of saying old things, in America it was more often an effort to make the *old ways* say new things.

The usual orientation for the discussion of such movements as neoclassicism and romanticism cannot therefore be applied without a great deal of limitation and modification when the scene is moved across the Atlantic. A new orientation must be found by an examination of the whole process of building a new literature rather than of that of reforming an old one. New terms must be discovered and new charts drawn.

A suggestion for this new orientation has already been noted in the urge to create and the urge to imitate. By its very nature, an emergent literature should be romantic because the opening of a new continent is a great adventure. The demand for a new national literature distinct from those of the old world is in itself a romantic motivation. On the other hand, the earliest writings of conscious art in a new civilization are likely to be imitative and deferential. The poles of reference for the romantic movement in America are therefore *imitation* and *nationalism*, existing contemporaneously rather than in sequence. The desire to create literature distinct from European importations, and better than any of them, was its primary incentive; the inevitable servility to European forms and modes, whether neoclassical or romantic, even to European materials and ideas, was its chief obstacle.

Even a casual reading of the periodicals between 1790 and 1830 will demonstrate that this view of the movement is historically accurate. One finds practically no articles dealing with problems of pure literary criticism before Bryant and Poe began to write in the 'thirties. The controversy between neoclassicism and romanticism, which was shaping the literatures of Europe, found no echo in our press. Our writers seem scarcely to have been aware of it, and they formed no schools in these terms. The radical Barlow and the conservative Dwight were literary bedfellows, and Cooper fought Scott's feudalism without being aware of his own debt to the romantic theory of the "Great Unknown."

On the other hand, it is quite easy to distinguish schools of critical thought in terms of imitation and nationalism. In the period between 1812 and 1825, American periodicals were crowded with articles proclaiming and demanding a "national literature." G. H. Orians has assembled an impressive list of such articles by Neal, Paulding, Ingersoll, Everett, Cooper,

Bryant, Longfellow, Flint, Channing, and a host of others. The rallying cry of early romanticism in this country is summed up by Walsh in 1827: "There is no objective more worthy the exercise of the highest attributes of the mind, than that of administering to the just pride of national character, inspiring a feeling for the national glory and inculcating a love of our country." And Emerson's *American Scholar*, ten years later, was a mature philosophical statement of the same defensive national pride.

III

In this new orientation of the romantic movement, the tendency toward imitation of European forms and modes takes the place, in America, of neoclassicism as the reactionary factor against which the movement developed. The model for imitation may be either romantic or neoclassic; the act of imitation puts the imitator into the class of reactionaries rather than into that of experimenters.

Any careful study of literary trends in the early days of American independence should start with an analysis of book importations and popular reading. This could be done by an examination of the catalogues of the early libraries and of booksellers, of excerpts from and notices in periodicals and newspapers, and of contemporary letters and journals. No such systematic study is available, but one can form general impressions from the evidence provided by such books as Mott's history of magazines, Raddin's study of Caritat's library, such biographies as Ellis' *Dennie*, Leary's *Freneau*, Cowie's *Trumbull*, and Adkins' *Halleck*, and from the published memoirs, letter collections, and journals of such men as Goodrich or Putnam. The impression that the reader of such sources will inevitably get is that few original books were published in this country, that periodicals and publishers followed the current English listings and republished popular work quickly, that the classics of English literature were still read but that books of only secondary literary interest were even more general, and that taste was largely dictated from London.

The eclectic character of American reprinting and reading during this period has frequently been noted. Importation and imitation alike reflected the judgment of the English upper middle class, and the popularity of a given author or work in the mother country or in France or Germany seems to have been the only and sufficient reason for introducing him or it to American readers by reprint or imitation.

The result was an undue degree of reverence for Dryden, Pope, Addison, and those other neoclassical authors who had become established as dictators of taste by a previous generation abroad. The American method of learning to write was still that proposed by Franklin in his youthful imitation of Addison: "By comparing my work afterwards with the original, I discovered many faults and amended them." Even Americans like Barlow and Hopkinson, who had radical things to say, felt that these things could not be made into literature unless they were coerced into the conventional forms of the epic, the satire, and the periodical essay.

Where departure was made from these fixed standards, it tended backward to the Elizabethans, now of established respectability, as in Godfrey's love lyrics, or into the late eighteenth-century or contemporary English romantics who were approved by bourgeois taste abroad. Such English nature poets as Cowper and Goldsmith enjoyed wide American popularity, and Dwight's *Greenfield Hill* is a good example of the direct imitation of this school. The more sentimental of the *fin de siècle* poets were likewise read and imitated: Burns, Campbell, the then popular James Montgomery, Samuel Rogers, and Tom Moore; as was the graveyard school: Blair, Young, and Gray. And, in the newer generation of English romantics, Byron, Hunt, and Wordsworth passed the dual test of popularity and propriety; whereas little attention was paid to Keats, Shelley, and even Coleridge, who was soon to be discovered by the Transcendentalists as a philosophical rather than as a literary influence. Freneau's "Beauties of Vera Cruz" and "The House of Night," Halleck's "Alnwick Castle," even Bryant's "Thanatopsis," can hardly lay claim to being fresh products of American soil.

Although there was comparatively little imitation of the familiar essay of Lamb and Hazlitt, the American periodical essay was as numerous as a family of guinea pigs and as strict in following the inheritance of dominant characteristics. Like its English parent, it was concerned with morals and manners, taste and character. Even the boisterous "Salmagundi" group could not break entirely with the precedents established by "Timothy Timbertoes," the "Visitant," and Brockden Brown's "Rhapsodist."

In fiction, Cooper's gesture of defiance in throwing aside an English novel, probably *Persuasion*, with the remark, "I could write a better book myself," is symptomatic of the formative period from 1790 to 1830. The result was little more than a transposition of the letters in the title to form *Precaution* and a similar but more clumsy treatment of English country life, which he had drawn from this and other reading and of which he knew nothing. Brown calls himself "a story telling moralist" and boasts that he employs "the European models merely for the improvement of his taste," but his novels, original and dynamic as they are in comparison with those of his contemporaries, are Godwinian and Gothic to an incongruous degree. Even the nationalistic Brackenridge wrote in 1795 from Pittsburgh, "Nature intended me for a writer, and it has always been my ambition. How often have I sighed for the garrets of London; where I have read histories, manners, and anecdotes of Otway, Dryden, and others, who have lived in the upper stories of buildings, writing paragraphs, or essays in prose and verse."

And the influence of Hallam's so-called "American Company" during the days of our youth guided our native drama into the molds of the popular English social comedy of Sheridan and Goldsmith and the sentimental melodrama of more antique ancestry.

In all such embryonic attempts to form a national literature prior to 1820, there was an almost complete absence of developed literary criteria. A largely indiscriminate copying of models, accidentally selected, cannot be said to provide a set of critical standards, whether of classicism or of romanticism, however much a given work may seem to belong to one school or the other. Imitation, as such, is a reactionary rather than a revolutionary force in literary history, and, as such, the seeming romantic elements which we have reviewed can be relegated to the class of spurious or at best secondary romanticism if they can be placed in that category at all.

VI

It was against this background, however, that the genuine American romantic movement came into being. In most of the writers mentioned above, as in their fellows whom we have not discussed, there is an element of impatience with their own imitation, on two counts: first, they had difficulty in adapting native American material to their models; and, second, the social, political, and religious ideas expressed in these models seemed narrow and reactionary. Against the trend of imitation can be set, even in our earliest literature, the romantic motivation of nationalism, which demanded the use of American materials and the expression of American ideas. The result was, in some cases, a strange and incongruous mixture, but the desire for novelty and freedom, which is characteristic of any romantic movement, is here apparent, even though in an elementary form.

The earlier writers were naïve in their belief that the task of adapting new materials to old forms was simple. Brown turned from "puerile superstition and exploded manners, Gothic castles and chimeras" to "the incidents of Indian hostility, and the perils of the wilderness" as more suitable means "of calling forth the passions and engaging the sympathy of the reader" in his stories of romantic terror. Barlow clothed his Adam in the costume of Columbus and gave him an Archangel Hesperus to take him to a height and point out to him the future glories of America. Tyler put the blunt Bob Acres into Yankee homespun and called him Jonathan. The banks of the Schuylkill and the Hudson were lined with sylvan bowers and peopled with imps and kelpies, while Drake, as late as 1835, cried out for "a seat on Appalachia's brow" (or one on the Palisades' lofty brow would do as well) so that he might "scan the glorious prospect round" and "sing the beauteous scenes of nature's loveliest land."

This desire to use familiar materials is a common characteristic of the romantic movement. Crabbe wrote of the village, Wordsworth of the country folk and the beauties of the Lakes. But it has an added significance in America as a basic and easily appreciated aspect of a growing national consciousness. Obvious as it is, it furnishes us with the first and most elementary factor in our own romantic movement.

There is but a short step from this demand for an objective treatment of the American landscape and the American people to an effort to explore and define the principles underlying an American national being. Without the traditions of race and habit, the only grounds our early writers could discover for national autonomy of mind and spirit lay in what they soon came to call "American principles." One should not merely accept these principles in theory; they must be in the very bone. "Her poets and artists," wrote Simms, "to feel her wants, her hopes, her triumphs, must be born of the soil and ardently devoted to its claims." Jonathan must not only wear homespun; he must speak to his servant as to an equal.

Yet the exact definition of these principles was vague. They constituted a common feeling rather than an agreement on a system of thought. Whether of political, economic, or religious implications, they invariably conveyed the concepts of novelty and freedom. Crèvecœur wrote, back in 1782: "The American is a new man, who acts upon new principles. . . . From involuntary idleness, servile dependence, penury, and useless labour, he has passed to toils of a very different nature, rewarded by ample subsistence."[1] "The leading distinctive principle of this country," added Cooper in 1838, "is connected with the fact that all political power is strictly a trust granted by the constituent to the representative."[2] And Channing gave the same concepts a moral and religious setting: "The great distinction of our country is, that we enjoy some peculiar advantages for understanding our own nature. . . . Man is not hidden from us by so many disguises as in the old world. The essential quality of all human beings, founded on the possession of a spiritual, progressive, immortal nature, is, we hope, better understood." [3] Liberty, equality, fraternity—the trio of Revolution —formed the tripod of democracy and erected a new man upon it. Whatever his race, creed, or color, he became an American as soon as he had absorbed the principles of democracy into his blood stream.

Four principal qualities made up this American democratic man. First, and most important, he was an intense individualist with a belief in his rights, his opportunities, his powers, and his destiny. Second, he had an almost equally intense social conscience, not in the modern sense of granting a common destiny to society as a state at a sacrifice of individualism, but in the sense that by developing his individualism he could help others do the same and lead society toward a perfection of the whole through a perfection of each of the parts. Third, he had a sound practical sense, born of his pioneering, which made him hospitable to "commonsense" philosophies from utilitarianism to pragmatism. And, finally, he offset this common sense by an idealism which shaped his religion and his ethics, his politics and his personal relationships, without ever becoming a systematic philosophy. The contradictions in these traits did not worry him because of his underlying certainty of inexhaustible spiritual and material resources. Rather the four added up to a buoyant nationalism which identified the destiny of the individual with that of the group, promised a vital present and a glowing future, and provided the instrument of common sense to make their attainment possible.

In Europe, these principles had been the stuff of revolution, the battle cry of the underprivileged. In America, they formed the established code of the ruling and the professional classes, whether of Federalist or Republican caste, Calvinist or Transcendentalist belief. For this reason, as Charvat has pointed out, the privileged classes, mainly men of legal or religious training, gave them a judicial and moral tone and brought literature close to the world of affairs on the one hand and to that of traditional religion on the other. The revolutionary code, stemming as it did from European disorder, had become the mark of respectability, the unique gift which America felt it her mission to contribute to the world currents of civilization.

The word "nationalism," when applied to this movement, has a meaning very different from that which it carries today. Recent events have given it the connotation of self-seeking, destructive imperialism. In the United States of 1840, its meaning was the contrary. Pride in the nation was pride in the democratic ideal, the property of the free man everywhere but native to America only, because there circumstances had provided the free environment necessary to its growth. The new American culture was to be different from any the world had ever known because it was founded on the political principle of the sovereignty of the people, the religious principle of liberty of conscience, and the economic principle of free use of apparently inexhaustible natural resources. In this ideal, America found the mainspring of its own romantic movement. The American man, once recognized and defined, must find his own means and his own forms of expression. That was the task which the authors of the period following the War of Independence set themselves.

V

By 1840, therefore, the romantic movement was fairly launched in America and was ready to provide the young nation with a literature of its own. The next two decades produced, for the first time on this side of the Atlantic, a half dozen or more writers worthy of a place in world literature. Obviously, tradition and originality had become reconciled.

The two trends which we have been following are still apparent in this mature literature. Each had deepened and become richer, more sure of itself, as the American democratic man gained confidence in himself. No longer was imitation a mere copying of models; no longer was nationalism a childish faith in the new nation. The one had become the tradition of conservatism, a deep awareness of the continuation of the culture of

Western Europe, and even of Asia, in this hemisphere; the other a bold and confident grappling with life's major problems in terms of the American experience.

Thus, in the perspective of a century, such writers as Longfellow and Lowell, who seemed in their own day to represent the culmination of the struggle toward a national literature in the romantic mode, appear to us in their truer colors as spokesmen for the culture of Europe transplanted to these shores. And such writers as Emerson, Thoreau, Melville, and Whitman, who seemed to their contemporaries to be eccentrics in many respects, protesting against currents of the times, reveal to us today the deeper forces of a romanticism at once indigenous and universal.

Enough has been said, I hope, to indicate that the search for the critical standards of romanticism in the United States as a historical movement must be undertaken with reference to the basic and self-conscious difference between that literature and those of Europe. A great deal of false speculation has resulted from the assumption on the part of historians that American literature, in the century between 1760 and 1860, was merely one more strand of European literature. Against the American background the movement developed a pattern of growth which should be and can be clearly distinguished from its European analogues.

NOTES

[1] St. Jean de Crèvecœur, *Letters from an American Farmer*, 1782.

[2] James Fenimore Cooper, *The American Democrat*, 1838.

[3] William Ellery Channing, "The Importance and Means of a National Literature," *Christian Examiner* VII, 269–295 (January, 1830).

After the Romantic Movement
1947

READ BEFORE THE AMERICAN LITERATURE
GROUP OF THE MODERN LANGUAGE ASSOCIA-
TION OF AMERICA IN DECEMBER, 1947, ON
A PROGRAM CHAIRED BY PERRY MILLER, AND
PAIRED WITH HENRY NASH SMITH ON THE
CONTRARY TENDENCY WHICH CAME TO EX-
PRESSION IN HIS *Virgin Land*.

MOST OF OUR LITERARY HISTORIANS are in agreement that the romantic movement which produced in Poe, Emerson, Hawthorne, Melville, and Whitman an American literary renaissance
about 1850–1855 was based mainly on political nationalism and
philosophical idealism. At least this assumption provides a convenient pole of reference for the critical discussion of these
and minor authors of the era. But for the period after 1870, the
corresponding pole of reference,—realism and its variations
down to something we have come to call naturalism—is less
adequate to the task of accounting for major authors even
though it describes minor authors and movements with some
success. I hope to show that a large part of the literature after
1870, and particularly the work of major authors, was the product of a movement actually counter to realism, although in some
respects it was an outgrowth of the realistic tendency.

In the romantic view of art, the accepted concepts of nature and of man's relationship to nature are of first importance
because, to the romantic, art takes its form from the artist's
view of the cosmos rather than from laws inherent in the creative process itself. The romantic theorists in America had de-

veloped a strong sense of the importance of man in the universe as a kind of arbiter between nature and God. They had learned from the teaching of the German, French, and English idealists to accept a provisional dualism by which man might, through his own efforts of insight, achieve a satisfying position and function for himself midway between the law of nature and the moral law. They had learned to maintain a sense of security and centrality in the universe by the assumption that seeming inconsistencies and contradictions on the plane of natural law were mere illusions caused by imperfect comprehension of a perfect moral law with which experience is in exact correspondence on the plane of the ideal.

The function of the artist, by this dispensation, was therefore to train his intuition so that he might see through the misleading illusions of experience and might translate the higher reality into terms of human comprehension. Nature thus furnished the language of his art, to be used freely as the higher reality became clearer.

This view of the function of the artist was in close accord with the democratic assumption of the importance of the individual, and the romantic movement reached a high level of achievement in Emerson, Thoreau, Melville, and Whitman, in whose work this assumption could be either asserted, as by Emerson, or challenged, as by Melville, without violating its validity. When Emerson wrote of the poet, "He is a sovereign and stands on the centre," he was stating the doctrine that Melville was using as the formula of tragic irony when he caused Ahab to throw the accumulated wrath of his obsessed personality against a nature which appeared malign because it did not submit to his will. Neither of them questioned the right of the individual to accept or to challenge his fate. Thus the whole range of literary interpretation was at the disposal of the romanticist because he assumed an egocentric universe. He stood secure on the ground of his own integrity because he had divine authorization to be a man.

When this concept of the artist was effectively challenged by the mechanistic views of nature which scientific thinking advanced toward the close of the century, romantic idealism in America and elsewhere rapidly disintegrated. Like all developments in our history, the change came suddenly and the contrast between the old and the new was violent. Those of our artists like Poe, Hawthorne, or Melville who could not face the dilemma into which they had reasoned themselves died or became silent. Poe made a final effort of adjustment to the new dispensation in *Eureka*, Hawthorne in his variations on the theme of the ancestral footstep, and Melville in *Pierre*. Only romantic artists of greater self-confidence, like Emerson and Whitman, or of less profound insight, like Longfellow and Lowell, could cling to the premises of romantic idealism and continue to produce; and their work—with the exception of Whitman's—became decreasingly important. In the coming generation, it is to those writers who accepted in some way the new cosmology, with its removal of man from the center of the universe, and who sought to construct a place and a function for the artist within its frame—to writers like Mark Twain, Henry James, Emily Dickinson, Sidney Lanier, William Dean Howells, Stephen Crane, and Henry Adams—that we must turn for the literary masterworks and dominant movements of the closing years of the century, rather than to those who, like Aldrich, Stedman, and a host of lesser men, clung to the remnants of romantic idealism and constructed from them an unsatisfying faith in ideality.

The first and easiest reaction to the loss of faith in man's centrality in the universe was a flat acceptance of the demotion. Mark Twain picked up in *A Connecticut Yankee* and *Pudd'nhead Wilson* the ambiguities which Melville had left in a hopeless tangle in *Pierre* and *The Confidence Man*, and ultimately managed to simplify the problem in his brief essay, "What is Man?" Unsound as this statement of a philosophic position may be as philosophy, it summarizes the dilemma of the modern American artist as the writers of his and succeeding generations came to see it. If man is merely a cog in the universal machine, it seems to follow that the artist has no function other than that of the recorder. The literal realism of

Howells was a logical consequence. Retaining from his romantic egocentrality only his consciousness, the artist now might describe the meaningless environment (in the sense of the world outside of his consciousness), but he was left no imaginative control over it.

This is, of course, an oversimplification of the problem, but I have deliberately so stated it because it seems to me that the common practice of literary historians of the period since 1870 is based on a realistic theory of art which in turn assumes a mechanistic view of nature. When the problem is examined more closely, it appears that this view of nature is inadequate as a description of the actual state of mind of our writers, particularly as we have just seen of those who came from or remained in the West. The most creative of our Western writers of these years were not satisfied with mere dismay at the growing disillusionment about them; they sought to construct new foundations for their thought and their art. The concept of the natural man thus persisted in writers from Freneau to Cooper to Mark Twain to Frank Norris to Steinbeck, taking new forms with the changing views of nature but growing rather than declining in intensity. On the moral plane, the American artist almost immediately sought an escape from his dilemma in the new mysticism of the superman, borrowed from Nietzsche, and his heroes plunged with Jack London's Martin Eden into a mid-ocean suicide of despair or with Norris' Magnus Derrick into a magnificent and hopeless revolt against the machine. This kind of writing is not realistic in any but technical respects; it marks rather the persistence of a romantic attitude and method in spite of science, equalitarian democracy, the frontier, and the industrial revolution. It is the expression of the dislocated ego of the artist in a mood of defiance. Henry Adams provided for it the two master symbols of the Dynamo and the Virgin.

The difference between this form of romantic primitivism and that of the earlier romantic movement is more significant than is the similarity between the two movements. Edmund

Wilson, in *Axel's Castle* and in later studies, has linked the two in an analysis of symbolism without perhaps giving enough attention to the consequences of the lack of moral certitude in the latter. The artist, with his anchor line in the moral law finally and completely severed, is set adrift. If he is unwilling to accept the role of the mere recorder of experience, if he persists in searching for meanings with the old romantic fervor even though he has thrown his quadrant overboard, he is driven in upon his own isolated consciousness with an intensity far greater than that of transcendental introspection. Rejecting the line of development suggested by the enviromental realism of Howells and exploited by regionalists and social critics from that day to this, he is left with the technique of internal analysis and the language of symbolism as instruments for probing his own consciousness in lieu of the cosmos. He is prepared to pick up the aestheticism of Poe, and, to a lesser extent, of Hawthorne, and to develop an art finally divorced from metaphysical and ethical significance. His attitude toward such values becomes either that of the skeptic or that of the mystic, or a combination of the two, neither one of which asks him to formulate philosophic problems clearly or to provide explicit answers for them. He may devote his entire attention to expression as an end in itself, and develop in his art a perfection of form and a complexity of technique, while his meanings become increasingly intricate and ambiguous.

It was this tendency rather than that of environmental realism that produced the outstanding American artists of the late nineteenth century and which provided the foundations for much of our contemporary writing, particularly our poetry and criticism. The writers of the East, like Emily Dickinson, Sidney Lanier, Henry James, Stephen Crane, and Henry Adams could not revert to the folk level of primitivism as did Mark Twain and the humorists. Those of them who wished to do so usually went West with Bret Harte and Artemus Ward and became recorders or humorists. Those of them who stayed in the East, those who, like Garland, Howells, and Twain himself, came

East, or those who went even farther East in a search for older cultures were all drawn ultimately into an aesthetic, surrealistic, or even antirealistic movement.

Perhaps the most elementary form that this movement may take is impressionism, and Garland is here a case in point. Garland was not himself aware of the consequences of his term "veritism" which he defined in his little book *Crumbling Idols* soon after the appearance of what has erroneously seemed to the critics a pure product of environmental realism, his *Main Travelled Roads*. He looked upon it merely as an extension of the "realism" of his master Howells, in that it preserved the scientific method but substituted truth for actuality as the goal of the artist. This is no trifling change. By truth he meant not only what was presented to the artist by life, but what the artist himself saw in the moment of presentation and what he supplied from his own consciousness in meeting it. Nature itself was no longer personal to him as it had been to romantics from Freneau to Emerson because he had rejected the principle of correspondence between the law of man (or God) and the law of things. But as he pushed nature away and made it almost wholly impersonal, his art became more intensely self-centered. As he walked through the gallery of the Columbian Exposition he was drawn to the impressionist painters of France, Russia, and Scandinavia and to their followers among the Americans. In the blue shadow, he saw more truth than could be found in the details of the Dutch and English schools. Committed as he was to the descriptive techniques of the new realism and inadequate as he was as an artist, by this essay he became one of the first Americans of this period to suggest an aesthetic answer to the moral dilemma of the American artist. In a brief moment of insight, he saw the artist as sovereign over the small island of his own consciousness and as legislator in the realms of color and form if not in those of good and evil.

To students of European literature of the late nineteenth century, Garland's late and tentative acceptance of impressionism should seem almost naïve. The movement away from the description of phenomena and toward internal analysis and pure expression has long been recognized as perhaps the dominant trend in the European literatures of the late nineteenth and the early twentieth centuries. To the historian of American literature of this period, with his fixed idea that only the environmental realist is the true American, it has seemed an alien and hostile element. Among its earlier professors, Henry James set the pattern of escape to the more sophisticated cultures of Europe; Emily Dickinson that for a hermitlike retreat behind a garden wall; Stephen Crane that for a futile effort to reconcile a concern for art with a participation in American life; and Henry Adams that for a retreat into pure aesthetic intellectuality. Yet we are still largely unreconciled to the kind of artist that our civilization produces at its best. The artists themselves invariably feel the rejection and seek some sort of retreat; and the historian of our literature accepts their alienation as evidence of their failure to become genuine parts of our literature and considers them in one or another fashion as alien or expatriate. The realism, regionalism, local color, democratic agrarianism, social criticism, and finally naturalism which Parrington and others have set up as descriptive categories for our literary history of this period will contain almost any number of minor authors, but will not describe these major figures. On the other hand, our nonacademic critics, becoming aware of the aesthetic significance of problems of personality, have had rather more success than have our scholars in discovering a historical context for such writers as Lanier, Dickinson, Adams, James, and Crane, and in reclaiming them for American literary history. J. G. Hüneker attempted to define impressionism in a Bohemian setting. Van Wyck Brooks pointed out that the "malady of the ideal," the division of personality which he found in Maurice de Guérin and Amiel, was present also in such American writers as Mark Twain, Henry James, and Emerson. H. L. Mencken early pointed out that Dreiser's art depended not so much on his detailed analysis of environment as on his mystical "groping toward a light but dimly seen." Spingarn, of American critics, most successfully defined the sphere of literature as limited to impressionism and expressionism. Edmund Wilson drew all such isolated recognitions of the movement into a single definition of symbolism and an ambitious attempt to give that movement historical significance by relating it to the earlier romantic and later symbolist movements in European literatures. And T. S. Eliot defined the perfect criticism as the statement in language of the structure of perceptions in a really appreciative mind, resulting in the development of sensibility.

I have said enough, I think, to set up the hypothesis that there were two main currents in our literature of the period from 1870 to the close of the century rather than merely the one— realism. I am suggesting that, in tracing the course of our literary history through this period and down to the present, we shift our emphasis for a time from the evidences of realism and its variations, and start afresh from the evidences of its contrary, by whatever term or terms we may describe it. Within the broad limits of this movement we may include impressionism, imagism, aestheticism, neo-Bohemianism, symbolism, and the metaphysical and analytical movements; in short, all those attitudes which take from science only its methods of analysis and symbolic representation and which direct attention to the human personality in itself rather than to the external world or to philosophical absolutes. Although this movement may be seen by hindsight to have been stirring in many of our major writers of the late nineteenth century, it was not articulated until Spingarn's lecture on "The New Criticism" in 1910, Ezra Pound's early essays, and finally The Sacred Wood of T. S. Eliot (1920). Its beginnings may therefore be sought out in the implicit literary attitudes of some of these earlier literary figures.

II

By the older dispensation, Emily Dickinson appears as a regionalist in that she is so completely the spokesman for the "decline of New England," but she fails as a typical regionalist in that she is not interested in her region as such. We recognize the intrinsic quality of her verse, while we are somewhat at a loss to account for it except as a sport. But, as George Whicher has pointed out, she is more significant for what she withdrew to than for what she withdrew from. With the positive faith of transcendentalism shaken, she could look upon heaven as on a map; and on God, Death, and Eternity as "integers of the mind." Her mature poems, as Whicher concludes, "show her weighing the data of consciousness, making distinctions and generalizations, and finally personifying the resultant isolated abstractions."[1] Her rejections of experience included not only the external world of society, but the internal world of systematic faith; her acceptances, the sensory impressions of nature, the unorganized intuitions of a highly personal sensitivity, and the analytical powers of her own mind. Her dependence on the dictionary for her revealing distortions of conventional meanings should perhaps be stressed more than it has. Noah Webster was finally her favorite author. The word for her was symbol, and by its manipulations, the truth as she recognized it within herself at a given point in space and a given instant in time, could be suddenly and vividly revealed.

An artist rather than a philosopher or critic, Emily Dickinson never stated explicitly and at length the poetic theory she developed and adopted for her own work, but the characteristics of the metaphysical poets are there, almost from the start, even though the evidence indicates that she did not know Donne, Herbert, and Vaughan, as did Emerson. The parallelism at this point is especially revealing because of the recent revival of interest in these British seventeenth-century poets. The metaphysicals were tossed, as was Emily Dickinson, between a disinterested universe on the one hand and a fading vision of heaven on the other. The resulting split of sensibilities, resort to "meditations," adoption of an analytical method of thinking, and the use of symbolic and formalized methods of expression which have been described by the critics as "metaphysical" are all so characteristic of the American writers we are discussing that the American movement might almost be described by the term "metaphysical" alone.

In this sense, Emily Dickinson was a modern metaphysical poet. Without any systematic study of the science of her day, she accepted the consequences of the subordination it assumed of the law of man to the law of things. Retaining from her transcendental inheritance the role of the artist as mediator, she pushed beyond Emerson to the complete isolation of the consciousness, and stood firmly on the ground of personal awareness. She accepted the impressions of nature as phenomena for aesthetic use and rejected the role of the realist as its mere recorder. Instead, she gave us the map of her highly individual consciousness, striving for expression through the deliberate manipulation of meaning and symbol rather than for communication. Hers was basically what American poetry has since largely become.

III

Lanier, on the other hand, was a less competent artist but a far more explicit formulator of doctrine than was Emily Dickinson. Neither his poetic theory nor his poetry give the impression of wholeness and aesthetic certainty that comes to us from the fragmentary work of Emily Dickinson, but because he elaborated his theory and then modified his art in so far as he could to conform to it, the tendencies at work in him are the more readily discernible.

Because he never allowed himself to become either skeptic or mystic, Lanier's views of man and the universe are relatively unimportant to our discussion. From romantic idealism he retained to the end of his life a faith in the ideal even after it no longer had the authority of an ethical system. His famous line, "Music is love in search of a word" could be taken as text for a discourse on the decline of romantic idealism into sentimentality; but it may also be taken as text for the new direction of his aesthetic thinking. If we translate it, "Art is the personality in search of expression," it places him immediately with the impressionists, the metaphysicals, and the symbolists; but such translation is admittedly a sloughing off of the remnants of transcendentalism which Lanier himself could not so easily let go. His theory pushed well beyond his art, and he is rightly accorded a higher place in our literary history as author of *The*

Science of English Verse than as author of "The Marshes of Glynn."

His theory is more important than is his poetry because it is the first thoroughgoing effort on the part of an American to make available to poetry the analytical method of science. Poe had attempted to do much the same thing in his day, but his accomplishment is not as impressive as is Lanier's, largely because science itself made such rapid progress between the 'forties and the 'eighties. Lanier's early poetry was Elizabethan, as was the early poetry of Keats, and in the same way. The romantic imagination took from the earlier poets their joy in sensuous impressions, but failed to take what the Elizabethans also had finally to offer: a disciplined aesthetic point of view and method. Later, when he prepared his Johns Hopkins lectures, Lanier's knowledge of English renaissance verse stood him in good stead, especially when it was corrected by the academic demands of a faculty already under German philological discipline and strong in its science departments. Lanier turned first to Puttenham rather than to Sidney for the inspiration of his poetic theory, and based his argument on the second book of *The Arte of English Poesie*, wherein its author discoursed "Of Proportion Poeticall," arguing that "the Philosopher gathers a triple proportion, to wit, the Arithmeticall, the Geometricall, and the Musicall." [2] In his effort to identify poetry as a branch of music, Lanier therefore sought in the discipline of mathematics the proportions of his art, and, leaving behind him Puttenham's rather elementary knowledge of mathematical science, undertook to study diligently the latest developments of the field as presented to him by his fellow lecturers at Hopkins, Sylvester in mathematics and Hastings in physics.

The effect of this theory on Lanier's later verse is the sloughing off of superficial Elizabethan and romantic conventions and a passionate effort to discipline sensory impressions, as they are received from nature by the sensitized consciousness, in an expression which uses rhythm and imagery in and for themselves. That Lanier did not succeed as fully as Emily Dickinson had with much less apparent struggle need not trouble us. Retain-

ing romantic idealism only as a basic philosophy, he tried with
the devotion of a zealot to make poetry, with the aid of science,
into a disciplined art, wholly valid within the limitations of impression and expression.

IV

In fiction, Henry James and Stephen Crane show almost
identical tendencies, and it is with James that the effort of some
of our literary historians to relate all of our late nineteenth-
century literature to the realistic movement becomes most obviously inadequate. His kinship with Howells, with whom he
is often paired in the histories, is limited to the adoption of a
dispassionate method of analysis. But he had no interest in environment except as it impinges on the sensibilities of his characters. So obsessed was he with the function of the artist that he
made it the central theme of numerous parables in short story
form. Although not all of his protagonists are practicing artists,
they usually discover what resolution they can for their divided
souls with the aid of aesthetic rather than ethical criteria. His
rejection of romantic idealism and his acceptance of deterministic
science did not lead him, as it did Howells, into a virtual sub-
mission as artist to the drift of things; rather, it stiffened his
aesthetic sense and challenged his conscience to make art itself
wholly valid. When he raised the question of the validity of
"the real thing" he found that even genuineness of character in
a model is inadequate to the purposes of the artist because it does
not allow enough plasticity in his material. James' artists, in their
consecration to the ideal—which is nothing more nor less than
the ideal of complete expression—are constantly finding that
life leaves them behind. This is the lesson of the master, but
James prefers to accept the choice somewhat ironically and to
devote himself to his ideal in spite of the divorce from life that
acceptance entails. His artists and his ladies are alike permitted
to concentrate on the golden bowls of their own personalities
and to ignore the inevitable flaw in each otherwise perfected
self or each otherwise complete experience. Once something approaching total awareness is achieved, life in its temporal and

spatial relationships is no longer significant. One loses one's role of ambassador and takes on that of cosmopolitan. Whether the place happens to be Rome, London, or Boston, one may move freely into a recreated past or into an imagined future where present life is reconstructed by idealization or memory or a combination of both. The personality is released—at a cost—from temporal and spatial bondage. His stories are perhaps little more than case histories of people who have chosen a variety of things, as Blackmur puts it, "advantageously chuckable for art." Irony or dismay at the price paid for such chucking is present in all of them, but only on occasion does he explore the vital flaw in the altar of personality each of his artists sets up. But when James probes deeply, as he came to do in his later stories, and reveals some of the dark recesses of the mind with almost Freudian implications, he is deserting his first province of the immediate consciousness and exploring a subconscious for which he has no adequate technique of analysis. Of such basic instincts as fear, ambition, or love, he had little firsthand knowledge.

I have purposely juggled some of James' most striking symbols to emphasize his kinship with Emily Dickinson on the one hand and with Stephen Crane on the other. Without the symbol, the impressionist would have little to say because it is the language of his art. In Stephen Crane, the symbol is developed to an even greater degree than in James, for Crane starts where James pauses, at the threshold of the unconscious. Cool and objective as his best stories are, their themes are finally referable to the single instinct of fear, or what modern psychiatry might prefer to call guilt. Working usually on smaller canvasses, Crane intensified his impressionistic technique because he was more keenly aware himself of the moment and its sensory impact, and his range was limited to his personal responses. He could not project himself, as could James, into the centers of fictional personalities like Isabel Archer or Milly Theale. His Maggie and Henry Fleming scarcely achieve sufficient existence to warrant their names, which in both cases were added after the stories had been fully conceived. They are merely girl and boy caught in the meshes of their own fears. In spite of the emphasis that historians put on the importance of these stories as social documents, neither tells much about environment in itself. Slums and bat-tlefield are mere settings for almost identical studies of the individual consciousness, robbed of self-directed motivation and swept along to defeat or victory as chance may direct. The personal crisis comes for Crane in an open boat or a lonely and ugly hotel—in places and at moments that have no meaning or value in themselves and are made significant only by the intense response of the virtually nameless character who stands at the center of the story. Only in instantaneous awareness of the sun or the sea, the dimly lighted room or the somber country-side, does Crane's art achieve near perfection. When he tried to extend it into more conventional plot narratives, it broke into unrelated pieces. But in those moments he reveals in near totality the single personality on the levels of both the conscious and the unconscious. In him, more than in any other nineteenth-century American writer, the artist justified himself, not to God, but to himself alone.

V

This concentration on a sort of generic self is perhaps the clue to the aesthetic significance of Henry Adams' dual master-piece, the *Education* and the *Chartres*. It has been relatively easy for critics to accept Dickinson, James, and Crane as literary artists, even though the effort to interpret their work in terms of realism has led to distortions. But in the case of Adams, we are totally unprepared to account for the aesthetic impact of his work because neither he nor his critics have presented it until very recently as art. There has been, ever since 1918 when the *Education* was first given to the public, a sort of semisecret, self-elected Henry Adams Society of enthusiasts for whom the reading of this book has been a major emotional experience and a determining influence on private thought. Only a handful of books in our literature—*Moby Dick, Leaves of Grass, Walden*—have seized the imaginations of their readers as have the *Education* and the *Chartres*. By the pragmatic test alone of impact on discriminating readers, these books stand a good chance of taking their place together as one of the major creative works in our literature.

Criticism up to this time has done little to account for or to test the value of their impressive influence. Adams taught history and made his first reputation as a historian. The *Education* and the *Chartres* were offered by him to historians as a professional challenge to their premises and their methods. The early reviewers, among whom were many of the distinguished historians of the day, took up the challenge and focused critical attention on this aspect of the problem. Their validity as interpretations of two eras was closely examined, and the value of their thesis that history must look to science for guidance was carefully weighed. Finally, the deterministic philosophy of the *Education* was analysed, restated, and evaluated as Adams' final position, while its skepticism was unappreciated and the mysticism of the *Chartres* was largely forgotten.

Adams emerged from this body of criticism as a brilliant but somewhat eccentric historian whose thought was certainly suggestive but in the end unsound. His intense self-centrality was taken as a disqualifying trait in the character of the scientific historian, his effort to interpret as well as to record the past by means of broad hypotheses was considered dangerous to objective truth, and his use of symbols to represent the components of his thesis seemed little more than amusing but incomprehensible whimsy. Even such former students as Henry Cabot Lodge and Henry Osborne Taylor, who at one time were profoundly influenced by him, were unwilling to come out in full support of this final tour de force. No one, it would seem— not even Adams himself—could explain the curious hold that these books had on thinking and feeling readers. At the same time that they were being dismissed by the authorities in Adams' own field, they were taking their places on an increasing number of shelves of essential reading, even for historians. Some of those who attacked them professionally were unwilling to part with them in their private and very personal libraries. To these readers, the *Education* and the *Chartres* were speaking as major works of art; and literary criticism is only now catching up with its public in a belated shock of recognition by Blackmur, Wilson, and some younger men. Just how great these books are, and in what ways, has yet to be measured, but the approach to our literary history which I have here suggested may, I hope, help in the task of literary reevaluation.[3]

First, it is necessary to exorcise the devil of failure—a theme upon which Adams himself harps continuously and which his critics have only too willingly taken as the starting point for evaluation. The author of the *Education* did not fail in any absolute sense. His failure was at least a successful protest against the demands of his inheritance and an overcoming of a temperamental sense of inadequacy. He failed only to conform to expectation on the one hand and to achieve the unachievable ambition that he set himself: the mastery of all knowledge and the solution of all human problems. All literary success—even Shakespeare's and Milton's—is in this sense failure, and it achieves its success by its very study of tragic failure. Adams did not fail.

Next, it is necessary to see him as a man of letters from the start. "If I write at all in my life out of the professional line," he told his brother in 1859, "it will probably be when I have something to say, and when I feel that my subject has got me as well as I the subject." [4] He wrote a multivolumed history, four biographies, two novels, at least two poems, hundreds of carefully composed letters, and numerous critical articles, the subjects of all of which obviously "got" him in exactly the sense he means. He then wrote two books which "got" him so completely that they set their own rules, developed their own form, and commanded their own readers in spite of his feeling that they were never completed.

Part of his sense of failure is doubtless attributable to this early realization that he was tempermentally an artist and thinker rather than a man of action in the family tradition. His detachment from the world of affairs was always defensive in tone but inescapable. He was surrounded by piles of the family papers as a child at Quincy, but he remembered rather the yellow light on the kitchen floor, the smell of rotting apples on the high shelf of his grandfather's closet. Affairs of moment transpiring at London during the Civil War or in Washington afterwards appeared to him as a pageant, the shapers of events as symbols of forces rather than as real men. When he wrote his history, for all its conscientious documentation from manuscript sources, it was, in the writing, a prose symphony with a carefully planned although unobtrusive thematic pattern, and when he wrote novels or biographies about people he knew, these people became almost impersonal agents, types of human conduct. His material in his earlier works was wholly drawn from those things about which an Adams was supposed to be concerned, but his view of it was always that of aesthetic detachment, never that of participation. He evaluted all things for their ultimate meanings and for their immediate impressions on his sensibilities. After the emotional crisis in his own life, this habit of mind was for the first time allowed full exercise. His first act was to symbolize death in the Rock Creek statue through the medium of his friend St. Gaudens; his last was to symbolize life by telling his own story as though he were writing of an actor playing the part he had lived.

Finally, the *Education* and the *Chartres* must themselves be defined in aesthetic terms. Adams gives us a hint in a preface to the former, which he wrote and Lodge signed at his request. He quotes a long paragraph from Chapter 29 in which he set himself no less than the task of stating the riddle of the Sphinx, if not of solving it. "Any schoolboy could see that man as a force must be measured by motion from a fixed point." He then arbitrarily selected a point from the twelfth century when, in the worship of the Virgin, man achieved Unity; a second from the present when man submitted to Multiplicity. "With the help of these two points of relation, he hoped to project his lines forward and backward indefinitely, subject to correction from any one who should know better." This statement has been taken as the announcement of an experiment in the application of mathematical physics to history; it is also the announcement of a plan for an epic of the mind.

What is this but a vast stage-setting for an imaginative explora-

tion of man's nature and destiny—a cosmology arbitrarily selected as Dante chose his Purgatory and Milton his Ptolemaic
cosmos. The specific points chosen are not important; there is
even much evidence to suggest that Adams weighed the possibility of using the Orient for his Unity rather than medieval
France, the Buddha rather than the Virgin. Nor is the particular
formula of the second law of thermodynamics in itself essential.
Living today, he might equally well have used Einstein rather
than Willard Gibbs to plot his books quite differently. They
would in the end have been the same, however, for he was
designing the aesthetic terms of a drama or epic of creation.
His stage was the cosmos, his characters the personifications of
ultimate forces, his themes the eternal and unanswered questions. His selection of St. Thomas and himself as protagonists
for the two acts of his drama was egotistic in a far more profound and legitimate sense than is the superficial egotism of
manner which offends some of his readers. For he, like other
characters in his cosmic drama, is a symbol rather than a fact.

Herein lies the final test of these books—in the adequacy of
their symbolism. They attempt on the grand scale what Crane,
Dickinson, and James were attempting in more detail—the symbolic representation of modern man adrift in an alien universe.
Their imaginative core lies in their intellectual awareness of
both the consciousness and the unconscious. They are studies
in sensibility, as is Joyce's *Ulysses* and Proust's *A la recherche
du temps perdu*. Their philosophic base lies in the mixture of
skepticism and mysticism which we have here taken as symptomatic of the aesthetic rather than the ethical approach to modern
literature. Their method is that of the impressionist, using the
evidences of the senses only as stimulators of aesthetic responses,
and that of the expressionist, giving shape to inner experience
by projecting its findings through the language of the symbol.
Only by recognizing the fact that there is a point at which the
realistic tendency in literature ceases to produce realism, and then
by attempting to define what it then actually does produce,
can we hope to provide a sound basis for the evaluation of what
became the dominant movement in our literature after 1930.

The formative phases of that movement lie in the major writers of the last years of the nineteenth century. It is in them that we first find faith in the aesthetic experience as an end in itself; the discipline of scientific analysis as applied to the work of art, thereby forming a reactionary or classical movement, did not develop until later.

NOTES

[1] George F. Whicher, *This Was a Poet, a Critical Biography of Emily Dickinson* (New York: Charles Scribner's Sons, 1938).

[2] George Puttenham, *The Arte of English Poesie* (London, 1811) p. 53. Cf. Lanier's preface to *The Science of English Verse*.

[3] This prediction has, of course, been richly fulfilled since this essay was written.

[4] *Letters of Henry Adams (1858–1891),* edited by Worthington Chauncey Ford (Boston: Houghton Mifflin Co., 1930), p. 51.

What Became of the Literary Radicals?

1946

A BY-PRODUCT OF THE CHAPTER ON "THE
BATTLE OF THE BOOKS" IN *Literary History of the United States.* PUBLISHED IN
The New Republic, LXIV (1946), 664–
666.

To THOSE OF US who were in college during World War I, the times seemed to be in a strange intellectual and literary ferment. Perhaps this is the normal experience of college, or of war; but if so, the absence of any such spirit among the young men of World War II was cause for comment. History was not repeating the pattern of a John Dos Passos in a John Hersey, nor of a Carl Sandburg in a Karl Shapiro. These new young men seemed wise before their time. If they protested, it was not against the sterile conservatism but against the callow childishness of their elders. For them there was no adolescent phase of storm and stress; they seemed mature at birth.

By contrast, their elders were, and still are, young men, even at sixty or seventy. The generation that found its spokesmen in such literary radicals as Randolph Bourne, Van Wyck Brooks, and H. L. Mencken, that marked its greatest triumph when Stuart Sherman deserted the ranks of the humanists to join the defenders of Dreiser, that argued the relationship of literature to life with the intensity of a debate on the atomic bomb—that generation is past. But those were not just any young men. They were—as they realized at the time—the heralds of a literary movement reaching maturity but not quite mature. There was, as Brooks said in 1915, "a nervous and acutely self-critical vitality" at work in those days, destroying the traditional concepts of American literature and culture and preparing for new creative efforts. His little book *America's Coming-of-Age* was a declaration of literary independence as historically significant for its day as was Emerson's *American Scholar* for the earlier renaissance. But this time American literature must tear itself free, not only from European, but from native-grown cultural conventions. If we today would understand the spirit of ripe age in our own young men, we should reexamine the spirit of raw youth in their elders. The revolt of the literary radicals, beginning about 1910 and extending, in its phase of protest, to about 1925, is a crucial chapter in our cultural history. What did these perennial adolescents revolt against? What did they call for? Did their revolt peter out or did it succeed?

At the time their challenge was thrown out, it sounded both new and startling, but it was neither. Behind it lay what Mencken called "the literary movement of the nineties"; before it lay the task of revising critical judgment of our cultural past so that living writers might honestly express what they lived.

Certainly there were many conventions that needed to be destroyed. The impasse which American literature had reached by 1910 is perhaps best illustrated in the confusion of William Dean Howells, the critical spokesman for the transition period between the time of Emerson and Longfellow and that of Dreiser and T. S. Eliot. Recognizing the force of the realistic movement which was sweeping through European literatures, he could never quite accept its full implications. In the last years of the old century, Howells welcomed the vitality of Stephen Crane's *Maggie* and Frank Norris' *McTeague*, but in his own work he made the mistake of assuming that American prosperity was American actuality. As a critic, he opened doors through which neither he himself nor any of his contemporaries could pass. The new movement lapsed because the American tradition, vital in its day, had become codified and restrictive and entrenched; the new forces in American life could not break through it. Young and fearless critics were needed—and they appeared.

II

Two of the most promising of the literary radicals of those war years, Randolph Bourne and Stuart Sherman, died before the phase of attack was over. Few people today even remember Bourne, the most nervous and self-critical of the group—its first leader and soon its anointed saint. For Bourne died early with a curse on his lips for the idealists who, under the guidance of Woodrow Wilson, had, he thought, led his country into what seemed to him a war for wealth and power. And those who remember Sherman think of him, not as a literary radical at all, but as a conservative who went over to the enemy—a kind of Benedict Arnold in reverse. But Sherman's discipleship to the humanists Babbitt and More was but a phase of his search for new ways of thinking. Always a literary radical at heart, he was fighting, as was Bourne, throughout his life for a reevaluation of values, and his move to a New York newspaper, where he was in the thick of the fight, was the most honest thing he ever did.

What these two might have accomplished had they survived the turbulent 'twenties and 'thirties may only be conjectured. What other literary radicals, who did survive, contributed to a revitalized interpretation of the American cultural past is a matter of record. Take Waldo Frank and Lewis Mumford, for example. In South America they ask today, "Have you any other writers of importance except Waldo Frank in North America?" And Lewis Mumford was but recently called to Europe to help plan the rebuilding of destroyed cities. No longer thought of in their own land as critics of literature, these two men have been acclaimed abroad as ambassadors of American culture. Yet it seems only yesterday that Frank's *Our America* (1919) and Mumford's *Golden Day* (1926) were shifting the crystal through which we view our cultural past and helping us to see Melville and Whitman in the high places formerly reserved for Longfellow and Lowell. In the 'thirties Frank was in Latin America and Spain and Russia, writing books about their civilizations, and Mumford was at home studying the technics of civilization. Each had chosen a specialty and each had developed an almost fanatic faith in his own solution to the riddle of contemporary civilization. Now builders rather than destroyers, they were little discussed in literary circles during those depression years.

There are two other literary radicals who have followed similar courses, but whose places in literary history are more secure because their devotion to literature has continued closer. H. L. Mencken spent his later years in the exploration of the American language, and Van Wyck Brooks that of American cultural history. Like Frank and Mumford, they both turned from the attack to the defense. Like them, they specialized their interests and developed their respective missions. Mencken in his study in Baltimore and Brooks in his country home in Connecticut were both for some years in virtual retirement from the literary forum. They were working at their elected tasks and hoping for enough time to complete them.

III

The appearance of *"Supplement One,"* a volume as substantial as the final edition of *The American Language* (1936) upon which it was hung, was testimony that Mencken's work was not yet done. That book was a beginning and not an end. Letters poured in daily to the Hollins Street address, and the files grew until a periodic inventory became necessary. But the masterwork itself was definitive in its way. Mencken had demonstrated that change is an essential element in a living language and should be encouraged rather than restrained. He had also demonstrated that language is an excellent index to the inner life of a people by rewriting the cultural history of America in the idiom of its popular expression. He called for one more reconsideration of the American tradition—and he supplied it.

One need not look far to discover the old fighting Mencken of the *Prejudices* in these flippant yet scholarly pages. For *The American Language* is its author's answer to his own challenge against complacency. Nor need one search the dusty and apparently dignified row of bound volumes of the old *American Mercury* to hear the wiry voice, to wince at shocking overstatement, to wriggle under digs at smugness and hypocrisy. The

literary radical who attacked the Christian moral code in its lat-
ter-day stiff formulation and who fought government by the
people in its leveling equalitarian phase was still in there, battling
with the weapons of irony and shock. The only difference is that
his blows are hammered at a single cause instead of being scattered. Red in the face with rage and protest, the reader of *The
American Language* lays down the book with the feeling that
here is a new kind of linguistic and historical anaylsis—in itself
almost as vital and organic a work of art as *Leaves of Grass*.

But the history of literary radicalism is even more fully illustrated by the career of Van Wyck Brooks. *The Flowering of
New England* (1936) won the Pulitzer Prize, was a Book-of-
the-Month selection and probably sold more copies than did any
other critical work on a literary subject in recent years. The
public liked it and read it, even though the academic historians
and critics were nonplussed and angry. If a work of history,
where were the footnotes and the quotation marks? If a work
of fiction, where were the plot and the characters? Was imagination running away with scholarly accuracy? To Brooks, this
was literary history and—become mild and conciliatory in these
later years—he supplied footnotes with an overgenerous hand
for the next of the series, *New England: Indian Summer* (1940),
but he did not alter his method or his intentions. He had set out
to answer his own early demand that the critics should supply
modern American writers with a "usable past." This could
only be accomplished by recreating the American aesthetic tradition in a living panorama drawn from letters and journals,
newspapers and playbills, novels and poems, paintings and music.
Other books were to supplement these two and recount the history of American creative activity—mainly literary—from the
days of Washington Irving to those of Van Wyck Brooks and
from the Boston of Lowell to the New Orleans of Cable and
the California of Mark Twain. American culture was to be re-
oriented in both time and place. This was the plan; the measure
of its execution will depend upon how far the imaginative vision
of a creative writer saturated in one part of his subject can be
stretched to all parts of it. Scholarship that depends upon crea-

tive imagination as one of its accepted tools may be sound scholarship, but only within the limits of the imaginative vision of the scholar. Let us not ask for too much.

These later books of Van Wyck Brooks are not literary history in the usual sense; nor are they social or cultural history as most other historians write it. The nearest approach to a description might be to call them the history of taste, but their eclectic quality and their long passages of literary criticism makes even this definition incomplete. For Brooks, the writer is always more interesting than the thing written; the general aesthetic environment more interesting than the individual writer. The one safe thing to say about these books is that they make important reading. They tell us things about our past that we should know and that could not be told in any other way so successfully.

Brooks' method is a direct response to his life's mission: to challenge the assumptions about the American tradition which had dominated our literature since its first "renaissance" in the days of Emerson and Lowell, and which by 1890 had seemed sterile and static; and then to reexamine our literary past in the context of the life out of which it had been created. This mission proceeded through three phases: an attack on accepted assumptions, a period of silence, an effort at reinterpretation. Here was literary radicalism passing through a cycle from destruction to construction, from attack to defense. Like Frank and Mumford and Mencken, Brooks elected his mission and specialized with the zeal of a convert.

IV

How then to evalute the work of the literary radicals, to chart the course and to define the scope of the movement? If these four survivors of the 'thirties may be taken as representative, their careers describe a cultural cycle. In the first place, they inherited the "literary movement of the 'nineties" rather than invented anything of their own. The emotional discovery of America—to use Sherman's phrase—had been slow in becoming articulate because, before 1910, its direction was uncertain and it was in conflict with too great an inertia of vested assumptions. But the literary radicals gave it voice, and for ten years or more their protests against complaisance and gentility seemed to be heard. In the teetering years between 1925 and 1933, they were quietly shifting from attack to defense while others fled. When "exiles" like MacLeish and Cowley and Hemingway began to return to a depression-ridden land, the full force of the movement was already being felt in renewed literary creation. The plays and poems and novels that appeared in such numbers during the 'thirties were grim rather than confident, but, because the old conventions had been so far weakened, they could be honest and they were strong.

Meanwhile, the survivors among the literary radicals, now no longer young in years, had each turned to his elected and ambitious task in the recreation of the American cultural tradition. Each made his distinctive contribution to the discovery of a past usable in the present. Rejected in their turn by the sage and disillusioned young men of the new generation, they cultivated their respective gardens.

That the literary radicals did not answer the questions they raised is matter of no moment; that their enthusiasms seem later a trifle callow is not important. They and their successors laid foundations for an indigenous culture in the excavations that they dug, and they were as much surprised as anyone at the buildings that were later erected. If American literature today is a dominant world literature—and there is every reason to believe that it is—these young men of the past must take no small share of the credit.

The Critical Movement in the Twentieth Century

1961

PUBLISHED AS "LITERATURE AND THE CRIT-
ICS" IN *American Perspectives*, EDITED BY
ROBERT E. SPILLER AND ERIC LARRABEE. CAM-
BRIDGE: HARVARD UNIVERSITY PRESS, 1961.

AN AWAKENING at the close of the nineteenth century to the inescapable role of major world power in a world but recently transformed by the latest revolution in science created by 1920 a self-conscious, self-critical, confused and violent, but finally triumphant literary renaissance, American in characteristics, universal in meaning and value. Like romantic movements in other times and places, this upsurge of literary power was both nationalistic and naturalistic: it drew its materials from its immediate culture, but it shared with other literatures of Western civilization the new view of man's relation to nature which modern scientific inquiry was unfolding. It rose to full expression by about 1935, and then was gradually defined and controlled by an analytical and critical reaction, thereby completing the full cycle of a literary movement.

In 1900 American literature was still a minor voice among the literatures of the world, with no more than a dozen or so masters to point to and a general level of mediocrity and derivitive ideas and modes in most of the current writers; by 1950 it had produced its own soul-searching and uncompromising interpretation of modern experience, and its current writers were read and studied in all literate quarters of the rapidly shrinking globe. The American people, by developing within its borders for the first time a vigorous creative and critical movement of national scope, had succeeded finally in destroying its complacent self-image as a colonial culture, and had substituted an image which was national only because it was a fully realized self-portrait of universal man. The story of how this transformation came about is too complex to be told here in full detail, but its main themes and stages of development can be traced in the work of those writers who were sufficiently conscious of their own aims and methods to express as well as to practice the literary theories of their times. It must be told therefore as a history of the literary criticism of an era, a people's view of its own expression of present and past experience through the writings of its most skilled and articulate interpreters.

II

The first phase of a major literary movement is likely to be romantic almost to the point of anarchism. Between 1910 and 1915, there was a stir on all our literary fronts. The reappearance of Dreiser's flagrantly naturalistic novel, *Sister Carrie*, virtually suppressed for a decade, was merely a symptom of a new freedom and vitality in fiction; the founding of specialized magazines like *Poetry* (Chicago) gave voice to an unexpected chorus; and an experimental theatre, widespread and amateur, came to Broadway to challenge the vested interests of the major producers. Scholars in the universities and colleges, and journalists in the marketplace, began to take note of developments in their own twentieth-century world and to tear at the barriers between past and present, "highbrow" and "lowbrow," national and international, tradition and originality. New magazines were founded and old ones reformed, poets once more became bards and took to the lecture platform to offer readings, original plays were offered to responsive audiences, and a new generation of critics and scholars began to examine seriously for the first time their own literature and culture.

Perhaps because of his very lack of connection with existing institutions and interests, Van Wyck Brooks was able in 1915 to announce the movement which everyone was beginning to feel but no one had yet quite defined. His little book, *America's Coming-of-Age*, created no great stir when it first appeared and has only recently been reprinted, but a search among contemporary documents reveals no better formulation of the critical issues of the day. It was, for the literary movement here under review, much what Wordsworth's Preface to *The Lyrical Ballads* was to the British and Emerson's *American Scholar* address was to the American romantic movements. In any case, it will here serve the historian's purpose of locating a point from which to study the interplay and movement of forces in the minds and affairs of men. It can be used to mark the summing up and restatement of the issue between literary idealism and realism of the late nineteenth century and as the announcement of the main action and reaction in the literary movement of the twentieth.

As in all such statements, the central plea of this book is that literature must periodically refresh itself by coming to terms with life in its own time and place. Specifically, Brooks argues that a tradition which he calls "Puritan" has consistently separated America's finest literary minds from the materials of life about them. The pattern of this division between ideals and facts, he believes, was set in Colonial days, and it persisted throughout the nineteenth century. "Transcendent theory," on the one hand, and "catchpenny reality," on the other, have divided American life between them ever since Jonathan Edwards took for his exclusive concern "the immanent eternal issues," and left to Benjamin Franklin the opportunism that originated in "the practical shifts of Puritan life" and which thereafter motivated American conduct in all practical affairs, particularly in business. This schism between the ideals of the intellectuals and the practices of the people accounts for America's failure to produce major literary figures, from Poe to Lowell and beyond, and especially for what Brooks feels to be the lack of vitality in the New England renaissance. Herein lies the difference between an Emerson who "never dreamed of

moulding society" and a Carlyle who "had the faculty of de-
vising and making intensely real and contagious a social ideal
the rudiments of which actually existed in the people he was
addressing." The inference is that "the more deeply and ur-
gently and organically you feel the pressure of society, the more
deeply and consciously and fruitfully you feel and you become yourself." The moral for twentieth-century American
literature is that our writers must concern themselves with
social ideals and social issues that "catch at the bottom of things,
like a dredging-machine" [1] before their writings can become
vital and authentic. The issue seemed to be one of social ethics
rather than of individual aesthetics. The road was at the fork: in
one direction lay social participation and responsibility arrived
at through realistic study and criticism and reform; in the other
lay alienation and aesthetic detachment. There is some hope
of healing the breach in American society, concludes Brooks,
because "It is true that under the glassy, brassy surface of American jocosity and business there is a pulp and a quick, and this
pulpy quick, this nervous and acutely self-critical vitality, is
in our day in a strange ferment." [2] But the American writer
has a further and more personal choice to make. He must decide whether to turn his art outside himself, identifying it
with the issues and reforms of his day, or to turn it inward on
the personal and subjective issues of his own mind and feelings.
Brooks, as the first major critic among the Literary Radicals,
cut the issue sharply for both the artist and his society. He made
it clear that the American artist in 1915 must help his society
come to terms with itself before he could come to terms with
his own art and use it for the expression of eternal verities and
and values.

This was a more basic kind of "realism" than that which the
earlier and milder radicals in literature like William Dean
Howells had launched against the entrenched "idealism" of the
acknowledged masters of the 'eighties and 'nineties. There had
been at least two quite contrary portraits of America presented
by the literature of the previous generation, that of the genteel
Eastern writers whose principal spokesmen had been James

Russell Lowell and Henry James, and that of the rebellious, continentally conscious group whose principal spokesmen had been Walt Whitman and Mark Twain. The plea for ideality as opposed to nationality was firmly presented by Lowell as early as 1849. "Literature survives," he wrote in a review of Longfellow's novel *Kavanagh,* "not because of its nationality, but in spite of it. . . . The only element of permanence which belongs to myth, legend, or history is exactly so much of each as refuses to be circumscribed by provincial boundaries." [8] To this position Whitman answered in the Preface to the 1855 edition of *Leaves of Grass:* "The American poets are to enclose old and new for America is the race of races. . . . As soon as histories are properly told there is no more need of romance. . . . The proof of a poet is that his country absorbs him as affectionately as he has absorbed it." [4]

At the close of the century this conflict between the genteel and the organic response of literature to American life had not been resolved. In spite of the efforts of W. D. Howells and the early realists to effect a reconciliation, the gap was growing wider. "Realism," he wrote, "is nothing more and nothing less than the truthful treatment of material," but he saw the truth of American democracy as quite different from that of the corrupt aristocracies of Europe, and he committed the logical fallacy of transferring this difference to the literature itself. In the United States, he argued, realism and idealism could survive together because "we have been now some hundred years building up a state on the affirmation of the essential equality of men. . . . These conditions invite the artist to the study and appreciation of the common, and to the portrayal in every art of those finer and higher aspects which unite rather than sever humanity. . . . The arts must become democratic, and then we shall have the expression of America in art." [5] Such an effort to reconcile the opposing views of the genteel idealist with the "barbaric yawp" of the true realist failed because it attempted to impose propriety on literature as well as on life, and the eruptive civilization of his times ignored his admonitions. The first critical spokesman for the new

literary movement had, long before 1900, sold out to the entrenched opposition, and the nineteenth century ended with
the genteel writers in full control.

Together with Dreiser's *Sister Carrie*, the year 1900 saw Edmund Clarence Stedman's *An American Anthology*, a garner-
ing of the poetic achievement of the past. "Our afterglow is
not discouraging," said the critic in his introduction, after
pointing out that the last of the literary masters of the older
generation was now dead. "We have a twilight interval, with
minor voices and their tentative modes and tones; still, the
dusk is not silent, and rest and shadow with music between the
dawns are a part of the liturgy of life, no less than passion and
achievement." [6]

A similar note of apology for the post-romantic generation
was sounded in 1903 by Professor William P. Trent of Columbia
in *A History of American Literature, 1607–1865:* "It is not
surprising that their performance is disappointing, especially
when it is compared with that of the writers who had been
permitted to grow up in the comparatively homogeneous and
unvulgarized New England of the first half of the century.
But in spite of all their disadvantages the newer writers . . .
upheld high ideals in a crass period, they profited from the les-
sons in literary art given by such British writers as Tennyson
and Thackeray," and "they helped greatly to educate and refine
their fellow-citizens." [7] And Professor Barrett Wendell of Harvard emphasized the same Anglicist and Brahmin prejudices,
the same belief that the primary purpose of literature is to refine the public morals, in *A Literary History of America*,
published in 1900. ". . . our main purpose . . . we should
constantly remember, is chiefly to discern what, if anything,
America has so far contributed to the literature of our ancestral English language." "The literary history of America is the
story, under new conditions, of those ideals which a common
language has compelled America, almost unawares, to share
with England. . . . The ideals which for three hundred years
America and England have cherished, alike yet apart, are ideals
of morality and of government,—of right and of rights. . . .

In the simple, hopeful literature of inexperienced, renascent New England . . . for a while, the warring ideals of democracy and of excellence were once reconciled, dwelling confidently together in some earthly semblance of peace." [8]

The first wave of the realist movement ended, therefore, in inadequacy so far as literary criticism was concerned, and during the first decade of the twentieth century the new forces went, as it were, underground. In evidence were, on the one hand, the "muck-raking" journalists and novelists like Lincoln Steffens and Upton Sinclair, whose work was subliterary at best, and, on the other, the editors and writers of the upper-class literary monthlies like *Atlantic, Harper's* and *Century*, which still dominated the literary marketplace. Mark Twain's humor soured into the caustic misanthropy of his later years, while Howells and James developed their art of sustained chronicles of "polite" behavior both at home and abroad. The stronger voices among the new writers, if heard at all, were as yet unrecognized as shapers of an awakening vitality in American letters.

III

The critics who led the revolt of 1910–1915 had in common only their impatience with the general state of stagnation that seemed to have settled on the American literary scene. Beyond this initial sharing of a common impulse, they broke up into a variety of schools and of species and subspecies. There was no one positive remedy upon which more than a handful could agree, although many saw "socialism" as a glorious sun on the horizon; nor did many of them think their problems through to a defined and stable position. The most that can be said of the situation is that it divided itself more or less along the lines of the classical emphases on Truth, Goodness, and Beauty, or according to the belief that the new order for American literature should seek its first foundations in an effort to understand and express the basic nature of things in its own time and place, in a reevaluation of its own experience according to revitalized ethical criteria, or in a fresh appreciation and analysis of literary

expression for its own sake. Convenient labels for these overlapping groups are: the Literary Radicals, the Neo-Humanists,
and the Aesthetic or Analytical Critics.

The Literary Radicals formed by far the largest group. Most
of them followed the line that Van Wyck Brooks was to define,
and proposed a more basic kind of "realism" than the descriptive and superficial method of Howells. This realism sought to
understand the nature of man and his universe in the light of
the new science, thus falling in with the naturalistic movement
in European literature, and, at the same time, to examine and
evaluate the principles and conditions of twentieth-century
American society as they actually were and not as a vague and
sentimental idealism would like them to be, thus identifying itself
with the social criticism by which the European movement was
so strongly motivated. In this group, literary criticism was hardly
distinguishable from metaphysical and social criticism. One may
divide its members into those whose social and political views in-
clined them to the Left or to the Right, but most of them were
content to espouse vague causes like "democracy," "socialism"—
even "anarchism"—rather than to conform, as their European
counterparts so soon did at their cost, to organized systems of
dogma and to political dictatorships. They were united only by
their primary belief that literature is never vital except when it
deals directly and critically with life.

The term "Literary Radical" was taken by Brooks from the
title of an unpublished novel about the then younger generation
by his friend Randolph Bourne, and it was to that physically
handicapped but intellectually dynamic young disciple and later
opponent of the philosopher John Dewey that the group first
looked for leadership. "He saw," wrote Brooks later, "that we
needed, first, a psychological interpretation of these younger
malcontents, secondly, a realistic study of our institutional life,
and finally, a general opening of the American mind to the
currents of contemporary desire and effort and experiment
abroad." [9] Bourne's own writings are scattered but incisive
fragments on literature and society, but when brought together
they provide a program of revolt for youth at a time when the

normal protest of a rising generation against its fathers was about to be magnified into a World War that cut civilization's future from its past. Mixing sociological with literary study, reading Dreiser and Dostoevski as well as Dickens, writing with equal insight on the cultural nationalism of the European countries and the raw cosmopolitanism of the American Midwest, Bourne saw in his world only uninhibited invitations to the mind of adventurous youth. Even though his naïveté was soon dashed by the issues of war, his early death left a challenge that more vigorous if perhaps more callous warriors like H. L. Mencken were to take up and carry forward.

With Mencken, the attack on the British-American genteel tradition became more virulent if not more profound. Perhaps because his grandfather had emigrated from Germany, perhaps because of an early study of Nietzsche, his thoughts and feelings were instinctively middle-European and his political philosophy pointed more toward Hitler than toward Lenin. In his series of *Prejudices*, starting in 1919, he centered his ire on Puritanism— defined much as Brooks had defined it—and on the "professors," any of those teachers of conformity, in school or out, who, he thought, substituted hypocrisy for honesty. He attacked the literary great and discovered and defended the literary underdog. Because his irony so far outdistanced his judgment, his importance as a critic is not so great as was his service as an irritant, but he did call attention to Dreiser, Hüneker, Conrad, and many other new voices in literature, in most cases supporting his views vigorously and for the right reasons. But the overall image of America that emerges from his collected writings is a caricature rather than a description: anti-British, anti-democratic, anti-respectable. Every stroke of his pen tended to bring the "lowbrow" up and the "highbrow" down, to force modern American man to view himself and his society honestly as products of human desires and weaknesses rather than as reflections of lofty and inflexible ideals.

He summed up the situation thus: "Romance, in American fiction, still means only a somewhat childish amorousness and sentimentality—the love affairs of Paul and Virginia, or the pale adulteries of their elders. And on the side of realism there is an almost equal vacuity. . . . They never penetrate beneath the flow of social concealments and urbanities to the passions that actually move men and women." [10] That this is so inaccurate a description of the literary situation some thirty years later is a circumstance for which H. L. Mencken is in no small degree responsible.

The ideas of the Literary Radicals produced a whole shelf of books of reevaluation and criticism of American life during the period between the outbreak of World War I in 1914 and the stock market crash in 1929. One popular form of the movement was the "debunking" biographies like H. S. Gorman's *A Victorian American–Henry Wadsworth Longfellow* or Lloyd Morris' *The Rebellious Puritan–Portrait of Mr. Hawthorne* in which an acknowledged master is reexamined "realistically," especially with respect to his private life and personal frustrations, and is thus reduced in stature. Another was the broad reevaluation of contemporary American society and the arts, like Waldo Frank's *Our America* or Harold Stearns' symposium *Civilization in the United States*, usually with a plea for reform of ideas and institutions as well as criticism of existing conditions. A third, and perhaps the most useful in the long run, was the attempt to discover America's "usable past" by a rejection of the assumed American tradition and a review of eighteenth- and nineteenth-century culture, again with a "realistic" point of view. Lewis Mumford's studies of architecture, *Sticks and Stones*, and of literature, *The Golden Day*, were perhaps as successful as any of the earlier attempts at historical reassessment. With the founding of the American Literature Group of the Modern Language Association in the early twenties, of the *Saturday Review of Literature* in 1924, and of the scholarly journal *American Literature* in 1929, the forum and the academy began to unite in a common effort. Carl Van Doren stepped down from his desk at Columbia to be literary editor of the *Nation* (1919–1922); Henry Canby came from New Haven to edit the *Saturday Review* for twelve years; and a previously unknown Vernon L. Parrington came out of the West with *Main Currents in Ameri-*

can Thought (1927–1930) to give a final academic sanction to the reexamination of America's literary past as expression of her main political and social tradition, which Professor Parrington defines as the democratic-agrarian philosophy of Thomas Jefferson in all its variations and contraries.

Between 1927 and 1933, the radical literary movement seems to have run its course, at least in its first phase of shock and reevaluation. Many of its leaders either died, like Bourne and Parrington; readjusted their sights—like Brooks, Mumford, and Mencken—before undertaking major works of synthesis, or identified their radicalism with one or another of the dogmatic ideologies—Freudianism, Marxism, Fascism—which were then being imported from Europe to absorb and channel American critical thinking. Its main drives of critical nationalism and philosophical naturalism were by this time incorporated into the new fiction, poetry, and drama which, by 1925, were already showing the full inspiration of the radical challenge in their free choice of materials from life, their uninhibited courage in dealing with previously forbidden themes, and their devastating critical candor. Theodore Dreiser, Sinclair Lewis, John Dos Passos, Eugene O'Neill, Carl Sandburg, and Robert Frost were among those who most directly profited from the interference run by the Literary Radicals.

Although sharing with this group an impatience with the conventionality of literary forms and modes at the turn of the century, the other two groups of critics that began to claim attention around 1910 were reactionary rather than experimental in their emphases. Both the Neo-Humanists and the Aesthetic-Analytical critics called for reexamination of standards and forms rather than for greater freedom in life and literature, the one for new and firmer ethical bases for art, and the other for more attention to art and the experience of art for its own sake.

When George Santayana wrote *The Genteel Tradition at Bay* in 1931, he was attacking the Neo-Humanists rather than the older defenders of ideality: "The humanists of the Renaissance were . . . pleasantly learned men, free from any kind of austerity, who, without quarreling with Christian dogma, treated it humanly, and partly by tolerance and partly by ridicule hoped to neutralize all its metaphysical and moral rigour." The new American humanists, on the other hand, seemed to be returning to the sources of the movement in the theocratic doctrines of Calvin. "Culture won't do, they must say, unless it be the one right culture: learning won't do, unless it fills out the one true philosophy." [11]

The new movement was signalized by the appearance in 1904 of the first volumes of Paul Elmer More's *Shelburne Essays,* which continued through 1909, when More became editor of the *Nation,* and then on for many years. These essays were followed by Irving Babbitt's *Literature and the American College* in 1908 and *The New Laokoön* in 1910, and by William Crary Brownell's *American Prose Masters* in 1909. By 1910 these philosopher-critics were apparently aware that they, and some younger men with them, were fellow workers in a cause. Their primary purpose was to attack what they thought to be the extreme pretensions of the new science, whether it appeared as philology in the college literature departments or as a sponsor of unethical conduct on the part of Theodore Dreiser's heroines. By offering a mechanistic natural law as the ultimate law of the universe, rather than the law of God or the will of man, science, they charged, was attacking human integrity at its roots and destroying literature along with life. Hoping to avoid the dogmatism of religion as well as that of science, these critics sought an answer to their problem in the middle ground of traditional human culture. They urged a return to introspection as a means of achieving knowledge and right conduct, substituting the "inner check" for the inner light, and human equilibrium for the extremes of theocracy and natural anarchy.

The sweet reasonableness of this position was not always reflected in the personal character and conduct of its proponents. Babbitt in particular was by temperament a warrior in the lists, fighting for his view of literature against Kittredge and the philologists as well as against Mencken and the Literary Radicals. More and Brownell, on the other hand, revealed some rather extreme romantic ideas in their essays on such American writers as Thoreau and Cooper. In the long run, it was not so much the rigid dogmatism without dogma for which they argued as their emphasis on the study of literature for the sake of its ideas that gave them a major role in American literary history. By 1930, when their leading disciple, Norman Foerster, garnered the best fruit of their thinking in *Humanism in America,* the movement itself had run its course. Like the Literary Radicals, the Neo-Humanists had served mainly to give literature a reason for feeling alive and important in a materialistic society.

The aesthetic movement in criticism was not at the start analytical or in any way associated with Neo-Humanism. James G. Huneker urged enjoyment as the aim of all the arts, and "John Charteris" of Willoughby Hall, the alter ego of that Southern gentleman, James Branch Cabell, suggested that all the auctorial virtues were "distinction and clarity, and beauty and symmetry, and tenderness and truth and urbanity." "So I in point of fact desire of literature, just as you guessed, precisely those things of which I most poignantly and most constantly feel the lack in my own life." [12] His plea that Romance, merely because it can exist only beyond life, contains a truth that is higher than that of Realism is a sensuous substitute for the ideality of Brooks' highbrows. An American version of Walter Pater, Cabell, with a few others, tried to lead the revolt down the primrose path of imaginative escape from reality.

It remained for J. E. Spingarn to offer a code and a discipline to all such vague searchings for the exclusive pleasures of art, and to cast the literary revolt into definitive terms as an aesthetic activity alone. American criticism "has neither inherited nor created a tradition of esthetic thought," he wrote in "The American Critic." For nearly all our critics, "a disconnected body of literary theories takes the place of a real philosophy of art. . . . Art has something else to give us; and to seek moral or economic theories in it is to seek moral or economic theories, but not art." Challenging at once the social concern of a Van Wyck Brooks, the moral anxiety of an Irving Babbitt, and the sensuous impressionism of a Cabell, Spingarn sums up the need of the American critic: "Only the drenching discipline that comes from mastery of the problems of esthetic thought can train us for the duty of interpreting the American literature of the future." [13]

IV

That future was becoming a present as Spingarn wrote, because the balance of forces of action and reaction in the decade 1925–1935 made it possible for the American writer of fiction, poetry, and drama to confront the materialism of his society and ask of it the ultimate questions about the worth and the destiny of man. American literature had really come of age.

The generation of Hemingway and Faulkner was far more sophisticated aesthetically than was that of Dreiser and Sandburg. The task of opening up the new material for shaping by new art forms had been completed by 1920. The even greater task of sharpening and refining the tools of a new art made its urgent demands. Simply because the situation required it, this generation developed the aesthetic detachment that art demands and that Spingarn had called for. In doing so, it took the first steps from revolt into reaction, from romantic exuberance into classical control. The peak of the movement was reached at that moment when the artist found himself both wholly within and wholly outside his material. This a dozen or more American writers succeeded in doing—among them O'Neill in *Mourning Becomes Electra*, Faulkner in *Absalom, Absalom!*, and T. S. Eliot in *Four Quartets*—but the moment passed.

By 1940 there was more than a war to declare the approaching end of a literary era. A new separation of the artist from his society was taking place at the very moment when they seemed in the best working rapport. It had been hinted in O'Neill's Hairy Ape who could not find the group to which he rightfully "belonged," in Hemingway's Jake Barnes who suffered a symbolic as well as a physical injury to separate him from his fellows, and in Wolfe's forever wandering and lost alter ego, Eugene Gant. In all these writers, the issue of alienation of the sensitive spirit from his society was a theme within the material itself.

When the artist finally achieved—first in poetry and criticism, much later in fiction and drama—the actual aesthetic detachment that O'Neill and Hemingway, and especially Wolfe, never quite sustained, he began a fatal separation from the material that gave life to his work. The reaction was in progress.

The theme of the alienation of the sensitive human spirit from the harsh realities of his world is, of course, common to the great literature of other times and places, including the American nineteenth-century renaissance, but it seemed, in the context of the modern machine and of American industrial supremacy, to force a rather special kind of escape in the twentieth-century group. Henry James, Gertrude Stein, and Ezra Pound had fled to Europe and settled there permanently well before World War I, and T. S. Eliot was soon to follow. Others, like Sherwood Anderson, Ernest Hemingway, and Archibald Mac-Leish, joined a widespread expatriate movement between the war and the depression, but returned to the United States by about 1930 to make their peace with its civilization.

Malcolm Cowley has described this migration in *Exile's Return* (1934) as motivated by three kinds of escape: into art, into the primitive, and into another land—presumably the continent of Europe. This explanation will do for those artists who took the third of these choices, but for the causes and meanings of the other two, one would better turn to Edmund Wilson's *Axel's Castle*, perhaps the best contemporary study of this problem of the alienated artist, a book which does for the literary reaction much of what Van Wyck Brooks' early books did for the literary revolt: it provides a summit from which the landscape may be surveyed before and after.

Taking as his text the long poem *Axel*, published by Villiers de l'Isle-Adam in 1890, Wilson presents a study of the Symbolist movement in contemporary European and American literature. This movement, he assumes, was based on the "renunciation of the experience of the outside world for the experience of the imagination alone." Poets, he finds, were particularly susceptible to this tendency because they seemed to have no place in "the utilitarian society which had been produced by the industrial revolution and the rise of the middle class." They might choose either the way of Axel (a retreat to the tower of their own sensibilities) or the way of Rimbaud (a retreat to distant and primitive lands). For both, the Symbol, including the entire art of language, becomes an instrument for concealing rather than revealing the outer reality, a screen around the inner world of the imagination, and a set of mechanical devices that can be used at will by the poet to satisfy his own needs. The symbols of the Symbolists are not, like those of Christianity, for example, representative of large and commonly held concepts; rather they are "usually chosen arbitrarily by the poet to stand for special ideas of his own—they are a sort of disguise for these ideas." [14] Of the six writers discussed by Wilson, two are French, two Irish, and two American—both of the latter having retreated to Europe, T. S. Eliot to London and Gertrude Stein to Paris. The movement, as he sees it, was international in character but had its roots in France. Why, then, is it important to American literary history or to the shaping of the American self-image?

The image of the alienated artist was already established long before 1930 as a characteristic American image, traceable to Poe, James, and innumerable minor writers of the nineteenth century. The Symbolist movement fell into this tradition and, once established on American soil by the expatriate or repatriated artist of the 'twenties and 'thirties, became the principal counter-image to that of the socially participating artist of the early years of the century. Much of this development can be traced to the influence of two literary women, Amy Lowell and Gertrude Stein, who had a far deeper and wider critical influence than the intrinsic merits of their own writing might warrant.

The influence of Amy Lowell was felt mainly through her sponsorship of the Imagist movement in the American poetry of the early 'twenties. At the time when Frost, Sandburg, Lindsay, and Masters were producing the bardic poetry of an aroused people, Amy Lowell set up the standard of a counter-movement. Stigmatized as the high priestess of a new poetic license known as free verse, she took pains in her own survey of the movement, *Tendencies in Modern American Poetry*

(1917), to stress the control and discipline that Imagism demanded. These poets, she felt, represented the third stage of the revolt, a stage in which poetry could "inherit in plenitude and calm" that for which the early and more stormy poets had fought. The rules that were to govern their performance emphasized the exact use of common language, the discovery of new rhythms, absolute freedom in choice of subject, and the use of images that could "render particulars exactly and not deal in vague generalities." Poetry, finally, must be "hard and clear, never blurred or indefinite"; it must be the product of concentration. Freedom of subject matter had been achieved and was to be maintained, but freedom of form was to be severely disciplined through control of language, image, and rhythm.

These first signs of reaction were simultaneous with the stormiest stages of the romantic movement, but again American literature was reflecting a European trend. American Imagism was but an echo of a recent movement in French poetry, and it was to France that America's other high priestess of the new order had retreated as early as 1902. Gertrude Stein had been thoroughly trained in scientific method at Radcliffe and at the Johns Hopkins medical school, and she knew and understood the new movements in painting. Approaching the problem of literary expression from the angle of the psychology of language, she was able to crack the rigid forms of normative grammar, syntax, and rhetoric, as Cézanne and Picasso were fracturing the conventional forms of painting. Words and images suddenly became mere colors on a palette to be applied as the aesthetic sense of the artist dictated. With this new fluidity of medium, she then turned to experiments of verbal expression. Never quite achieving the aesthetic control for which she pleaded, she was able nevertheless to communicate her principles to those who were finer artists than she—among them Ezra Pound, Sherwood Anderson, Ernest Hemingway, and, at one remove, T. S. Eliot and William Faulkner. Surely the place of this lifelong expatriate in American literary history has been underestimated. Her *Three Lives* (1909), apparently anarchic in concept and discursive in style, is the focal book of the new order in American prose and poetic arts. It released the scientific principles of form as Dreiser's *Sister Carrie* had released the new material. It was an elementary textbook for the American Symbolists.

After a brief flirtation with the Imagists, in 1908 America's most technically gifted and experimental poet, Ezra Pound, took up what he hoped would be a permanent residence in Europe. Between 1920 and 1924 he was in Paris in close association with the expatriate groups of all countries at the modest salon of Gertrude and Leo Stein. Soon thereafter he moved to Rapallo, Italy, and associated himself with the rising fascism which he found congenial to a theory of "usury" he had even by then developed to the point of fanaticism. Apparently a follower of fads, Pound in perspective appears not only as a naturally gifted poet, but as a consistent advocate and student of the basic requirements of his craft. "Great literature," he wrote in 1931, "is simply language charged with meaning to the utmost possible degree." [15] His experiments in poetry, from the simple early verse to the complicated *Cantos* of recent years, are all exercises in the use of language as form. Whatever posterity may think of his political and economic views, it cannot escape the facts of his inherent poetic gifts and his major contribution to an understanding of the principles and possibilities of language when released and controlled by modern science. Pound became for subsequent American writers the model of the alienated artist who achieved success by devotion to the requirements of his art, and who found his relation to society by rejecting it. His critical detachment from American life was so complete as to make his social thinking absurd, but his position supreme as lord of the tower of Edmund Wilson's Axel.

In acknowledging Pound as his master, T. S. Eliot was marking the beginning rather than the end of his poetic career. In him the alienated artist perfected his role. Eliot's is a deeper and broader mind than those of his contemporaries and followers. Profiting from Pound's experiments in language and the uses of the past, he knew what to take and what to leave. His earliest published poems reveal a long technical and philosophical apprenticeship. An isolated artist in that he has held firmly to the necessary alienation of the artist-role, he has never allowed himself to lose touch with the society of his day and with its underlying ethical structure.

There has never been any question in Eliot's mind about the reactionary character of his own thought. Admitting in one place that he began as a disciple of Irving Babbitt and in another that he is a Royalist, an Anglo-Catholic, and a Classicist, he insists time and again that literature must be judged by moral, religious, and even political as well as aesthetic standards. The reading of "great" literature is only one of many ways that an individual may use in cultivating his own intellectual and spiritual growth, and there is for him a right and a wrong in his measurement of what is great. But to recognize the close interrelationship of the parts of experience is not to confuse the various functions of the human intelligence. He differs finally from Babbitt in that the latter speaks of "humanism *and* religion"; whereas Eliot recognizes an alternative of religion *or* humanism. When he says, "The 'greatness' of literature cannot be determined solely by literary standards," he adds, "though we must remember that whether it is literature or not can be determined only by literary standards." [16]

Eliot's literary conservatism is therefore parallel with his general conservatism as an individual, but it is none the less distinct. For him art is a special kind of experience and should not be confused with other kinds. It is complete in itself. What one believes as a man does not make poetry; it merely supplies the material for the maker. "The poet makes poetry, the metaphysician makes metaphysics, the bee makes honey, the spider secretes a filament; you can hardly say that any of these agents believes: he merely does." Eliot himself as a poet and critic is careful to make and to judge poetry as poetry, and not to inject into it his own emotions. Not until it becomes a total "objective correlative" of life is it good art, as *Hamlet* is not a good play because Shakespeare is obviously feeling more in this case than his medium will allow him to express.[17] Eliot is unhappy about most literature since the seventeenth century because he finds that somehow there occurred at that time a "dissociation of sensibility," a break between the capacity to experience and the adequacy of the medium to contain the expression. "While the language became more refined, the feelings became more crude." He himself went back to the English Metaphysicals to learn his art, as Emerson and Emily Dickinson had before him, and he has in effect dismissed the whole romantic movement and all that it stands for. As one trained in philosophy, he is able to separate the aesthetic from other functions of his mind without involving the other functions immediately, a feat that even Pound has never quite been able to accomplish satisfactorily. Without becoming an analytical critic, Eliot provided the platform on which the analysis of meaning could become a specialization in itself; and without alienating the artist in himself from the rest of his personality, he distinguished the artist-role so clearly and completely from other roles that he prepared the way for a total alienation. His importance to American literary history lies both in his general conservatism and in the autonomy he provides for the aesthetic function of the artist and critic alike.

Some critics, like Kenneth Burke and Yvor Winters, have likewise attempted to distinguish the special role of the artist without destroying the interdependence of art and ethics, but others have been willing to take the next step and complete the separation. By 1939, with the founding of the *Kenyon Review* by John Crowe Ransom, the analytical reaction was ready to take command of the literary situation in the United States, and the main dynamic phase of the twentieth-century literary movement was over.

V

Meanwhile, naturalism had shown signs of exhaustion even before the outbreak of World War II. Chief symptoms of the decline of this romantic and organic impulse lay in the search for authority, the willingness to subordinate free inquiry to dogma in literature as well as in politics, religion, and other aspects of human thought. Eliot's turn to the Anglican Church and Pound's identification with the cause of Italian fascism were only extreme examples of a general movement in the 'thirties toward conservatism and conformity among American writers. Those who did not become expatriated or did not remain so were attracted by the extremist movements of communism and fascism at home. Acceptance of the doctrine of Marx in its most dogmatic form became the badge of the "radical" critic of 1930–1940. V. F. Calverton's *The Liberation of American Literature* (1932) and Granville Hicks' *The Great Tradition* (1933) demonstrated what can happen to a socio-literary approach like Parrington's when the Marxian dialectic is substituted for Jeffersonian liberalism. James T. Farrell's *A Note on Literary Criticism* (1936) and Edmund Wilson's *To The Finland Station* (1940) attempted to discover the relation of American life to the new ideology while avoiding the excessive dogmatism and political commitment of the extremists. Magazines were taken over by control groups of both the political Left and Right, and writers of fiction, poetry, and drama, as well as of criticism, became critics of the democratic tradition and the capitalistic order rather than, like the earlier Literary Radicals, advocates at most of reform. Anti-Americanism and ideological conformity were characteristics of many of the naturalistic writers and critics by 1940. The symbolism of the Spanish Civil War as an uprising of the so-called "Democratic front" against the threat of fascism brought the new alignment to a head; the signing of the Russo-German Pact broke the spell. By 1940, the advocates of literature as the expression of the forces at work in American society were a scattered and self-defeated army.

The purists, on the other hand, who had long been advocating a new separation of literature and society, began at the same time to find refuge in the aesthetic-linguistic-psychological emphases of Stein, Pound, Eliot, and a revived Henry James. The metaphysical or Symbolist movement in American poetry and the analytical or "New" movement in American criticism began to take root in American soil in the 'thirties, and by 1945 it had become the dominant school. Only then did it begin to show any marked influence on the American drama and novel, as Freudian analysis offered fiction an apparently systematic symbolism. Those writers and critics who felt the need for orthodoxy and authority—and who among the American writers in the postwar period did not?—found in a kind of aesthetic existentialism an escape from the dilemma of social and political conformity. The "New" critics took over, and the dominant literary image of America began to be drawn by a highly intellectual and aesthetically sensitive coterie.

The result was a major contribution by America to world literature in the form of a literary reaction, as the American literary revolt had contributed its major writers to the naturalistic movement in world literature in the early years of the century. The existence of several schools of criticism like the Southern Agrarians or Fugitives (Ransom, Tate, Cleanth Brooks, R. P. Warren, etc.), and the Chicago School, as well as of individualists like Burke, Winters, and Blackmur, does not prevent these critics from accepting a strong common core of orthodoxy. Instead of a central principle of organic process, they substitute a central principle of organic form, which throws the critical emphasis away from problems of social context and of historical or biographical causation and onto problems of structure, texture, and meaning in the work of art itself. Language and symbol are embraced in the single concept of metaphor, and literature becomes a substitute for rather than an involvement in life. The central doctrine of the movement is expressed by W. K. Wimsatt, Jr. and Cleanth Brooks in their *Literary Criticism, A Short History*, published in 1957. " 'Form' in fact embraces and penetrates 'message' in a way that constitutes a deeper and more substantial meaning than either abstract message or *separable ornament*." [18] Escaping from the conflicts and complexities of modern life, the new analytical criticism supplies a "job of work" to be done and the tools, mainly of rhetoric, with which to do it.

It is too soon, perhaps, to sum up the achievements of these analytical critics, but some of their contributions are already apparent. They have developed in the cultivated reader a much sharper sense of the values in the work of art with which he is dealing; they have singled out and set in a permanent gallery some of the really great and nearly forgotten or misinterpreted works of the American literary imagination; and they have stimulation and guided a whole generation of new writers. Many of their judgments of their contemporaries—particularly of writers like Wolfe, O'Neill, and Dos Passos, who are remarkable for their vitality rather than for their refinement of sensibilities—have probably been too much hampered by dogmatism to stand the test of time, but any lack in this respect is more than compensated for by their aid in the reevaluation of earlier authors like Hawthorne, Melville, Stephen Crane, and Henry James, and by their insights into such highly tempered contemporaries as Hart Crane, Faulkner, Eliot and Wallace Stevens.

It is not too soon, however, to recognize in this reactionary movement a return to the status of separation of literature and American life which aroused the concern of the Literary Radicals of the early years of the century. The gigantic swing of the great mass of the American people away from drama, fiction, and poetry to other media such as movies, television, and radio would indicate an increasing need for mass expression that written literature is failing to supply. The trend of historians and social scientists away from studies of economic and political causation to studies of human behavior itself as the best index to culture would suggest a way of approaching the larger problems of literary meaning that the techniques of the analytical critics are entirely inadequate to cope with. Minority groups such as Jews, Catholics, Negroes, and recent cultural migrants from Western Europe and the Orient are producing a large proportion—and perhaps the most vital part—of a literature that was once Protestant, Anglo-Saxon, and middle-class. The literary image of the America of the second half of the twentieth century is already beginning to take recognizable form as something quite different from the images of either rebellion or conformity discussed in the preceding pages, but it is too soon to attempt to describe it, much less to evaluate its worth or indicate its direction.

NOTES

[1] Van Wyck Brooks, *America's Coming-of-Age* (New York: B. W. Huebsch, 1915), pp. 81–82, 92, 170.

[2] *Ibid.*, p. 161.

[3] James Russell Lowell, Review of Longfellow's novel, *Kavanagh*, *North American Review*, LXIX (July, 1849), 202, 206–207.

[4] Walt Whitman, Preface to 1855 edition, *Leaves of Grass* (Garden City: Doubleday, Doran, 1931), pp. 488–507.

[5] W. D. Howells, *Criticism and Fiction* (New York: Harper and Brothers, 1891), pp. 73, 139–140.

[6] E. C. Stedman, *An American Anthology* (Boston: Houghton Mifflin Co., 1900), p. xxviii.

[7] William P. Trent, *A History of American Literature, 1607–1865* (New York: D. Appleton, 1903), pp. 462–463.

[8] Barrett Wendell, *A Literary History of America* (New York: Charles Scribner's Sons, 1900), pp. 10, 521–530.

[9] Randolph Bourne, *History of a Literary Radical, and Other Essays*, ed. Van Wyck Brooks (New York: B. W. Huebsch, 1920), p. 24.

[10] H. L. Mencken, *A Book of Prefaces* (New York: Alfred A. Knopf, 1917), pp. 275–276.

[11] George Santayana, *The Genteel Tradition at Bay* (New York: Charles Scribner's Sons, 1931), pp. 4–5, 23.

[12] James Branch Cabell, *Beyond Life* (New York: Robert M. McBride, 1919), pp. 342, 355.

[13] J. E. Spingarn, "The American Critic," *Creative Criticism and Other Essays* (New York: Harcourt, Brace and Co., 1931), pp. 123–147, 93.

[14] Edmund Wilson, *Axel's Castle* (New York: Charles Scribner's Sons, 1931), pp. 257–258, 268, 20.

[15] Ezra Pound, *How to Read* (LeBeausset [Var] France, 1932), p. 17.

[16] T. S. Eliot, *Selected Essays* (New York: Harcourt, Brace and Co., 1932), p. 343.

[17] *Ibid.*, pp. 118, 124–125.

[18] W. K. Wimsatt, Jr. and Cleanth Brooks, *Literary Criticism, A Short History* (New York: Alfred A. Knopf, 1957), p. 748.

The Alchemy of Literature
1958

READ AT BEDFORD COLLEGE, UNIVERSITY OF
LONDON, AND SUBSEQUENTLY BEFORE STU-
DENT GROUPS IN ENGLAND, FRANCE, GER-
MANY, AND THE SCANDINAVIAN COUNTRIES
DURING APRIL, MAY, AND JUNE, 1959. PUB-
LISHED (IN GERMAN) IN *Zwei Völker im
Gespräch*. FRANKFURT: WALTER PLATA,
1961; II, 106–125.

IN THE FEW WEEKS that I have been in England, I have been
impressed again by both the similarities and the differences in
the cultures and in the literatures of our two peoples. At one
minute I feel that we are virtually the same and at another that
we are less alike than are the tall, blond Nordic and the short,
dark Polynesian. If my remarks reflect some of this ambivalence,
please blame it on my pure British ancestry, separated by nine
generations from what I still cannot avoid calling the "Mother
Country."

I should like therefore to avoid this issue as such and to
probe rather to some of the underlying factors upon which national differences and similarities in culture and literature are
based; and then to apply what I may discover to the work of
three contemporary Americans, John Dos Passos, Eugene
O'Neill, and Ernest Hemingway, as a means of testing the
principles involved.

First, some of the factors upon which such differences and
similarities are not based:

They are not, I think, based on language except as language
is, like literature, an expression of a culture. Nothing is more

misleading than the similarities in the English language as spoken in England and in America. The word "automobile," for example, will call up in an Englishman's mind a compact, probably black, mechanism capable of passing its brother between two almost touching hedgerows; the same word will suggest to an American a chrome-trimmed, three-toned mechanical elephant sweeping down a six-lane dual turnpike at seventy miles an hour with flat unhedged fields on both sides. The words "comfortable home heating" might suggest to an Englishman the analogy of a piece of steak seared to a crisp brown on at least one side, but still red and juicy within; to an American, an oven roast, done all the way through. And so forth. It is not so much the similarities in the words as the differences in underlying concepts which really matter. And one wonders just what subtle differences there are between us when we use such words as "family," "education," "national safety," "economic stability," "political necessity," and many others which seem to mean the same things to both of us. We are perhaps safer with the Chinese where differences in language and race are so dramatic that the danger lies the other way about: in not recognizing our common humanity.

Nor are our differences based—at the opposite end of the spectrum—on the universals of our common humanity: on "love," "pride," "ambition," "faith," "despair." Literature is primarily and ultimately concerned with such basic factors as these, of course, but the simple statement of them: "I love you," "Death comes to all alike," "Have faith; do not despair," are mere colorless platitudes unless the truths which they affirm have been rediscovered in the contexts of living cultures. Hamlet's love for Ophelia and Frederic Henry's love for Catherine Barkley in Hemingway's *Farewell to Arms* may be essentially the same emotion, but we are interested in them only because these authors, by their skill, have rediscovered certain universals in totally different times, places, and circumstances.

As students of the art of literature, we are specialists in the study of these differences. We are not so much concerned that all great works of literature say essentially the same few things and that all the really important words are virtually common to all languages; we are fascinated by the constant miracle which art performs in confronting the infinite diversities and complexities of human experience and reducing them to comprehension through expression. It is the alchemy which literature ever and again performs in transforming the dross of our daily lives to gold rather than the gold itself which challenges our curiosity and provokes our study. I do not apologize, therefore, in asking you to consider with me the problem of how and to what extent American literature is a unique art expressing a unique culture even though it may use essentially your language and give expression to your deepest motives as human beings. If we are to understand each other better, we must learn to distinguish the cultural differences between us where they exist, and there is no better medium for making them clear than the best works of literary art.

In urging the use of literature rather than documentary record as a means of understanding a national culture, I realize that I am in danger of falling into one of the commonest errors made by all those who dare to explore the quicksands of international cultural relations. The temptation is to assume that a novelist, for example, who gives an intimate and detailed portrait—or what seems to be a portrait—of the people and events of a small country town in Ohio or Cornwall or Provence is primarily interested in leaving an accurate record of life in that time and place for the future use of historians. Quite the contrary. If he is a true artist, he will distort every fact and twist every scrap of data that falls under his creative hand. Even if he is technically what is known as a "realist," the reality he produces can be no more than a semblance; if it is actually a true record, if it is really realism, it cannot be art; for the primary function of art is to comment on life implicitly through the use of symbols and not to record life explicitly through the use of photographic reproductions. Not without reason does such a novelist, however he may be indebted to his own observation and experience, put a warning on his half-title page that no person or event in his tale is to be taken literally. Such warning is more than his escape from

legal entanglement; it is his declaration of professional commitment as an artist to the truth of the imagination and to that
truth only. Whether he be an optimistic dreamer who can see
no evil or a sour satirist for whom nothing is good, his right
to express his own subjective interpretations of his experience
is the same. The London of Dickens, the Mississippi of Faulkner,
and the Russia of Dostoevski are all based on fact, but they are
all massive distortions of evidence to convey the visions of great
creative imaginations. They are, in the final analysis, the stuff of
which myth rather than history is made.

I do not wish to belabor this point, and I would not do so
were not the error involved in the use of art as document so
nearly universal. Only recently one of the great American
foundations prepared a list and a library of three hundred and
fifty books under the general title "Panorama of America" as
a contribution to the better understanding of American culture
abroad, but failure to distinguish art from document led to an
indiscriminate confusion in the list as a whole as to whether it
was intended as an objective description of American life or a
subjective commentary on American ideas and values. It was
part one and part the other, but there was insufficient editorial
guidance to make always clear which was which.

A good example of this same kind of confusion was the reception even in America of such books as Sinclair Lewis' *Babbitt*
and John Steinbeck's *Grapes of Wrath* as accurate pictures of
American social conditions. The alarming suggestion has been
made in Carl Anderson's study of the reception of American
literature in Sweden that the Nobel Prize was awarded to Lewis
in part because he presented an unfavorable picture of American
life which the Swedes had learned from the Norwegian Knut
Hamsun, rather than for the artistic achievement of the American author. The same mistake of confusing politics with art
was made by the Russians in rejecting the honor which Pasternak
brought them. Fortunately, in each of these American cases we
have a sociological study of essentially the same problem with
which the novel deals—the Lynds' *Middletown* for *Babbitt*, and
Carey McWilliams' *Factories in the Field* for *Grapes of Wrath*

—and we can check data against literary treatment. Lewis' hero becomes a protest against the pettiness and frustration of little men everywhere, and Steinbeck's Joad family a modern example of man's eternal wanderlust, of the theme of restless migration which is found in the Odyssey and the Old Testament. In each case, the initial suggestion for the novel came from indignation at what were sociological facts in the immediate environment of the author, but in each the resulting novel is a literary comment on, rather than a documentary record of, experience—a distortion if not a total reversal of the evidence.

II

What then can—and must—literature do that document cannot do about a nation's culture? Because the idiom which it uses is the language of symbols rather than that of direct discourse, it works from immediate facts into general representations, and develops, through this use of symbols, out of the experience of the now a view of experience that can be shared by people in different countries who speak different languages, as well as by people of the past and of the future. Thus the symbol raises an experience from the level of fact to the level of general concept, of values, of norms, of ideals. A very simple example of this process would be the flag or the cross or any other of the familiar and traditional symbols which have grown out of specific experiences of the past, but have taken on larger meanings so that they can be applied to many different circumstances involving common values or common criteria of judgment of human experience. The flag will lift us above our selfish and personal concerns and make us think of the common good; the cross will make us realize that great goals can be achieved paradoxically through sacrifice. And the difference between these so-to-speak public symbols and the private symbols of such a complex and brilliant poet as the author of *The Waste Land* is one of degree rather than, as Edmund Wilson would have us believe, one of kind. If we do not at once comprehend a poet's private world of concept and value through his personally created symbols, the loss is ours and not his. In time, we will learn.

The creative writer not only develops individual symbols in some such fashion as this, but he organizes them into patterns and something emerges that critics have called "symbolic form." This is a kind of organization over which the artist rather than the statesman or the military man can alone exercise control. He can arrange his experiences in such a way that they have special meanings for him, and these meanings can be conveyed to others by reference to the symbols he has used. Little by little a form or structure, or an interrelationship of ideas and values begins to emerge until there is developed a body of mythology like those associated with the Christian story or with the classical culture of Greece. We Americans have already developed such a body of myths and symbols associated with the founding of our country, from the fundamental ideas of the founders and from such personalities as Washington, Jefferson, and Lincoln. We have even erected a kind of temple to each of these three in our national capital. Thus we are developing an heroic struc- ture, a structure of symbolic form, that we can place between our experience and our understanding of it.

We need not intellectualize this structure in order to share in its meaning; we need not say that each of these symbols means so and so and that they add up to this meaning or that. In fact, it is better if we allow them to remain largely connotative in their meaning. A repetition of these patterns of symbolic form which we thus learn to understand and take for granted forms a myth or tradition which can then be infinitely varied as new experiences are related to it.

The existence of such a tradition or mythology in American literature is a relatively new development in our cultural his- tory. Only as recently as 1915, Van Wyck Brooks was deplor- ing our lack of a "usable past" much as Emerson did in his "American Scholar" address of almost a century earlier. Wash- ing Irving, Fenimore Cooper, and others of our early writers had no such structural background to be shared with their readers, against which to play the lights and shadows and variations of their symbolic interpretations of the meanings of their times.

Because of this lack, they turned for a referent to the cultures of Europe, cultures which were not products of that time and that place. Their structures were not symbolic expressions of the experience of the Western continent, of life in the wilderness, of the building and expansion of a new civilization. The day-by-day events and thoughts which came to these early writers and to their readers were alien to the cultures against which they were forced by circumstances to play their symbolic interpretations of the meaning of life. This is the reason, I think, that our early writers were so much concerned with what we called nationalism in literature. They were not unduly chauvinistic; they had a practical problem of their craft to meet and solve. They could either plunge into the immediate experience, as did Jefferson or Tom Paine or Franklin, without trying to reduce it to symbolic form; or they could try, as did Irving and some others, to borrow their symbolic forms elsewhere, from the Gothic romance of Germany or the nature poetry of England, transplanting medieval castles and nightingales to the banks of the Schuylkill in Pennsylvania, where they felt very uncomfortable. They had no other alternatives, because they were faced with a problem that only time could solve.

But time has by now solved that problem, and American literature today has a tradition with its own system of symbolic expression—a tradition that has developed out of the unique American experience itself. We Americans have our own problem of reconciling the present with the past and giving it literary expression, for ours is a transplanted culture. We have brought the liberal eighteenth-century ideals of Western Europe to a new environment, and we have tried to make them work in the belief that they might have a better chance in a less complicated situation. In the process, we have made our lives as complicated as European lives ever were. We have not escaped our problem. But we still feel that they can and should work in the highly complex, machine-made society of the twentieth century. No wonder we are in for a massive sense of frustration and defeat. The longer we live and the more complicated our society becomes, the wider is the discrepancy between the ideals of our founders, the ideals of our tradition, the ideals of our mythology, and their full realization in the actualities of our modern life.

It is the task—an increasingly difficult task—of our American literature to discover and organize new sets of symbols to bridge the gap between the experience we now have and our basic assumptions—to make that experience vivid and organized and comprehensible to us so that we can live in it understandingly. That is what our writers have been trying to do as our civilization has settled down in the twentieth century and admitted that it is urban and industrial rather than rural and agrarian as it was in the earlier days; that the United States is actually one of the great world powers and not a group of colonies of a European power. As we have come to recognize these facts, our literary men have slowly learned how to extract from them meaningful symbols and how to organize these symbols into a workable pattern to which we can relate our daily experience. Thus the new literature which has developed from a special set of American facts is comprehensible and useful not only to us but to all those who share our experience even in part. Because Western European man has gone through a similar transition into the terms of modern living, American literature has something special to say to Europeans as well, something perhaps that their own literature cannot say as clearly. The violence of the struggle to be born into the modern age is much more elemental in a Cooper or a Mark Twain or a Hemingway than it is in a Joyce or a Proust or a Kafka. The very absence of sophistication makes the essential factors in the experience more clear and sharp. No wonder American literature is being looked to by the critics of France, Germany, Norway, and England for a symbolic interpretation and criticism which they can use for themselves in so far as they share the experience of the modern mechanized world and the alienation from the past which it implies.

The human problem in this mechanized world is not new: it is that man's scientific knowledge has outdistanced his ability to cope with his experience and control his behavior morally. The American experience merely presents this paradox more dramatically, in a more extreme form than do some others. America's ideals of democracy have been so clearly stated as a working philosophy that their contrast to the materialism of its economy of abundance is particularly striking. We see the misery of our condition, whether that of the poor whites or Negroes in the Mississippi of Faulkner, that of the congested streets of the New York of Dos Passos, or that of the small Midwestern town of Sinclair Lewis with its narrow and shallow lives. We see all this misery and we see the selfishness of our conduct about it, the fact that we do so little to correct it, and we stand helpless until a literary man comes to us and reveals for us the ultimate human values and the human meanings involved in our situation. Then we realize that this is nothing new, our perplexity differs little from that of the Romans in the time of Augustus, of the Englishmen in the time of Elizabeth, of any great civilization at a time of great powers and crises. There have always been poverty and riches, love and hate, ambition and despair, jealousy and revenge and compassion and peace, even though each new people on the earth must face the problem anew.

The civilization of the United States in the twentieth century presents this basic human situation in terms so new that they require a completely new literary response. Tradition can help very little. Toward the end of the nineteenth century our writers began to realize this fact and went to work on the job of making the modern problem intelligible to us by a process of developing from it its own system of symbolic expression.

III

The first attacks were direct. Genteel writers like Longfellow, Lowell, and their followers who had for so long controlled the literary market were still being read, but people were showing signs of becoming impatient with them because they did not seem to come to grips with life. Then, at the beginning of this century, Theodore Dreiser took a fresh look at life and said, "Let's see it straight; let's take a few simple characters, people that we know, and present them logically and honestly and let the story tell itself." He used his own family, his sisters, his brother, his father and his mother, his friends, all the people he knew, people with whom he had been in contact in his jobs as delivery boy or newspaper writer, and he made stories of them by changing them only a little. He was skimming over the surface of the problem in such novels as *Sister Carrie* and *Jennie Gerhardt* and the trilogy about the Philadelphia financier Yerkes, who became Frank Cowperwood in *The Financier, The Titan,* and *The Stoic.*

Here was the beginning of a new process of symbolization of actual life. These characters were themselves but they were generalized, they were typified as Cooper's Leather-Stocking had been. Each of them became an anybody: Clyde Griffith of *An American Tragedy* became American youth, Cowperwood became the American entrepreneur. Because each of Dreiser's characters has a particular and then a general meaning, they are each a symbol of ideality as well as a semblance of reality.

The next step came with Sinclair Lewis, who took off from Dreiser's beginnings by saying, in effect, "I was born and brought up in a small town in Minnesota; I've been to Chicago and throughout the Middle West; I like to write about the people I know best; their problems are my problems. I will present these people, but I will also reveal them in their mean little inner selves." He added to Dreiser's direct method the more sophisticated instrument of satire, a method which often reveals truth by presenting its opposite. This put a finer edge on his inquiry, but it also increased the chances of misunderstanding his method. He manipulated the truth enough to make his characters look in upon themselves. As in a distorted mirror, they saw their traits exaggerated so that their weaknesses and extravagances stood out. A book like *Arrowsmith* or *Babbitt* is a more generalized statement in symbolic form than is a book like *Sister Carrie* or *An American Tragedy.* The conflict in Dr. Martin Arrowsmith between a life of pure research and the commercialization of his profession is a personal, a modern, a universal problem, but it is distinctively American in the context of the culture which here gives it shape.

By the mid-1920's most of the literary spadework had been

done and there were a great many important new American writers ready to make their contributions to the new literature. I will conclude by choosing somewhat arbitrarily three of them, as representative of different ways of performing the role of the literary artist, and ask each one of the three the same series of questions: "How do you go about this process of generalizing in such a way that the values and the meanings of American life can be better understood? And how successful have you been? If you have failed, in what ways have you failed to perform this alchemy and become a great writer, the bard of your culture? Is there a Shakespeare among you and your fellows, and if not, why not?"

John Dos Passos is a writer of Spanish extraction although an American citizen. Whatever the cause, there is basic in his writing a sense of alienation and protest. It may or may not be this attitude which has separated him from the society of his day, from the normal pattern of family life, and which has given him special desires and needs, powerful emotions which intensified his concern for all aspects of experience. His life was divided, as were the lives of all of his generation, into three parts: an era before the First World War, experience in the war, and an aftermath of adjustment to the postwar society. The pattern of life that we see in Dos Passos was common to many of the writers of his generation, even in such details as serving in an ambulance unit rather than in the regular army, becoming, so to speak, an observer rather than a participant, and then coming back to throw himself into the social situation in the United States between wars, identifying himself with the radical social movement as editor of *The Masses,* organ of the extreme leftist group. All this experience culminated in the great trilogy, *U.S.A.* But no sooner was this novel written than, to our surprise, we see him denying his radicalism and, in many people's minds, becoming a turncoat, defending through the later years a conservative political philosophy. But we must remember that we are not here concerned with Dos Passos as a politician or an agitator. Because the idiom of his thought was mainly political, his journalistic and literary work deals with political material, and it was his business as an artist to reflect and to interpret the political currents and crises of his time.

Because his material is impersonal, even though his feeling about it is not, Dos Passos makes a good writer to take as illustrative of our first stage in our theory of the literary process. We can see him responding vividly and immediately to the social life about him, trying to work out a system of symbolic form against which to throw the likeness of his experience, experimenting with all the new techniques he could discover, and finally writing a series of stories that embody these symbolic forms and give them permanence like a bit of plastic hardening into a fixed shape after it has been mixed and stirred and then set.

Dos Passos starts with a disgust at man, which probably, as we have seen, arises largely from his experiences as a youth and in the war. Naturally, his first attack was a direct one. He wrote a novel of three soldiers, presumably himself and two others, and told of their reactions to the war. Like Dreiser, he took a familiar situation and raised it from the ground just enough to gain perspective on it. These three soldiers become three types of reaction to the war situation. Dos Passos seems to have originated this particular device, but it has been copied by a great many other writers of war stories.

In his next step, after an experiment with a very different sort of form in *Manhattan Transfer*, Dos Passos moved toward symbolic structure with the great trilogy *U.S.A.* Here he took a full cross section of American life and revealed its dismay and decay and disease, as he saw it, by the use of three or four experimental technical devices. The first of these he calls the "Newsreel," in which he clips the headlines from newspapers and mixes them with scraps of news stories and bits of popular songs. In each of these Newsreels, which are inner chapters of his novel, the popular song is used in rhythmic accompaniment as the news items follow one another—none of them complete—in a kind of movie technique, a series of flashed pictures. In this way, the reader gets a feeling of what is going on in the country without pausing to focus on any specific facts or events long enough to become wholly aware of them. Then, in what

Dos Passos calls the "Camera Eye," he is plunged into the contrary kind of experience, that which starts in the subconscious, in the complex self-awareness of the individual. In these passages, Dos Passos uses incidents remembered from his childhood or from the war, such as the occasion when the taking over of the ambulance corps by the Red Cross was interrupted by a shower of shells and all the Red Cross majors took to hiding. He pulled this relatively unimportant incident out of his memory and put it into his story in order to give another dimension to his sense and the reader's of what was going on in the times. A third device is that of the biography of prominent persons such as Roosevelt or Veblen, businessmen and politicians and radicals, people who were shaping the times. And finally there is his story itself, an interlocking series of narratives about individuals who are exaggerated examples of American types presented in a kind of Sinclair Lewis vein of satire, but with less sympathy. There is little or no plot as the paths of these people cross and crisscross and recross one another in a tangle of episodes, their lives coming and going on a dead level. These three related novels cover the entire war experience: before the war, during the war, and after the war. In raising the experience of an era and a civilization up to the level of symbolic form, Dos Passos is successful, but his success does not extend to a full realization of the meaning of the form he has constructed. He leaves the reader about where he found him except that he has given him a much fuller sensory and emotional realization of the events which have been narrated. But he does not quite say why or what is universal about them. The only generalization to which his art can be related is the Marxist ideology, which Dos Passos himself apparently never fully accepted and which he rejected within not too long a time after writing this novel. One is left with only a kind of sentimental humanitarianism to temper despair as a basic philosophy underpinning the literary form.

It is no wonder that in later life Dos Passos felt that he must get another intellectual foundation for his work. He then wrote the trilogy that he finally called *District of Columbia*, a series of novels in which he attacked first communism, then fascism,

and finally the New Deal, a study of the microcosm of Washing-
ington, D.C., to offset that of the macrocosm of the United
States as a whole in *U.S.A.* In doing so, he wiped out all contemporary political possibilities and left himself and his readers
only the inherited American tradition of Thomas Jefferson.
But because again his ultimate frame of reference was political,
it was logical for him to desert fiction for history and to write
books about the American past. After almost achieving the
level of great literature, Dos Passos lost his grip on the problem
and slipped farther and farther away from mastery of the
literary alchemist's art.

IV

Eugene O'Neill went further than Dos Passos in literary development. He was somewhat older than either of our other
two authors, but not enough older to prevent his being essentially a member of the same generation. He also had a stormy
youth in a family that was disordered. As we know from
O'Neill's play, *Long Day's Journey into Night*, which is largely
but not strictly autobiographical, his home was disrupted by
the efforts of his father and mother to escape from themselves
through the artificial means of alcohol and drugs. As this is the
great tragedy of his life, it probably stimulated him to run off
to sea, led to his adventures in far places, and might even have
had something to do with his physical breakdown, his time in the
hospital, and his final return. It was the source of his struggle
all through his life to become adjusted to himself, to his intense
emotions, and to the society of his day.

In his early plays O'Neill is concerned with people who, like
himself, are unhappy and discontented with life, but they could
also be grouped according to the social problems with which
they deal. For instance, there are plays on the Negro question,
like *The Emperor Jones* and *All God's Chillun Got Wings;*
there are plays on the lot of the worker versus the lot of the
capitalist, like *The Hairy Ape* and *Marco Millions;* and there are
plays on the decay of domestic morals, especially in family life,
like *Beyond the Horizon, Desire Under the Elms,* and *Strange*

Interlude. He wrote many plays which examine the American family and ask what is happening to it. They are suggestive of Ibsen, who was much concerned with this kind of problem. And finally there was a series of plays on the failure of the American ideal, like *A Touch of the Poet,* although *The Iceman Cometh* might be included in this category; and O'Neill planned many more.

There is no doubt that O'Neill was concerned throughout his life with social problems as such, but in each case in which he deals with one of them and starts creating symbols for his facts, his problem becomes personal rather than social. His symbols are the symbols of psychology rather than of sociology, and his characters represent the plight of individual men in modern society rather than the plight of man in general in modern society in general as is the case with Dos Passos.

O'Neill has used two major techniques for accomplishing this aim, two kinds of art, in one of which he leans slightly more toward the facts and in the other of which he leans more toward the symbols. The two kinds are sometimes called naturalism and expressionism, but they often merge. In plays like *Desire Under the Elms* or *Beyond the Horizon,* he deals with a single situation and a single problem, and his characters are individuals first and symbols only secondarily. In other plays, however, his process of symbolization goes so far that his characters lose almost all sense of life and become nothing but puppets, walking symbols. Among such plays are *The Emperor Jones,* where a Negro porter who becomes the ruler of a small island is little more than a symbol of the primitive instincts that underlie the civilization of all of us, and *The Hairy Ape,* where the stoker Yank is the essential hairy ape in all men. No one thinks of him as a real person from the beginning of the play to the end, although the process of his reversion to type is the main point of the play. These are both early plays, but even toward the end of his career, in *The Iceman Cometh,* O'Neill told his story through characters who are much more symbols than they are individuals. In each case, he succeeded in escaping from reality into illusion, from fact into meaning, by raising the individual's problem (often his own) from the immediate and circumstantial to the general. This accomplishment becomes most impressive and moving in the last of his plays, the one unpublished and unproduced at the time of his death and later produced in Stockholm and elsewhere in Europe and America, *Long Day's Journey into Night*. This is the story of his own family, and here he confronts the problem of his youth most directly and deeply: how to deal with the people who gave him birth, who shaped his early life for him, and yet whom he had to reject in order to become a man in his own right. It is that rejection, which we see happening in the play, that allowed him to realize the great artist that was in him. And yet even so great an achievement is imperfect. One cannot help feeling that, in this most nearly perfect of modern tragedies, O'Neill was still so much wrapped up in his own emotions, and his problems were so intensely personal and psychological, that he fell short of the social perspective of a Dos Passos or a Sinclair Lewis on the one hand and of the aesthetic perspective of a T. S. Eliot or a Faulkner on the other. In this play there is insufficient relief from the dead weight of tragedy because there is too much life, too little art.

V

My third choice should be an author who achieved success in the respects in which Dos Passos and O'Neill fell short of it, in discovering the full sociological and psychological meanings of his symbolic forms. But I have already said that I do not believe that we have produced a modern American Shakespeare. We must still be satisfied with approximations, and Ernest Hemingway will serve to suggest the next stage in artistic development.

Hemingway was neither completely absorbed in the social life of his time, although he was strongly drawn into it, nor in the psychological problems of the age, although he was very much drawn to them also. Of our three, he is the one who most nearly succeeded in extricating himself from the tangle of contemporary emotions through symbol, through the use of symbolic form, and who developed the purest art. I have chosen him rather than Faulkner or Eliot, whom some might claim as greater artists, because he presents the same problem as they but in a simpler form. I can illustrate, I think, the process of distillation of life into art better with an uncomplex artist like Hemingway than I could with a more complex artist like Faulkner or Eliot, either of whom would involve us in many other considerations before we could get to the crux of our problem.

At the heart of all of Hemingway's stories is a boy in the woods of northern Michigan. This boy, Nick Adams, is his fictionalized self, and he puts him through many of his own experiences, experiences with pain, with death, with life as he himself met it. In every incident, we feel the sensitivity of this boy as he grows into young manhood in Hemingway's first volume of short stories, published first in Paris under the title *in our time*. Between the stories, which are not otherwise connected, are camera-eye interludes similar to those of Dos Passos to link them to the subconscious awareness of the same sensitive human being, the boy. Under various names, Nick, grown-up, is in all of Hemingway's stories.

Although Hemingway's first mature novel, *The Sun Also Rises*, states his basic attitudes toward life as fully as anything he ever wrote, it is not as focused on a single character as are most of his later stories. Jake Barnes has been wounded by the war and faces sterility in love and death. The narrative is centered on him as much as on anyone, but almost equally important are Lady Brett Ashley, whose affairs with the various characters provide much of the action, the American Jew Robert Cohn, the Spanish bullfighter Pedro Romero, and the others of their expatriate, pleasure-seeking set. Written in the cynical vein of the passage from Ecclesiastes that supplies the title, the novel also states Hemingway's basic stoicism, the belief that only in love and death is complete self-realization attainable. At the same time that it is revealing human nature on as base and sensuous a level as would seem possible, it comments on the dilemma of an entire generation by use of the "wasteland" themes of sterility and ritualistic killing which were also effectively used by Eliot and others. Much more effectively than Scott Fitzgerald or any other of the "Lost Generation,"

Hemingway in this novel summed up the meaning of life this side of Paradise. Confronting the fact that man in modern society has failed, and is in danger of even more serious failure, the artist in Hemingway, in his passion, his dismay at this knowledge, is able to free himself so completely from personal involvement that he can see his people coldly and clearly, confront them with the ultimate dilemmas of love and death, and present them in a symbolic structure more nearly perfect than anything which Dos Passos or O'Neill was able to achieve.

The symbolism of *The Sun Also Rises* is not as obvious nor as fully developed as it was to become in Hemingway's later stories. In *A Farewell to Arms*, the Hemingway theme is concentrated with white-hot intensity on the central characters, Frederic Henry and Catherine Barkley, and the symbolic use of the elements—water, rain, plain, mountain—becomes much more confident and effective. As a work of art, this is probably Hemingway's best novel, but *For Whom the Bell Tolls* is more revealing of his intentions and methods because it is more complex. Here the Hemingway hero, Robert Jordan, finds himself caught in the central political problem of the day, the choice between communism and fascism as they work out their destinies on the mountain battlegrounds of Spain, but social issues as such are subordinated to the personal crisis in the life of one man: the necessity that he should realize himself fully in love and courage before accepting death. The two levels upon which the novel is written, the narrative and the symbolic, are clearly stated in the title, for the symbol of the bell which tolls for all alike could have purely political significance (it is impossible to escape the crises of the times) or merely personal meaning (anything that happens to anyone anywhere in the world is a part of each of us when we have realized, through love and death, our basic kinship with our fellows). To the elemental symbols are added those of the bell, the bridge, the cave, Maria's close-cropped hair, the earthy Pilar and the cringing Pablo, in an intricate web of implied significances which gives the story an entire world of meaning quite apart from its narrative action.

I cannot, of course, discuss all of Hemingway's work, but I

would like to conclude with brief mention of one of his longer short stories, "The Snows of Kilimanjaro," a more skillful symbolic structure even than *The Old Man and the Sea*. Here the Hemingway hero faces death from an infected leg on the African plain while contemplating the unattainable white peak of the mountain of his spiritual yearning. So sharply does the symbolic structure represent the two levels of human experience that the story even has two endings. While death comes in the most sordid and undramatic way that cynicism could devise, the spirit is freed by the arrival of the rescue plane and a true death is realized by a symbolic crash against the white peak. The narrative and the symbolic structures so exactly coincide that not a word in the story could be disturbed without destroying the whole.

Yet this particular story could not have been written by anyone but a middle-aged twentieth-century American on safari in Africa, escaping what he felt to be a wasted life in a modern mechanized world. The airplane, symbol of that mechanical world, is also the agent which, in his imagination, rescues his soul by lifting him from the level plain of his futility and crashing him against the remote and timeless ice-capped mountain. This ability to write on two levels of experience at the same time and to blend the dual vision into a single integral whole is, I suppose, the test of art: it must be intensely real at the same time that it escapes from reality. In order to present a society or a culture, it must transcend at the same time that it fully comprehends the issues and the complex and confused forces at work among a people at a given time and place. It would seem that a generation of American artists in fiction and drama and poetry has come close to achieving that high aim. Perhaps we should turn more to them and less to the historians and sociologists for the meaning of that complex and vital culture which has taken shape in our time beyond the Western horizon.

Tragedy and Romanticism
in Modern American Literature
1962

PREPARED FOR THE COLLEGE OF WOOSTER, OHIO, AND READ BEFORE THE JAPANESE AMERICAN LITERATURE SOCIETY IN TOKYO, AT THE UNIVERSITY OF TEXAS, AND ELSEWHERE.

THE RISE AND FALL of the romantic movement in American literature has never been satisfactorily charted. Norman Foerster many years ago in his classic anthology, *American Poetry and Prose*, described a movement, closely related to romanticism in Europe, in the first half of the nineteenth century and followed by what he called "realism" in the second half. Most literary historians have since followed his lead and have made pretty good sense of the group that centered in Concord and Cambridge in the 'forties and 'fifties, but only recently have they begun to gain a perspective on the course of American literary history since then.

To achieve such perspective, we must find ways of identifying masterpieces of the recent past and then construct a frame of reference in which these masterpieces may take their respective places. May I suggest two hypotheses out of which such a frame of reference might be developed? These are that literary history is marked by the cyclic recurrence of high moments of romantic intensity, with their valleys of intellectual and critical analysis between, and that literature reaches its highest intensity in those expressions of the tragic issue between Man and Destiny which these moments seem to produce.

A few years ago a leading critic wrote: "The poets of the seventeenth century . . . possessed a mechanism of sensibility which could devour any kind of experience. . . . In the seventeenth century a dissociation of sensibility set in. . . . While the language became more refined, the feeling became more crude." [1] This is T. S. Eliot's way of proposing that Donne or Herbert or Marvell could hold the mirror of his own complex, ironic, and intellectual sensibility up to experience and record the resulting image without becoming himself involved in the complexities. In other words, the seventeenth-century metaphysical poet had achieved a nearly perfect stasis in art, when the poem itself *is* the experience rather than the fluent expression of something in life that had happened previously.

One can agree that such a moment represents the full maturity of art in any one particular cycle of its development without taking the next step with Eliot and deploring the breakdown of the highly sophisticated equilibrium which produced it and somehow disparaging all that came after. For that same moment was preliminary to the dawn of what we have come to think of as the greatest of all ages in English poetry, the age of the romantic movement. It was another century before the dissociation of sensibility which Eliot so accurately described could produce a Keats and a Coleridge, a Shelley and a Browning, a Poe and a Whitman. There was an era of even colder and more classic intellectuality to be passed through before the emotions of poets were free to flow again and another cycle of romantic expression was to evolve. What happened was perhaps not so much a breakdown of sensibility as the breakthrough of the creative imagination. In the romantic view—the view of Coleridge and Wordsworth and Emerson—the poet is the maker, the doer, the agent of life. "Poetry," said Wordsworth, is "emotion recollected in tranquillity." And before Coleridge will answer the question, "What is poetry?" he identifies it with the question, "What is a poet?" and refers it to "the poetic genius itself, which sustains and modifies the images, thoughts, and emotions of the poet's own mind." And Emerson takes the final step toward the freedom of the imagination. Poetry, he says, was all written before time was—"The poet is the sayer, the namer, and represents beauty. He is a sovereign, and stands on the centre." [2]

In thus recognizing his own kinship with John Donne and the English Metaphysicals, Eliot was therefore helping us to fix a moment in literary history: the end of one romantic movement and perhaps, in due course, the beginning of another. For the equilibrium of the poetic sensibility which he recognized in Donne—and in himself—came at the close of the Elizabethan age as well as before that of Wordsworth and Coleridge, and it can be understood rather better as the final phase of one great creative era than as the beginning of another. Chaucer and Shakespeare, Spenser and Milton all lay in the past, with Milton's work but barely done. Chaucer had no such delicately poised poetic sensibility as Eliot describes, nor had Shakespeare; in Spenser it was but imperfectly developed, and only in Milton did it reach the poise and detachment, even in part, of the Metaphysicals. The eighteenth century thought of Chaucer as a primitive and Shakespeare as an excusable "original" genius. When Dryden and Pope were the masters, most of Shakespeare's great plays had to be rewritten. A literary historian of the year 1700 could—if he had had the perspective—look back on the earlier romantic movement in English literary history which had produced these masterpieces and trace its rise in the primitive Chaucer, its fulfillment and maturity in the four great tragedies of Shakespeare, and its afterglow in the very sensibility that Eliot describes. For that was, as historians are fond of saying, a kind of watershed in English literary history. The poetic imagination of Renaissance man had broken free of the tragic issue of Man versus Fate and had produced a memorable spate of literary masterpieces.

All of this may seem a roundabout way of stressing the nature and the importance of Eliot's recognition of his own position in American literary history. This is not, of course, what he was intending to do; but this, it seems to me, is what he did and did supremely well. For these essays in the slim volume of 1920, *The Sacred Wood*, together with its poetic accompaniment of two years later, *The Waste Land*, mark the culmination—and therefore the beginning of the end—of a great romantic movement, not only in American literature but in the literature of Western Europe. For, whether we call it a breakdown of the sensibility, as Eliot would, or a breakthrough of the imagination, as Wordsworth would, we can all agree that something happened in the seventeenth century which has apparently by now nearly run its course and which has shaped the literary history of all the Western world, including the United States.

II

These few very general speculations on how literary history is shaped around the rise and fall of romantic movements, when man has sought fresh forms of expression in order to intensify his awareness of life and its deepest problems and meanings, should give us a start in dealing with the nature and the value of the American writers of today and of the recent past. For, if we can identify the whole of our national literary history with a single romantic movement, we can stand at mid-twentieth century, like the mythical literary historian of 1700, on the watershed of a moment of static sensibility, with the surging forces of the creative imagination in the past on one side, and presumably in the future on the other. Even though we can afford to concern ourselves with the first part of this story—the forces which brought American literature to its present state of achievement—the identification of our present position with that of a kind of harvest time or maturity in a life cycle should give us a way of understanding better the masterpieces of which that literature is composed.

As we take our stand thus in the present and seek out the recognizable masterpieces of our literary past, the first fact that must impress us is that we find not one but two eras of great achievement in that history, a romantic fulfillment in the East—mainly in New England—which came just before the Civil War and apparently did not survive it, and a second era

of even greater achievement approximately between the two
World Wars and embracing the entire continental nation.

Because the culture of Western Europe was brought to our
shores in two great waves, we need not assume that there were
two romantic movements in the country between 1800 and
the present. These were merely two stages in a single process,
but a process that reached two peaks of fulfillment. The years
just before the Civil War brought the movement to a head in
the eastern seaboard states; it was then diffused over the continent as the West was opened by the great migrations and
immigrations of the mid-nineteenth century; and it reached a
second climax in the recent past.

The definition of the first of these—that Golden Day just
before the Civil War—has been attempted by many of our
literary historians, but the most thorough and convincing interpretation so far is of the late F. O. Matthiessen in his masterly
book, *The American Renaissance*. Mr. Matthiessen notes in his
preface an amazing concentration of masterpieces by a few
authors in the five years 1850–1855. Emerson, Melville, Hawthorne, and Thoreau all produced major works in this short
period, and Whitman capped the climax with the first edition
of *Leaves of Grass* in 1855. Poe's only excuse for not being of
this company was that he died in 1849 when he was obviously
at the climax of his literary life, and Cooper and Irving, who
both died in the 'fifties, were of a slightly earlier generation but
produced up to the end of their lives—the one in 1851 and the
other in 1859.

Such a conjunction of planets was of course not an accident.
There were many forces of thought and influence from the
time and the environment that brought these great books together, but the interaction of these forces is so complex that
the whole problem can probably never be solved. But Matthiessen went a long way toward its solution by focusing on the
central theme that all five of his writers had in common. This
was the tragic vision of life in the New World and the modern
age. Tragedy had given classical Greece and Elizabethan England their greatest literary achievements; and its rediscovery in

the American nineteenth century brought depth and power to the work of a new group of writers.

The key, then, to greatness in romantic art would seem to be the rediscovery of the tragic issue and the ways to give it expression. Aristotle defined the problem for the Greek drama only after several generations of dramatists had extracted it from the experience of Athenian civilization, and subsequent artists have tended to substitute imitation of Aristotle's ideas for the reexperiencing which is the source of all great art. As the biologist would say, the tragic sense is an "acquired characteristic," which cannot be inherited. It may be that tragedy is always present when, as one critic put it, "that which can't be, must be," but never does that issue recur in exactly the same terms. Man must forever challenge life into awarding him a personal triumph over fate, and he must always rediscover the truth that only as Man—as humanity and not as an individual— he can survive. Or, as Matthiessen said, "The creation of tragedy demands of its author a mature understanding of the relation of the individual to society, and, more especially, of the nature of good and evil. . . . For the hero of tragedy is never merely an individual, he is a man in action, in conflict with other individuals in a definite social order. . . . Tragedy . . . is built on the experienced realization that man is radically imperfect. Confronting this fact, tragedy must likewise contain a recognition that man, pitiful as he may be in his finite weakness, is still capable of apprehending perfection." [3]

Thus, bringing the tragic issue and the American experience to a single focus in the mid-nineteenth century east-coast United States, Matthiessen established a moment in literary history from which other historians could trace the lines of force which led up to and away from this climax in an evolutionary curve.

The application of the same critical method to the problem of modern American literature is more complicated but should be equally revealing. If we think of it as part of this same cycle, the curve must inevitably be downward. This is the error made by Lewis Mumford in his 1936 book, *The Golden Day*, and it runs through most histories of American literature down to

the otherwise excellent *Literature and the American Tradition*
of Leon Howard of a year or so ago. All evidence seems to indicate that the romantic movement suddenly declined and dis-
sipated with the Civil War and the opening of the West. Is
everything that has been written since some sort of aftermath
or reaction to this surge of force? Have we been for a century
in some sort of literary doldrums, or has there been another
rise to a romantic climax in terms of the expanding continental
nation, the rise of the United States to the stature of a world
power, our tremendous and heterogeneous population increase,
and the realignment of all Western thinking to the new universe
of concepts, habits, and beliefs that modern science and technology have unfolded?

III

For a long time, American literary historians were content
with the theory of decline, with a resulting depreciation of all
late nineteenth- and all twentieth-century American writers.
The thwarted-genius theory of Mark Twain was matched by
the man-without-a-country theory of Henry James. Howells
was accepted as honest but dull, and Emily Dickinson was a
sort of moth in the flame, while the bearded poets from Bryant
to Longfellow lined every schoolroom wall and the so-called
"hard-boiled school of American fiction" (which grouped
Faulkner with Erskine Caldwell and James M. Cain) was read
furtively and shuddered at publicly. It took recognition abroad
—and in far more than the British Isles—to shake us into an
awareness that twentieth-century American writers had again
come to grips with basic issues and had worked out new ways
of giving them expression. The award of the Nobel Prize to
Sinclair Lewis in 1930 was, as Lewis himself generously admitted
in his acceptance speech, an award to a national literary awakening rather than to a single writer. The judges had decided in
advance to give the prize for the first time to an American and
had narrowed the choice to Lewis and Dreiser. Lewis won by
one vote.

But even before this token recognition, contemporary American writers were being translated in Scandinavia, the continental European countries, South America, and the Orient. While we were apologizing for the supposed crudities and pessimism of our Faulkners, our Hemingways, and our O'Neills, their works were being translated, read, and played in all parts of the world to an extent that had never previously been true of any American writer.

Before we take a closer look at a few of the major authors who may provide us with the evidence to prove this hypothesis, we must recall one more salient fact: by the twentieth century the mode of tragedy had changed, not only in America but in all of Western culture as well. Perhaps the best definition of this change is given by Northrop Frye in his book, *Anatomy of Criticism*. Identifying classical tragedy with the high or near God-like status of the hero, he shows how modern tragedy has gradually become more social, and how its hero has tended to descend to the level of common humanity—or even below. The pity and fear of the earlier tragedy has now become a "central tradition of sophisticated pathos" or "the study of the isolated mind, the story of how someone recognizably like ourselves is broken by a conflict between the inner and the outer world, between imaginative reality and the sort of reality which is established by a social consensus." [4] This Mr. Frye calls "the low mimetic mode" as against the "high mimetic mode" of Shakespearean tragedy; but the tragic issue is still present in that its resolution in the defeat of a single person by the inevitable march of fate or circumstance relieves the reader of his own tensions by restoring his faith in the persistence of humanity or of moral law in some form, whatever may happen to the single individual. This is what Faulkner seems to mean also when he expressed in his Stockholm address his belief that man would not only endure—he would prevail.

IV

It had not seemed, in 1900 when Theodore Dreiser, the son of a German immigrant, wrote his first novel, that the country was approaching a moment of tragic crisis in its literary history.

The Spanish war had just been won, and American power had at last stretched out into both the Atlantic and the Pacific beyond its continental boundaries. The vast resources of that continent, so long untapped, were now being poured into the greatest industrial economy that man had yet known. The poor of Europe and of Asia were swarming into our cities and spreading over our countryside in their frustrated passion for comfort and life. Technology had opened new doors to man's power over the forces of nature. Infinite resources, improved knowledge, and inexhaustible energy seemed to promise an era of power and plenty.

But it is always at moments of hope and fulfillment in his history that man has come up short to confront his fate, and it is then that the great tragedies are written. So Aeschylus, so Shakespeare, and now so the modern American writer discovered in his mass power the defeat of his personal will. Only at such times of romantic achievement does the tragic issue come sharply into focus.

In two essays written some years later—"Life, Art and America" and "The Essential Tragedy of Life," both included in his volume of miscellanies called *Hey Rub-a-Dub-Dub*—Dreiser has attempted to define that issue. The spirit of the rebel is in every word that this ill-educated, powerful, thoroughly though clumsily articulate son of a German peasant Catholic immigrant in Chicago has to say. The first of these essays (which is the last in his book) is a challenge to what he thinks of as the materialism, the prudery, and the conformity of the average American. "For after all," he cries, "the great business of life and mind is life. . . . The individual should question the things he sees—not some things, but everything—stand, as it were, in the centre of this whirling storm of contradiction which we know as life, and ask of it its source and its import."

Planting himself firmly, therefore, as Emerson had before him, at the heart of American experience in his own time, Dreiser discovered a very different universe of thought and feeling from that of the Concord sage. Yet, in his own "original and radical" way, he rediscovered the tragic vision much as Melville or

Shakespeare might have done if they had lived in a modern world of science and technology and in the teeming and expansive United States of 1931. "To me the most astonishing thing," Dreiser says, "in connection with man is . . . that whereas in reality he is . . . a structure of brief import and minute social or any other form of energy, left by his loving Creator to contest in the most drastic and often fatal way with thousands . . . still he has this astonishing power of viewing himself as a tremendous force in himself, a god, a hero, an enduring and undying figure of glory and beauty—as significant almost as the Creator Himself, in whose image and likeness he is supposed to be made!" [5]

The new tragic dialectic according to Dreiser is a circumstantial, mechanistic determinism, symbolized in the findings of modern chemistry which always had a strong attraction for him and which became in his cosmography the equivalent of the Greek Fate. Chemistry, he believed, shows that man is "merely —and, what is worse accidentally so—an evolved arrangement of attractions and repulsions." These are determined by the "chemisms" which become the shaping factors for motivation in his fiction and for which he was always, without success, seeking authority from many scientific friends.

Dreiser's heroes and heroines are not noble persons fallen from high estate through some twist of fate like those of the classic drama. As Northrop Frye might state the case, they are not cast in the high mimetic mode. They are helpless men and women, boys and girls, reduced to the lowest common denominator of human consciousness and tossed and buffeted by meaningless forces directed by chance alone. Carrie, in her rocking chair at the end of his first novel, still dreams of unattainable beauty while her former lover dies in a cheap lodging house nearby. "Oh, Carrie, Carrie! Oh, blind strivings of the human heart! . . . Know, then, that for you is neither surfeit nor content. In your rocking-chair, by your window dreaming, you shall long, alone. In your rocking-chair, by your window, shall you dream such happiness as you may never feel." [6]

This is the tragic dilemma as seen in the low mimetic mode,

unfulfilled in action, as it was in most of Dreiser's novels because he was so emotionally engrossed himself in his characters
that he fell short of the necessary aesthetic perspective to withdraw from them and see them as symbols of a larger truth. In
only one, the story of Clyde Griffith, did he push beyond his
own sentimental involvement into a tragic resolution, and even
then with only partial success. *An American Tragedy* is important to our speculations about this second renaissance in
American literature, more for what it attempted than for what
it achieved; for it is American and it is tragedy. The basic formula of tragedy is still there: Man, as individual, still believes
that he may conquer and consume all of life; and still it is his
destiny to perish, while man, as humanity, in general, survives
or even as Faulkner was later to put it, "prevails." It is this sense
of the survival of larger values in the face of individual defeat
that gives to tragic recognition its dignity, whether its mode
be high or low.

Dreiser's shortcomings as a tragic writer are not, as so often
is said, primarily his clumsy and undistinguished style or his
ordinary and uninteresting people, but rather his failure to attain
sufficient aesthetic perspective on his profound and passionate
understanding of life's paradox. His strength, on the other hand,
is that he broke through the complex and richly varied, hurry-
ing, hetereogeneous urban life of his time and place to the
simple and single truth of man's tragic dilemma, of which the
terms alone change from age to age. It was he who turned to
science, not for new truth, but for the idiom in which the men
of his day had come to examine and report on a truth older
than time. He was in America, as Zola was in France and Dostoevski in Russia, the master of naturalistic tragedy. From him
a whole generation of American writers learned a new art and
inaugurated a new literary era.

The major writers of that era pursue the way that he opened
for them. They see life in his idiom, modified in each by his
own insights and experience, but still basically a battle of individual man, reduced in size and in his own sense of impor-

tance, with a universe which is far more complex, arbitrary and impersonal than any previous generations of men had ever dreamed. But still they proclaim—rather in their images, rhythms, and larger symbols than in any overt exposition of ideas—the eternal recurrence of man's puny but heroic challenge and destiny's cold answer. In the escape from the petty, the personal, and the passionate into a larger truth comes the sense of relief from tension which the Greeks called "catharsis."

V

The view of life which is thus so powerfully, although murkily, expressed by Dreiser comes into sharper focus in the plays of Eugene O'Neill. This is partly because drama is a sharper, leaner form than the novel anyway, but it is also because O'Neill is willing to use his art as a means of withdrawing just far enough from his subject to see its form and to understand its meaning more clearly than Dreiser, in his overwhelming pity for his characters, was able to do. This he does mainly by using the dramatic masque and other kinds of expressionistic technique.

But first his meaning: in his earlier plays, like the symbolic *Emperor Jones* and *The Hairy Ape* and in the somewhat more realistic *Desire Under the Elms*, he seems merely distressed that man has somehow lost his bearings. Yank, the perennial O'Neill essential Man, struggles futilely to find out where he "belongs" in an unfriendly world of rejections—even in his attempt to identify with a huge gorilla at the zoo—and in the saga of the Cabot farm the ancient passions of greed and jealousy seem to rise out of the soil itself, to mingle with the blood of hungry and thwarted people, and then to sink back into the soil again with their total destruction. There is little to temper the elemental struggle of the single man, bound by his biological urges and his sociological ties, to find himself in some world of larger meaning. This is pure philosophical naturalism, whether expressed directly in what would seem to be almost a case record or indirectly in types and symbols and stylized action. The tragic vision is present in its modern form: the average man struggles to assert his dreams and his hopes but is pushed back by the indifferent forces of nature within and without him.

In his next group of plays, from *The Great God Brown* through *Mourning Becomes Electra,* O'Neill did two things to broaden and deepen his art: he turned to the Greek drama for modes and devices and to modern depth psychology for a new idiom in which to define his meaning. The tragic masque of Greek drama became the symbol of man's conscious personality, allowing the world of subconscious drives and inhibitions to flow and surge at will. By this device, used overtly in *The Great God Brown* and in a somewhat different way in *Lazarus Laughed,* and implicitly in *Strange Interlude* and *Electra,* O'Neill could present at least two lives for each of his characters aurally and visually on the stage. Nina could be her own self-willed "persona" as the passionate and thwarted wife of Gordon Evans and, at the same time, a guilt-ridden vampire sucking the lifeblood of all the men who came into her sphere; and Dion Anthony's mask could be his wife's love-object rather than Dion himself, an object transferrable to another after its owner's death. Thus the dramatist could state in his own medium the essential duality of experience: its supposed "reality" which reduces human beings to their elemental state as parts of impersonal nature and therefore dooms them to destruction, and its other level of "illusion" which, because identified with the wills and the dreams of individual men and women, becomes for each of them the only reality they can accept.

After a silence of some years, O'Neill finally offered in 1946 *The Iceman Cometh,* a tragedy in the realistic setting of Harry Hope's waterside saloon, in which his theme of the necessity of illusion is stated with maximum emphasis and clarity. There is no doubt now what O'Neill believes and there is no weakness in his techniques for expressing it. Hickey is not a tragic hero in the classical sense; he is merely the lodestone that draws together the tragic issues in the lives of all he meets. Each is his own tragic hero; each must live by his own illusions, even though they be induced by drink, drugs, or sexual indulgence.

The only reality is death—that is, the return to a common source of life and meaning in an impersonal nature.

With his faith in the power—or, at least, the necessity—of the human imagination to create a world with which to offset the relentless grinding of chance and fate, O'Neill finally undertook to explore his own childhood and, from it, to reach out to other aspects of American life. The undertaking was too much for him, but it resulted in at least one great play, *Long Day's Journey into Night,* and several others which were less perfect in conception or execution. But this one play is the fullest and clearest statement of modern naturalistic tragedy that we have. With it, American literature reached a new focus of meaning and expression.

But even at this peak of performance, O'Neill suffered from some of the crudities as well as enjoying all of the power of Dreiser. His language is not distinguished, his dramatic forms are often experimental and sprawling, his characters are not subtle, and his meaning is perhaps all too explicit for a refined and perfected art. But the same things were said of Shakespeare and Chaucer by some of the eighteenth-century critics.

VI

Ernest Hemingway in fiction and Robert Frost in poetry help us take the next step toward a disciplined art of naturalistic import. One could work out in some detail Frost's basic acceptance of the determinism of natural law and man's defiant will to retain his right to live by his illusions in narrative poem after narrative poem—the two tramps in mud-time, the hired man who came home to die, Job and Jonah arguing the causes of reason and mercy with a strangely futile God—but Frost is, I feel, primarily a lyric poet and I can illustrate my point best by what is perhaps his most famous poem. One does not need a John Ciardi analysis to get the full point of the repeated last line of the third stanza of "Stopping by Woods on a Snowy Evening," with its use of identical words to express the two levels of human experience. First we have a farmer on a snowy road, stopping briefly and then remembering how far he is from home and food and fire; and then, in exactly the same words, we have the human soul contemplating what there is for him to do with the days and years that stretch out between the moment of living and the eternity of death. Do we need more explication than this? Or has the dilemma of modern man as yet had a more satisfying expression in art?

More cynically perhaps, but no less explicitly, man's use of his imagination to create a world acceptable to his illusions of his own importance makes it possible for the typical Hemingway hero to face life and death with equal equanimity. Whether it be Jake Barnes, whose impotence ironically enables him to appreciate the lost soul of the Lady Brett Ashley; Frederic Henry, whose cowardice brings him the realization of life in love and death in the rain; or Robert Jordan, who has, before he must blow up the bridge, three days in which to fulfill his world of illusion before death creeps up behind him; there is here the same interpretation of the inevitability of natural law pitted against man's need to live by his imagination, even by his mechanically induced illusions. Perhaps not Hemingway's best, because it is his least subtle expression of this tragic view of life, is *The Old Man and the Sea*, a brilliant gem of almost overt allegory. The Old Man's victory in defeat is symbolized at the end by the skeleton of his giant marlin. He had his illusion and his life was done.

It is not hard to see what is happening as we move from one of these authors to the next—even though I should have discussed Frost before O'Neill if I had observed a strict chronological order, but literary history does not happen quite so logically, and contrary factors within any one literary movement are always present at the same time. The tragic soul is essentially the same in all of these authors; it is merely the modern way of facing the eternal riddle of Man versus Fate; but its expression in art runs the full spectrum from emotional involvement to intellectual and aesthetic detachment, and the age as a whole tends to move from the one position to the other. Hemingway as a man was far more deeply involved than Dreiser in tragedy itself, but he had an aesthetic perspective that Dreiser largely lacked. Economy of style, irony of point of view, subtlety of characterization, and wealth of controlled symbolism all made it possible for him to achieve a degree of technical perfection which was beyond the reach of the pioneering Dreiser. As our authors moved beyond tragedy itself to the detachment of tragic irony, American literature was moving through the climax of its second renaissance.

Faulkner's first important novel, *The Sound and the Fury*, appeared in 1929, his *Absalom, Absalom!* in 1936, and he was still producing prolifically at the time of his death in 1962. We need not here examine the meaning and form of this staggering achievement of the man who is generally held in other lands to be our greatest writer of fiction in order to appreciate his philosophical stand on a simple base of naturalistic determinism as well as the mature sophistication of his art form which is vastly more complex, intricate, devious, colorful, and obscure than that of any other modern American writer except perhaps Eliot. Futhermore, he is a humorist, the first among those writers I have discussed.

Faulkner had from the start the most heartrending and immediate tragic vision of any recent American author—so much so that he had to tear his own personal and racial inheritance down to the ground in order to extract from it the mystery of all life. There is no doubt of his tragic intensity; but there is also no doubt that his art, more than that of any other of this group, has provided him with aesthetic perspective. His is the fully ripened grain, heavy with August heat. He alone of these writers could say with Melville's Ishmael, "One did survive the wreck. . . . I was he whom the Fates ordained." His is the irony of intellectual detachment as well as the tragedy of emotional involvement. For this reason, he finally left tragedy, at least in the series of novels that deal with the Snopes family, and discovered the silvery laughter of the comic spirit, grotesque and ribald. The tragic tension had broken; the irony had taken over—not only for Faulkner but perhaps for all of modern American literature as well.

And now we are back again to T. S. Eliot with his "objective correlative," his "ideal order of existing monuments," and his reassociation of the sensibility into a modern metaphysical poetry: and the second renaissance in American literature moves into its reactionary phase and is over as a romantic movement. From tragic irony, Eliot moved, in his later plays, into a phase of tragicomedy, and as his critical theories took hold, American literature became more and more intellectual, complex, and static. The romantic movement was over at long last, as that earlier romanticism of the Elizabethan days had moved into its later phases with the metaphysical poetry of the seventeenth century. Was this another watershed in literary history—a beginning as well as an end?

NOTES

[1] T. S. Eliot, *Selected Essays* (New York: Harcourt, Brace and Co., 1950), p. 247.

[2] R. W. Emerson, *Complete Works*, Centenary Edition (Boston: Houghton, Mifflin Co., 1903–1904), III, 7.

[3] F. O. Matthiessen, *American Renaissance* (New York: Oxford University Press, 1941), pp. 179–180.

[4] Northrop Frye, *Anatomy of Criticism* (Princeton: Princeton University Press, 1957), p. 39.

[5] Theodore Dreiser, *Hey Rub-a-Dub-Dub* (New York: Boni and Liveright, 1920), pp. 243, 257.

[6] Theodore Dreiser, *Sister Carrie* (Cleveland: The World Publishing Co., 1927), p. 557.

III

Science and Literature

1939

FROM THE INAUGURAL ADDRESS AT THE
FIRST MEETING OF THE ENGLISH INSTITUTE,
COLUMBIA UNIVERSITY, NEW YORK. PUB-
LISHED AS THE INTRODUCTION TO THE *Eng-
lish Institute Annual, 1939* IN 1940.

AMONG THE IDEALS which our profession has always held before it has been to learn from science the techniques which make
for precision and thoroughness but to use them for humane
enlightenment: a difficult and often divided task, surely, but
one to which as a group we have been committed for more than
half a century. There is now no turning back. We can add to
what we have learned, and we can adjust ourselves to new
times and new ways; but these fifty and more years, with their
gallery of masters from Bright to Kittredge, are our heritage.

Why, then, should I and more than a few others have sensed
during the past six or more years a growing feeling of restlessness among our associates, a testing of new attitudes, a searching
for new materials, and an experimenting with new methods?
There seems to have developed a loss of confidence in old tasks
and old ways of performing them together with a spirit of
adventure and experimentation in our research. We should be
in an unhealthy state if we felt no such stirrings, but we seem
to be experiencing even more of them than we might normally
expect from a living and growing organism.

Part of our restlessness is caused, I feel sure, by a rebellion in
certain quarters against what might be called a bondage to science which seems to endanger our humanity and devotion to

our art. That revolt has been a vitalizing experience and will carry us yet further with it. A renewed stress on criticism and on appreciation (will someone find a better word?), rather than on mere fact-finding, has served to illuminate much seemingly useless data. But even if we retain our link with science, our way is not too clearly charted. I wonder whether we are not sharing with our fellow workers in the natural and social sciences some skepticism about the certainties which the nineteenth and early twentieth centuries attributed to what they knew as science. If we be allowed to question the physicists, the botanists, and the economists concerning their hypotheses and techniques, which might be sufficient to turn an occasional extremist into a mystic, surely we should experience a twinge of doubt about our methods in so far as they are "scientific." We may well be suspicious of ourselves if we find that we move too easily about our own preserve.

I cannot even enumerate all the evidences that I observe with respect to our skepticism and our growth, but here are a few: It has seemed to me that since 1933 our scholars have been devoting more and more attention to the seventeenth-, eighteenth-, nineteenth-, and even twentieth-century literatures. New methods for the reproduction and preservation of books and manuscripts (notably the microfilm and the ultraviolet ray) have greatly increased our stores of materials and their availability. Libraries, both public and private, have collected and arranged for our use materials that before were buried or unknown and have appointed special staffs to promote research. Projects have become far too large for the resources of any individual, and our scholars have formed into groups for cooperative attack upon them. Foundations have provided subsidies for undertakings which previously would have been impossible. New techniques have been developed for dealing cooperatively and individually with these new problems. Standards for editorial, bibliographical, and textual work have been adapted to the requirements of research in recent literature, as well as in the older works, and have become even more exacting than they were. The contemporary unrest in philosophy has infected our criticism, and the aesthetic substructure of literary art has been tentatively reexamined. The impact of psychology has been felt in biography and literary history, and the lives of many authors have been reinterpreted. Our scholars have recognized the revolution which has taken place in the study of history and have admitted social and economic determinants as sources for the creation of literary art. These changes have been widely reflected in revised curricula, which attempt to link literary study with history, philosophy, and the social sciences, as well as with linguistics; but in the higher levels of study and research they are equally important, although their influence is not always as obvious. Our task is to discover whether they are sporadic and miscellaneous in character or are various evidences of some central trend or force operating in the whole field.

Some order may be obtained by listing these changes under three heads: a great increase in available material; a revision of techniques for dealing with it; and a reexamination of theories of the origin and evolution of literary art. But even such classification leaves a sense of anarchy. We have not yet learned the relationship between our traditional problems and methods and this sudden expansion of our range. One thing is certain, however: we cannot move into the future with closed minds as to the limits of our field, the kind and scope of problems with which we should deal, and the techniques which we should use. I seriously doubt whether the firm faith in mastered techniques and defined objectives which found expression in the 1933 meeting of the Modern Language Association is as general or as unshakable today as it seemed then to be. And I am prepared to welcome the change, even at a sacrifice of some of our old confidence.

Perhaps the chief reason for our change of attitude is that many of our scholars have taken up the challenge of contemporary science and philosophy. Recent meetings of the Modern Language Association have given unmistakable evidence of a movement in this direction. There have been fewer papers of a mere factual nature dealing with minor problems and a great increase of speculative and broadly critical studies. Together with a recognition that literature, as an art, has functions and immunities not enjoyed by some other activities of human nature, there seems to be a general awakening to a realization that the science of today is not the science of the ninteenth century and that something more is demanded from it than the careful analysis of set problems with the accurate recording of findings. The speculative science of the present is more like that of the Renaissance, and we can no longer call ourselves "scientific" when we are merely objective in our attitude toward our materials and meticulous in our dealing with them.

A link with contemporary science can help us to understand the origin and evolution of art and can supply us with improved techniques for our work if we open our minds to its influence. We have been too narrowly concerned with "what" and "who" questions and too little with "why" and "how." What was the date of the first quarto of *Hamlet?* Who was the author of *Piers Plowman?* Which was the earlier version of Keats' *Hyperion?* What was the source of Poe's *Murders in the Rue Morgue?* Such questions of detailed fact are of the greatest importance, as it was important for scientists like Agassiz to classify fishes and for the chemical elements to be isolated and exactly counted. Our philological techniques were developed from their foundations in linguistic science to solve such problems and to give us data previously unknown. "A New Source for *Paradise Lost*," "Some Unpublished Letters from Goethe to Carlyle," and "The Text of Chaucer's *Canterbury Tales*" are typical titles of that period. But even with such data in hand we were still confronted by the mystery of literary creation, and our techniques were unequal to the task of resolving it. Few newly discovered laws governing the composition of poetry have been revealed to us, and little insight has been gained into the nature of the imagination and its relationship to reason. While science has marched on to new methods of studying the composition and functions of the galaxies, the subvisible organisms of biology, and the nature of the human mind and nervous system, we have continued to limit ourselves largely to the accumulation of more and more data about dead authors and their work, without even seeking for causes, relationships, and results outside the field of a frequently petty problem, objectively and narrowly defined. A theory like that of the communal origin of the ballad is rare enough almost to prove the rule. We have had few techniques adequate to sift and interpret our ever accumulating data. Our conception of the possible service of science to our investigations has been too restricted; the hiatus between our reported facts and our creative criticism has been too great.

Much of the fault lies with science itself. In its effort to be accurate it had to stress objectivity, and a means was transformed into an end. Observable data outside the human mind could be classified and defined, whereas the thoughts and emotions of human beings were beyond the reaches of sensuous experience. The phenomena with which the students of literature must deal could not be submitted to the microscope and the telescope. They could not be taken into the laboratory, subjected to formulated tests, analyzed and compared. The *Ode to a Grecian Urn* would reveal little under the microscope, and in a test tube *The Legend of Good Women* would have little response to a Bunsen burner. But modern science has moved beyond such limitations. Animal magnetism, phrenology, political economy, dismal as they all now are, prepared the way for Gestalt psychology and the researches in economics and the new physics which are making such progress today, much as astrology and alchemy opened the territories of the earlier sciences, now legitimized and established. This is dangerous and unproven territory still, but it must be the field of our future researches if we, too, are to move forward. We cannot afford to break our bond with science, but we must share with the science of today more of the skepticism and self-questioning which have so decreased its confidence and so increased its range and power.

If this is to be our mood, there are certain attitudes from which we must free our minds. The most depressing is the conviction that all important work has been done. I know very little about the Elizabethan field, but I recall that almost two decades ago the most distinguished and industrious of the elder scholars under whom I studied likened his generation to the gleaners who search for the scattered grains in a field after the reapers and the harvesters have passed. But I have been unable to observe any cessation of important work even on Shakespeare, a subject which above others should have long since been exhausted if Shakespearean scholars are only gleaners. And I need hardly call your attention again to the virtual rediscovery of the Victorian, the American, and even the seventeenth- and eighteenth-century English periods. If the gleaners have passed, surely someone has appeared to plow, fertilize, and replant the old fields, as well as to clear new ones. The living human mind is incapable of exhausting its curiosity about any realm of its knowledge.

We must also abandon the theory that we have vested rights in problems for research if we are to be pioneers rather than misers. For years we have hesitated to follow the lead of other groups and to encourage our members to advertise the work which they are doing, in order that the work rather than they might be advanced. There is a curious notion embedded in the minds of some literary scholars that only one book may be written on any subject and that secrecy is of the utmost importance while any investigation is in progress. I am glad to say that as a professional group we seem to be outgrowing this particular kind of childishness. We are sharing our kiddie cars so that we may learn from one another the muscular control necessary for the piloting of Atlantic clippers. The work of Professors Leisy, Paine, and more recently Osborn, in reporting research in progress is a good omen. Surely the field of literary scholarship, in which the personal interpretation of data is always more important than the data itself, can afford the excitement and stimulation of open competition. One of the principal functions of our institute must be to encourage interchange of ideas and materials if it is to succeed.

A third obstacle to our progress has been our fear of dealing with modern and contemporary literatures—a fear based on the contradictory pleas that the problems involved are too chaotic and that they are too simple. A really scientific attitude would convince us that the more evidence obtainable on any problem, the more likely it would be to lend itself to a solution; and surely the more immediate our sources, the more evidence they should afford of the principles and laws governing their appearance. The study of the work of John Steinbeck should in some respects lead to more valuable conclusions than could the study of the work of Shakespeare, however inferior the former may be as an artist. If our objective be to assemble new facts and to reap reward for our industry, the earlier fields lend themselves to more exact and exacting discipline. But if we are searching for principles and laws, if we are asking "why?" and "how?" surely we cannot afford to close our minds to the problems of literary creation itself and the materials which we see in expression immediately around us. The scientists do not reject a new comet or living animals as being too readily accessible for study.

But perhaps the most serious obstacle to progress in our field is our too great eagerness to restrict our work to linguistics and to philology in the narrow sense of the term. The forms and idioms of expression are and probably always will be our primary, but they should not be our exclusive, concern. Form is but the outward clothing of substance. A work of art is a living organism and must be examined in terms of its being as well as in those of its appearance. Science, as we define it today, does not demand the objectivity, the exclusively analytical approach, the narrow specialization within sharply defined boundaries which the science of the past generation emphasized. No wonder that some of us are eager to break a bondage which cuts us off from the vital center of our material by "no trespassing" signs. That bondage has made much of our work impeccably accurate and completely inconsequential. But no such restrictions are demanded by the speculative science of today. Perhaps we should inquire further into the revised hypotheses and techniques that modern science has developed, even to its own confusion, before we reject it as an ally.

Much progress will have been made when we have revised our definition of the word "source." There seems to be a general assumption that a source is one work of literature that has forced another and later work into a similar mold with itself.

But Lowes, Parrington, and many others have recently made it clear that only a small part of the complex background of any literary creation is to be found in other works of literature. Backgrounds can no longer be studied as backdrops; they are sources. So, too, are the unspoken emotional experiences of the writer and the thought currents of the age in which he lives. We must learn more about authors than they know about themselves. Behind the initial impact of their writing is a complex network of forces of many kinds which cause that writing to find expression. A bibliography of an author is not a mere list of titles and dates; it is the record of a creative evolution. By exploring all possible sources in the consciousness of the writer and of the age in which he lives we may hope to penetrate a little further into the creative imagination, always our ultimate concern. The history of its expression in significant and beautiful writing is the history of literature, as yet largely unwritten.

In conclusion, a spirit of adventure in scholarship such as this may easily lead into romantic generalization and unfounded dogmatism. In a little-known story Lewis Carroll tells of his excitement over the discovery of an unusual sign over a shop door announcing a dealer in "Romancement"—a new and exciting commodity certainly, but one difficult to pass over the counter. Upon a second examination, however, the word "Romancement" broke down into "Roman cement." Because we are aware of the novelties still available to us, the new fields to be explored, the new techniques to be developed, the new problems and attitudes to be evolved, we need not wander vaguely into "romancement." We may still retain our reverence for the cement of facts and our faith in accuracy and thoroughness. But perhaps we should learn better to discriminate between significant and irrelevant facts, and with our fellow scientists in other fields should explore more profoundly into causes. The phrase "source hunting" today means more than the search for the influence of one book upon another. It leads us to all the forces which operate in the creative imagination and bring into expression a work of art.

Value and Method in American Studies
1958

WRITTEN AS THE SUMMARY CONCLUDING CHAPTER OF *Studies in American Culture*, EDITED BY JOSEPH J. KWIATT AND MARY C. TURPIE. MINNEAPOLIS: THE UNIVERSITY OF MINNESOTA PRESS, 1960. REVISED FOR THE ANNUAL MEETING OF THE GESELLSCHAFT FÜR AMERIKANISCHE STUDIEN IN MAY, 1959, AND PUBLISHED IN THE PRESENT VERSION IN THEIR *Jahrbuch*.

AMERICAN STUDIES as a separate academic program in the universities of the United States began as a series of rebellions in the various established disciplines, primarily in those of English and history. In the departments of English language and literature, the discontent which took shape in the nineteen twenties and 'thirties was three-pronged: against the assumption that American literature, because it is largely written in the English language, is merely an inferior branch of English literature; against the assumption that serious research can be done only in literature prior to the year 1800; and against the domination of historical philology in literary study to the detriment of sociological, psychological, philosophical, and aesthetic approaches. William G. Crane, in a report to the National Council of Teachers of English in 1948, found that the college teaching of American literature could be traced back to 1890 and before, but that the subject did not begin to have a place of its own in the curriculum until after 1918 and was not generally recognized for at least another decade. The American Literature Group of the Modern

Language Association was founded after World War I, and *American Literature* as a separate scholarly journal began publication in 1929. Mr. Crane concludes his historical survey with the comment: "In 1938–39 only a few institutions, notably the University of Chicago, George Washington University, Harvard University, the University of Pennsylvania, the University of Wisconsin, and Yale University, made provision for graduate work in American culture or American Civilization, although this type of work was to become the most striking feature of the study of American literature in the decade which followed." [1] The program at the University of Minnesota was initiated in 1945 and 1946, and other programs followed rapidly.

The reasons for the steady growth of this movement in literary study are complex, but an examination of the scholarly books and articles of the period shows a close relationship between it and the shift of emphasis from the linguistic and belles lettristic approaches to those of cultural and intellectual history. Vernon L. Parrington's *Main Currents in American Thought* appeared in 1927, ten years after the first volumes of *The Cambridge History of American Literature*, and the work of such radicals in the philosophy and method of literary study as Babbitt, Lovejoy, Manly, and Lowes began to be reflected in the reexamination of American as well as English authors, their thought, and their backgrounds. Even more important, scholars in American literature began to show a heretical interest in such historians as Turner, Beard, McMaster, and Schlesinger and to reshape their literary interpretations around dynamic theories of historical evolution in both the individual and the group. A theory of literary history which was based mainly on a linguistic tradition and which sought to explain a work of literary art by reference solely to its "sources" in other works of art began to give way to a theory which saw literature as the direct product of the circumstances, both within and without the experience of the writer, that had brought his artistic expression to fulfillment.

In this discovery lay a new approach to the study of literature in the English language, but an approach which had its history in the thought of Herder, Taine, Brandes, and other European literary historians. This approach sharply distinguished those works which were the productions of artists who had participated in the shaping of a civilization on the North American continent from those of artists who had remained in the British Isles. American literature in itself and in relation to its culture suddenly became a legitimate field for serious scholarly devotion.

This change of emphasis was greatly aided, if not actually caused, by basic shifts in scientific thinking from the systems of analysis and classification of data current in the nineteenth century and earlier to the organic systems developed mainly by modern physics and biology. New theories of the character and functions of nature itself began to be reflected in theories of literary production, and students of American literature, partly because they were exploring a virtually new culture, were perhaps more generally adventurous in their speculations and their methods than most scholars in fields where historical philology had for so long held undisputed sway. Literary Americanists needed a new orientation for their thinking in order to justify their very existence. Scholars like Norman Foerster, H. L. Mencken, Van Wyck Brooks, V. L. Parrington, and F. O. Matthiessen were too independent and original for the ranks of the Modern Language Association, while scholars who remained within the guild but fought for the new dispensation—men like Arthur H. Quinn, Jay B. Hubbell, Stanley Williams, Kenneth Murdock, Ralph L. Rusk, and myself—developed the needed agencies and instruments for the new scholarship and produced major works in literary history in the new idiom. The appearance of the *Literary History of the United States* and the founding of the American Studies Association, with its official organ *American Quarterly*, were almost simultaneous at midcentury.

The contribution of the guild of American historians to the American Studies movement followed similar lines and was, in somewhat the same fashion, a by-product of the new science. Scholars in general American history had, however, one advantage over their literary brethren: American history had been recognized from the start as a legitimate field for special research. The narrative historians Bancroft, Parkman, Prescott, and Motley told the American story for itself and without apology, even though they saw it chiefly in the context of the expansion of European power, and the "objective" constitutional and military historians like Henry Adams, Channing, and Hildreth applied the new German documentary techniques to American sources without inhibition. The revolution was apparent more in changing theories and methods of historiography than in a shift to the American field as such.

It was important however in both ways. F. J. Turner's frontier thesis explained American devolpment as an indigenous growth rather than as an importation, but it also pioneered in the application of economic determinism to historical data. Schlesinger's restudy of immigration, Beard's of the framing of the Constitution, Becker's of the Declaration of Independence, and the new surveys of Morison, Commager, Nevins, and others were only a few of the many reinterpretations of old facts in terms of immediate environmental causation. To these men, literature was one of the many sources of documentation for movements which embraced the entire human experience in any given time and place. They were drawn to the literary historians at about the same time that the literary historians were turning to them and for much the same reason, a desire to broaden their field of inquiry, their methods, and their range of usable data.

Meanwhile, parallel revolutions were taking place in the scholarly study of the social sciences and of the other arts— revolutions which are still in progress and which need not be discussed at length here. The general historians were soon aware of sources of fresh and dynamic thought among their colleagues in economics, political science, and sociology, whereas the literary historians found their interest in recent developments and in environmental causation echoed among the historians of painting, sculpture, architecture, and the minor and "useful" arts. Both groups found the philosophers turning from the classical forms of their subject to pragmatism and experimentalism and from traditional histories of pure philosophy to a type of intellectual history which was firmly anchored to the time, the place, the group, and the thinker.

American Studies as a movement caused none of these trends, but by 1935 it was providing a convenient point of focus for all of them. The prestige of the United States as a world power encouraged the study of its culture, and the strong movements away from overspecialization and toward cooperation among the academic disciplines made the creation of interdepartmental programs in this and similar fields virtually inevitable. Harvard led the way in 1936 with a graduate program in the History of American Civilization, and Pennsylvania, Wisconsin, Yale, and other universities followed.

II

At first these alliances could be described as little more than loose confederations or extensions of the programs of single departments, usually of literature or history. There was little if any feeling that a new subject or a new discipline was in the making. Courses were often grouped merely because they could be described as "American" and their synthesis was left wholly to the student. Administrative committees seldom met and often took little responsibility either for the program or its students. Doctors of Philosophy were thrown out into the academic world without status or job and usually drifted back into conventional channels for their careers. There were few new journals ready to publish experimental scholarship in interdisciplinary problems, and the established journals were largely inhospitable and suspicious.

But the movement needed a rationale as well as a history, and progress toward this end came from general trends in the scholarly world rather than from within the American Studies movement itself. As modern science learned to deal with problems of human nature and human culture rather than merely with the physical world and its biological and economic manifestations, the study of American Civilization gradually began to develop meanings and methods of its own. It is still far from the goal of systematic research to which all scholarship tends to aspire, but it has recently shown signs of moving toward larger syntheses.

Two such movements have had increasing influence in reshaping our definition of American culture and in developing methods for its study. On the one hand, some of the trends which began to bear directly on the problem of understanding American or any other modern culture were to be found in the so-called "behavioral sciences"—sociology, cultural anthropology, and psychology, both social and individual; and on the other hand, contributing trends were to be found in the new analytical methods of criticizing sophisticated works of art and literature and the new techniques for analysing and interpreting mass or popular culture, many of them developed by the folklorists and by the students of the new rhetoric, or linguistic analysis, and of semantics. Cross-cultural indexing of artifacts and documents, psychological analysis of group and individual motivation, content analysis of communication documents, and studies in myth and symbol as basic rather than idiosyncratic formulations of experience began to supplement the older methods of the physical and social scientists and of the general and art historians. Again, American Studies, by offering a limited body of closely related data in the history of the culture of a nation which had developed wholly in the modern era, provided a convenient focus for research and teaching. Modern scholarship was regaining slowly the conception of total cultures which had inspired humanistic scholarship from classical times through the Renaissance but which had been lost in the disintegrative tendencies of modern scientific research; and, even more important, it was learning to apply this conception to modern cultures. American humanistic scholarship began to realize that an immediate culture of recent development and a high degree of sophistication as well as complexity was available to them for examination: the culture of the United States as a political unit, of the North American continent as a geographical unit, and of the people who settled and developed this area in the three hundred and fifty years from 1600 to 1950 as a cultural group. In spite of the difficulties inherent in the problem and the variety among the proposed methods of dealing with it, there seemed at last to be here something of a single and legitimate field for scholarly research as well as a convenient pedagogical device for liberalizing higher education.

The problem of developing suitable methods for such research was, however, very far from solved. In fact, the failure of the movement to settle on a generally accepted method of dealing with its diversified materials—far from being a weakness—appeared as one of its major strengths. It could remain experimental and exploratory; it could still act as the yeast rather than the dough of the academic staff of life, research. American Studies still could, and should, be thought of in the plural as a mixture of different ways of dealing with the same material, but the mixture had tended to become chemical rather than mechanical; that is, its components could now merge in a more integrated whole because each gave up a part of its own identity in becoming a facet of the general enterprise. Since about 1945, the study of American Civilization had become not so much a new discipline as a new focus for the higher study of human habits, ideals, and achievements by a variety of methods. As a branch of humanistic scholarship it was learning to apply the principles and methods of traditional humanism to modern problems and thus to answer in part the criticism that the humanities, alone of the great divisions of learning, are wholly lost in the past.

III

I hope that you will pardon me if, at this point, I turn from a general discussion of our problem and describe, by way of example, a specific experiment in which I had a part. At the University of Pennsylvania, where I have shared in the growth of one of the earlier and more consistently experimental programs in American Studies, we began to feel a few years ago that the movement had reached a stage in its development where a concerted attack on the heart of the problem might prove feasible. Up to this time, all of our thinking had been from the circumference of the circle in toward the center; we had been asking what each of the various disciplines might do to synthesize their concepts and their methods toward the common objective of studying American Civilization. We now proposed to set up a quite different hypothesis and attempt to reverse the direction of our thinking, i.e., to work from the center of the circle out toward the circumference. What would happen, we asked, if we merely assumed that there is such a thing as American civilization in the Gestalt sense and that our sole need was to learn how to isolate it, understand it, evaluate it, and recount its history? To test this question we projected an open seminar, of the nature of an intellectual laboratory, in order to bring together in a common inquiry a group of people who shared an interest in this central problem, regardless of the disciplines which claimed their primary allegiances.

In 1954, a generous grant from the Carnegie Corporation of New York made such an experiment possible. Professor Thomas C. Cochran, an economic historian, and I, who claim allegiance to the discipline of literary history, decided to join forces and offer a seminar for graduate students, resident faculty, and visiting scholars. In the fall of that year, about a dozen people met around a table to undertake the inquiry. About half of them were graduate students working for the American Civilization doctorate; the rest were advanced scholars of various ages and interests. Professor Hellmut Bock of the University of Kiel was our European visitor that year and joined in most of our sessions. We also had such visitors as the novelist-critic James T. Farrell, the sociologist Robert K. Merton, the psychologist Robert B. MacLeod, and the philosopher Richard Brandt. Several members of the resident faculty were regulars, and others came sporadically. The laboratory work was done mainly by the graduate students; the direction and discussion came rather more from the senior participants.

Our first task was to select a general problem which could be dealt with by a variety of methods; we finally settled on the use of concepts of value and value systems as indices to the nature of culture, especially that of the United States in the twentieth century. At the start, we agreed that we could detect the presence of a value concept where there was evidence of a choice and that we should deal with such instances objectively and without imposing upon them any evaluation of our own. Society obviously functions through the choices of both individuals and groups, and mass or individual expressions of such choices in popular and sophisticated forms of art are therefore evidences of value concepts and systems, or "clusters" as we came to call them. Surely here if anywhere, the students of literature, social history, art, philosophy, language, economics—almost anything—could find common ground by jointly examining the same evidences in a contemporary culture. As my colleague in the seminar, Dr. Cochran, was well versed in modern literary theory, and as my field of specialization has always been social criticism, we anticipated—and in fact developed—no personal clash in directing the group.

Nevertheless, we had not been in session more than a month before a deep schism appeared, and, as the year progressed, the group split more and more definitely into two parties: those who were primarily concerned with the nature of society itself as the embodiment of a culture and those who were concerned with the expression of the culture in mass media or individual art. This difference might well have been and remained little more than a division of effort toward a common aim, the one group describing the culture through the evidences of social data and the other through those of various media expressions, had not the split becomes final in the refusal of either group to admit the validity of the method of the other. That which we may call the "social" group maintained that the method of content analysis should be applied with complete objectivity to public documents, advertisements, literary works, and all other forms of expression, without allowing any hierarchy of values other than that of their degree of abstraction; whereas the "literary" group maintained that the element of discrimination in, say, a first-rate novel lifted it and all the values in it to a different plane from those found in, say, the advertisements of a brand of toothpaste to be found in the three top mass-circulation periodicals of a given year. The "literary" group were of course at fault, because they were violating one of the basic assumptions agreed upon at the start: namely, that the principle of relative evaluation should not be applied to values themselves. Their error had been to agree to any such proposition because, by doing so, they relegated all art to the role of social documentation and eliminated the subjective elements of intuition, insight, imagination—call it what you will—which are the very essence of all aesthetic expression and without which art as such is nonexistent. How, then, could a culture be described if its students were forbidden to deal with art as art?

The seminar was highly useful in educating its participants, and it produced several original and excellent doctoral dissertations, but its group findings, if any, will and should of course never be published. Nor was the experiment repeated, as the schism had, by June, become rather painful to all concerned and a year's cooling-off was needed. Then Professor Cochran reopened the experiment alone and offered a faculty-student seminar in the problem of social change as discovered through content analysis of value and other evidences; and in the following year, I took over with a seminar on the relation of literature to society through transformations of social data into popular and formal art by the use of myth and symbol. We both had profited by our first experiment, and we never gave up our common conviction that the study of value concepts and clusters is one of the most fruitful ways of exploring a culture, but our differences became increasingly fixed: he moving with the sociologists toward more objective and scientific analyses, I moving with the psychological critics more toward the formulation of hierarchies of value as expressed in the myth-making functions of both popular and sophisticated art; he concerning himself with such problems as population shifts and changes and the roles of the entrepreneur and other social types, I concerning myself more and more with the creative process itself and with the mysterious and disturbing violations of human experience to which the human imagination, whether group or individual, is so universally addicted.

I have discussed this rather personal experience in some detail both because it seems to me an evidence of the American habit of learning by doing and because I feel that we uncovered not only a difference among ourselves at a particular university but a basic dualism in the larger problem with which I am dealing today. This dualism was well stated and explored by Professor Henry Nash Smith of the University of California in a recent article.[2] Dr. Smith is especially qualified to speak on this question because he was the first American to take a doctoral degree in the History of American Civilization as such. Only those who, like him, have committed themselves professionally to the movement by taking a higher degree in American Studies can realize the full urgency of the problem of unity; and there are by now a constantly increasing number of brilliant young scholars who are so committed. No normal mind can long remain a mere confederation of ideas. Whatever the value of loose organization in a curriculum, the human spirit to its credit will always demand an organizing principle and a unity of goal in its thinking and in its action. When the first Ph.D. in American Studies or American Civilization was awarded, the happy days of intellectual anarchy and free adventure were over. A moral commitment had been made.

That commitment is deeply evident in Dr. Smith's clear presentation of the central problem of the movement. To him "American Studies" means one thing only, a concern for an increased understanding of American culture. The existence of such a culture is assumed; he has defined it as "the way in which subjective experience is organized." There remains only to discover who has done the organizing, exactly what components have been organized into a single whole, and how to study the result.

The tacit assumption in this essay that a single method, although not yet in sight, would be desirable for research in American Studies, springs from the desire to find an organic unity in the subject itself rather than merely a synthesis in the mind of the student. To appreciate the difference in attitude of the scholar trained in one of the older disciplines with that of the product of the new program, one need only turn to Tremaine McDowell's statement of a decade ago: "The discipline of American Studies is the intellectual process whereby a student assimilates the complicated and often contradictory details of

American civilization . . . whereby he fashions out of them a
picture of these United States. In doing so, he reduces diversity
to some degree of unity." [3] Compare this descriptive procedure
with Dr. Smith's focus on a single problem, i.e., the relationship
of Mark Twain to his writing and to the context of his culture.
The conclusion is that which we arrived at in our Pennsylvania
seminar. "It may turn out," says Dr. Smith, "that one of the
distinctive fields of American Studies is precisely this ambiguous
relation between works of art and the culture in which they
occur." The difference is not so much that between two scholar-
colleagues as between the pioneer and devoted proponent of a
movement and its committed product, a difference between
1948 and 1958.

Even though Dr. Smith's findings are, at least for the present,
largely negative, his basic but unanswered question may provide
a plan for the movement as a whole: "To find out what was
happening to the man and to the society we have to ask questions which lead simultaneously to literary analysis and to analysis of social change," and he recognizes that "the development of
a method for American Studies is bound up with the effort to
resolve the dilemma posed by the dualism which separates social
facts from aesthetic values." [4] This is where the movement
started, with history as the spokesman for the social approach
moving toward literature as the spokesman for the aesthetic,
and literature toward history, but now they have met and are
engaged in a common enterprise, they are faced with a tough
and resistant inner dualism.

Upon the nature of this dualism will rest the future of American Studies in America. Is it one of basic disciplinary distinction
or one of different approaches to a common problem? Is not the
movement taken by the social historian from the level of fact
and opinion of the society as a whole, through its image-making
propensity, up (or down) to the level of value and myth
merely the reverse in direction of that taken by the literary or
art critic who starts on the level of the mind and the imagination and moves through value and myth to the materials of actual

life from which aesthetic expression is derived? Should the two not meet somewhere in a realm of values and images, which could express both the social realities and the covert dreams of the total culture? Many scholars in American Studies turn, as does Dr. Smith, to the cultural anthropologists for a solution of this kind, only to find that methods which seem to meet both sets of requirements when applied to the simple cultures of primitive people break down when confronted by complex cultures into the conventional methods of the sociologists or the folklorists. Others turn to modern methods of critical and textual analysis only to be confronted by the web-spinning activities of the aesthetic purists among the new critics.

IV

What, then, is the hope for the future of American Studies in the United States? Or in Germany? Or in Japan? Perhaps it lies in the acceptance of the humanist contention that life is and always must remain dual. Man constantly aspires to monism, whether of God or Nature, and as constantly fails. The human consciousness, to be whole, must participate in the divine and in the material, but cannot identify itself wholly with either and remain human. As American Studies began with a flirtation between literary and historical studies, it would seem now in danger of ending in a divorce, because it asks that union to become total unity. With increased understanding of each other, differences rather than similarities become important in making or breaking a dynamic cooperation.

Another way of stating the problem is to think of a stereopticon viewer which achieves a three-dimensional effect by allowing two angles of vision to focus simultaneously on a single object. Perhaps the two kinds of reality—that of the imagination and that of the reason—really are both real, both essential to human culture in its more complex forms. Perhaps what is needed is a tolerant relationship of cooperation between the two disciplines, that dealing with art and that dealing with society, and a willingness on the part of each to move from the level of fact to the level of value. Perhaps the limitation of scholarship in American Studies to one method and one kind of material would spell defeat, self-inflicted.

The irony of the present situation in social and humanistic scholarship in the United States is that the trend is counter to any such cooperation. The desire to achieve objective, "scientific" validity is once more separating them—not only in American Studies, but in other branches of research as well. The social scientist strives to isolate the social fact from its cause and its consequence so that it may stand up and be counted; and the literary critic strives to free the work of art from both intention and affect so that its supposed meaning may be read from its own being, the text, unconfused by what are considered to be extraneous circumstances. Not only is the artist once more being deliberately alienated from his society, but society is being deliberately robbed of its aesthetic experience. Values themselves, in the social science definition, are all of one level of worth although they may exist in a hierarchy of abstraction. Content—whether social or aesthetic—becomes form, and form becomes content; the dialectical relationship between them is ignored or suppressed. Quantification, objectivity, and system are once more pushing the humanities and the social sciences apart, and American Studies may fall between.

Dr. Smith has thoroughly considered this problem in the article to which I have referred, and has provided a clear estimate of what internal analysis in literary criticism (the "New" criticism) and quantification in social science research (content analysis) are accomplishing separately and are failing to accomplish together. William K. Wimsatt, Jr. and Monroe Beardsley make the case for literary criticism when they say, "The Intentional Fallacy is a confusion between the poem and its origins. . . . The Affective Fallacy is a confusion between the poem and its results. . . . The outcome of either fallacy, the Intentional or the Affective, is that the poem itself, as an object of specifically critical judgment, tends to disappear." [5] Bernard Berelson speaks similarly for the social sciences when he defines content analysis as "a research technique for the objective, systematic, and quantitative description of the manifest content of communication." [6] In both cases the process is that of arbitrarily isolating and delimiting elements of subjective experience in order to approximate the precision and accuracy demanded by science. In both, the endeavor is doomed to failure if regarded as more than a provisional operation to suggest rather than to prove hypotheses. Both are highly useful within these limits, but are misleading if strained beyond them.

The difficulty on both sides of the dilemma is of course that, in an effort to be objective and scientific on the one hand and aesthetically pure on the other—in short, to achieve a validity above experience—both positions tend to confuse means with ends. What is only a method, a provisional isolation of an entity for purposes of analysis, attains the finality of verifiable truth. The method of content analysis can be successfully applied to elements which are not really objective and quantitative, such as values, images, and ideas, if the categories developed are recognized as quantitative only in their expression and not in any absolute sense and if the results are regarded as suggestive rather than as scientifically valid. In spite of the advances in the techniques of psychological analysis in recent years, human thinking and feeling are still very far from submitting to the conquests of exact human knowledge. In both the individual and the social mind, there are vast areas which are, and will remain as long as anyone can foresee, purely qualitative and susceptible only to intuitive rather than logical methods of understanding and evaluation. Bernard Berelson somewhat reluctantly admits the usefulness of "qualitative" as well as quantitative analysis, especially for meanings which are largely connotative, but warns that it too has a responsibility for sharpening categories and hypotheses and for avoiding "impressionistic and ambiguous formulations." He does not, however, develop the positive usefulness of such analysis for purely speculative explorations into the realms of social metaphor, myth, and ritual. Presumably he would not approve such formulations as Malinowski's imaginative as well as scientific study of the mind and habits of the primitive Trobriand Islanders,[7] Constance Rourke's attempt to probe the roots of American culture by exposing folk elements which underlie a complex and rapidly changing modern civilization on the move,[8] and the broad revelation of a national character in the generalization of David Riesman and his associates that modern times have witnessed a shift of emphasis from the "inner" to the "other" directed man.[9] All such speculative studies are suspect by the purists among research scholars because their hypotheses cannot be submitted to factual and quantitative validation; but it is just this quality which allows them to impinge on the realm of the human imagination and thereby provide possible meeting grounds for the student of the arts.

On the other hand, there is nothing in the procedures of the "New" critics which would prevent the application of their insights to the total product of the artist, to the creative processes that underlie his work, and to his biographical and social conditioning as well as to the isolated work of art if the fact of isolation be accepted only as a provisional condition of the analytical process and not as an end in itself. This, of course, the purists among the "New" critics could not allow, but there are increasing signs of restlessness among them and of desire to relate their findings, in the way that Mr. Allen Tate has attempted to relate Southern literature to broader and deeper contexts of experience than can be found in a single poem, novel, painting, play, or composition. Their sometimes violent and unreasoning antihistoricism, as found in many of their so-called histories of criticism as well as in their individual analyses, must give way to a recognition of the validity of content study *through* as well as *in* form, and the larger relationships between life and art, experience and expression. If the doors are once more opened, as they were for Goethe, Lessing, Coleridge, and Arnold, on the speculative exploration of the realm of imagination, myth, and metaphor that exists in the creative process as well as in the work of art, the literary critic might recapture his right to conversation with the more speculative of the social scientists.

It must be admitted that the urge toward final and tenable results is today so strong in all fields of scholarly research, and the desire of social scientists, and even of humanists, to become as accurate and predictable as the physical and natural scientists is so impelling that a move in the direction of intuitive and non-quantitative methods may be increasingly unlikely. If this trend continues, American Studies may well become a branch of sociology and move with the purists in that field into severely limited and definable areas of research or it may dissolve with the New Criticism into the vacuum of pure literary analysis. But the literary, cultural, and intellectual historians, who have always had a stake in pure speculation in spite of repeated efforts—and repeated failures—to reduce their discipline to a science, are likely to protest. The latest committee attempt on their part to explore the methodology of their craft, far from reducing history to a mere analytical description of society, concluded with the suggestion that "the use of social science approaches focused attention on the aspects of the event that reveal the major dynamics of the culture" and predicts that "when the United States is even two hundred years old instead of a hundred and seventy . . . broader and less detailed syntheses will be demanded by the exigencies of space and time, and it will be up to the historian to . . . avail himself of the aid offered by the social scientist." [10]

The scholar in American Studies, devoted as he is to a specific field of data and to a single large historical event—American Civilization, both in its development and in its present status—is more free to explore and experiment with methodology than are the scholars who are committed to specific disciplines. By learning to use the techniques of both types of analysis, that of the social scientists and that of the literary and art critics, but by refusing to be confined to the end proposed by the purists in either field, he may discover broader and deeper truths about man's experience in a single time and place than would be available to the more specialized researcher. He might also, by analogy, understand better man's experience in other times and places and, by generalizing, the nature of culture itself. The movement should not give in wholly to the historians and, through them, to the formalizing and limiting methods of the social sciences, nor should it renounce history and move into formal literary and art criticism. Its role is still, and probably should remain, that of the mediator; but in filling this role, it can develop even further than it has during the past decade toward self-esteem and precision in carrying out its specific if not specialized task. That task is the understanding of the culture of the United States, and there is no one research method competent to accomplish it alone. A focus on aims does not necessarily mean a limitation on means.

NOTES

¹ Committee on the College Study of American Literature and Culture; William G. Crane, Chairman. *American Literature in the College Curriculum* (Chicago: National Council of Teachers of English, 1948), p. 19.

² *American Quarterly*, IX, Part 2 (Summer, 1957).

³ Tremaine McDowell, *American Studies* (Minneapolis: University of Minnesota Press, 1948), p. 33.

⁴ Smith, H. N., *op. cit.* pp. 199, 202, 207.

⁵ William K. Wimsatt, Jr., *The Verbal Icon* (New York: The Noonday Press, 1958), p. 21.

⁶ Bernard Berelson, *Content Analysis in Communication Research* (Glencoe, Ill.: The Free Press, 1952), p. 18.

⁷ Bronislaw Malinowski, *Magic, Science, and Religion* (Glencoe, Ill.: The Free Press, 1948; reprinted in Doubleday Anchor Books, 1954).

⁸ Constance Rourke, *The Roots of American Culture* (New York: Harcourt, Brace and Co., 1942).

⁹ David Riesman and others, *The Lonely Crowd* (New Haven: Yale University Press, 1953; reprinted in Doubleday Anchor Books, 1954).

¹⁰ Thomas C. Cochran and others, *The Social Science in Historical Study*. A Report of the Committee on Historiography. Bulletin 64 (New York: Social Science Research Council, 1954), pp. 163, 171.

A Letter to American Literary Historians
1958

WRITTEN FROM LONDON TO PROFESSOR
WALTER BLAIR, THEN CHAIRMAN OF THE
AMERICAN LITERATURE GROUP OF THE MOD-
ERN LANGUAGE ASSOCIATION OF AMERICA,
AND READ BY HIM AT THE ANNUAL LUNCH-
EON OF THE GROUP.

I HAVE BEEN so closely associated with the activities of the American Literature Group in literary history and bibliography since
the 1920's that I cannot refrain from expressing my pleasure at
this new spurt of interest and energy in the perennial reinterpretation of our literary past. Not only must each generation write
its own literary history, as the editors of the 1948 *Literary History of the United States* assumed, but each group and each individual who develops a hypothesis and a method must be
allowed to make his own contribution in his own way; for the
writing of history is never done as long as anyone can read new
meanings into his own life by studying the reflection of the
present in the mirror of the past. As long as we are vitally concerned with the problems of the relationship of the now to
the then, the work of art to the artist, and literature to its society, our historical scholarship will be alive; as soon as we feel
that we have answered all such questions, we will become mori-
bund. The danger in a work like *The Cambridge History of
American Literature* or the *Literary History of the United
States,* or any massive synthesis, is that it can act as a deterrent to
intellectual curiosity by giving a false sense of a false finality.

Of the making of histories there is no end, and much scholarship of the right kind is the very lifeblood of a culture.

As I look back on the movement which, from my point of view at least, culminated in the *Literary History of the United States*, I see it as the scholarly part of the so-called renaissance of the second and third decades of this century. America's cultural "coming-of-age" in that era is now a generally accepted historical fact. The completion of the historical process which established one of the modern world powers on this North American continent and gave it full political, economic, and intellectual self-awareness found expression, in the years 1912 to 1920, in the poetry, fiction, and criticism of a major group of writers. The same movement brought a new crop of literary histories by Quinn, Boynton, Cairns, Van Doren, Foerster, and Parrington to assert a vigorous nationalism instead of the lingering colonialism of our then elder statesmen. Strongly influenced by the economic determinism and the intellectual challenge of the "new" history, they stressed the social and philosophical contexts of American writings in order to establish firmly the integration of our literary past with the forces which had shaped our civilization.

The *Literary History of the United States* attempted to sum up the achievement and point of view of this generation of scholars, but it also challenged their limitations in three important ways: by a series of "instrument" chapters, by emphasis on the masterwork and the major writer, and by examining the relationships of American to European as well as to English literatures and cultures.

In the "instrument" chapters it related the work of art to the factors of environment which immediately conditioned it— the processes in the making and the consumption of the literary product per se. In so doing, it raised in specific terms that could be understood by the social scientists the problems of the direct relationship of literature to the culture of which it is a major expression. Even now, this kind of sociology of literature is still in its infancy, but at least we understand better than we did in

1940 just how the presence or absence of publishers, periodicals, copyright laws, circulating libraries, booksellers, educational institutions, theatres, and other such agencies are essentials of the form and direction of any literary development.

At the other extreme, the *Literary History of the United States* proposed that the meaning of a national literature can best be sought in its masterworks and its major authors rather than in the clusters of minor and subliterary productions which are the delight of the social or intellectual historian. Selecting somewhat arbitrarily the authors and books which our generation had come to agree upon as our highest literary achievements, it discovered two peaks of performance in the periods 1835–1855 and 1915–1935, and it then subordinated all other aspects of the history to the task of explaining and evaluating the cultural processes which thus culminated. By pointing to the need for fresh study of the really important literary works and authors in themselves as well as in their contexts, it suggested a kind of analytical and evaluative criticism at that time none too common among us.

It is in these two respects that the *Literary History of the United States* predicted the two major trends in our scholarship of the past two decades. The new criticism (I do not use the term in a special sense) has sharpened the tools of analysis and has discovered in the psychology of the work of art and of the creative process new and important bases for aesthetic understanding. By turning attention from the causes of literary production to the results in the literary product itself, a whole generation of critics has taught us how to write the chapters on masterworks and major authors around which the architecture of the next literary history must be constructed.

On the other hand, the American studies movement (again, I use the term in a general sense) has taught us that a culture is to be discovered as much in the composite imagination of a people as in their habits of economic and political behavior. Largely with the help of the cultural anthropologists, the social scientists of the present are beginning to study mature and sophisticated cultures as configurations of social consent, habit, and communal expression in much the same way that primitive societies have been so successfully interpreted. Again, we have barely made a start in developing the needed methods for this kind of study, but it is surely here that the literary historians of the future will find the mortar with which to weld the bricks of their aesthetic analyses of masterworks into the story of the historical development of our national culture.

A third respect in which the *Literary History of the United States* opened doors which have subsequently been widened was in calling attention to the increasing interdependence of American and European literatures and cultures. Some historical critics today even go so far as to say that national and racial factors are no longer of importance in the modern world of swift and easy intercommunication—that what we need is a history of modern rather than of American literature. They may be right, for it is increasingly difficult to assign nationality to such writers as Joyce, Proust, Kafka, Eliot, Auden, and Pasternak, but such a view tends to forget the breakup of the vast colonial empires of the nineteenth century and the simultaneous growth of local, racial, and national movements toward self-determination which are now apparent in all parts of the world. This is not the place to discuss so broad and so controversial a problem, but I would like to conclude by expressing the view that the new literary history must retain a sense of the autonomy of the immediate cultural context of every work of art if it is to be history at all. There is no historical continuity in art as such. Masterworks are related to masterworks in a realm that knows no time or place. For the historian, even the great work of art is the expression of a culture at a specific moment in its development, and only in the progress of human society will he discover the process which culminates from time to time in supreme aesthetic fulfillment.

If another literary history is needed for another time, it will not result from the anti-historicism of some of our literary critics or from the anti-aestheticism which has infected some of our social scientists. It will come rather from those who have learned to use judiciously the insights and the methods of both the analytical critics and the behavioral scientists and who can apply the findings of both groups to the task of telling once again what our literary achievement really is and how it came to be what it is.

The Province of Literary History

1963

WRITTEN FOR *The Aims and Methods of Scholarship in Modern Languages and Literatures.* EDITED BY JAMES THORPE. NEW YORK: MODERN LANGUAGE ASSOCIATION OF AMERICA, 1963.

LITERARY HISTORY is concerned with describing and explaining the expression *in literature* of a people during a period of time, in a place, and usually in a specific language. It differs from other kinds of history to the degree that literature is a distinctive kind of expression. We need not stop to define the word "literature" further except to note that it will be used in this essay to mean an art—the art of the word—rather than merely any given body of preserved writings.

Literary history is *not* the history of language, although the language in which a work of literature is written is perhaps its primary determinant, and the work of the historical philologist and the linguistic analyst must have reached a stage of clear definition before the work of the literary historian may begin.

It is *not* textual analysis, although it must start with the assumptions that certain texts are authentic and others are not, and that some are better than others; and it must depend upon textual analysis or criticism to explain the relationships between two texts of the same literary work or the texts of any two or more literary works.

Nor is it literary criticism, although it must depend upon the literary critic to identify and to evaluate the works of literature with which it is to deal, to eliminate from its consideration as literature those writings which are not literature, and to establish the necessary hierarchies and other relationships in terms of value of the literary works which it is to use as data in its historical account.

The literary historian may—in fact, he must to a greater or lesser degree—be trained as a linguist, a textual critic, and a literary critic, but in his role as literary historian he has a separate and quite precise function. He must answer such questions as *how? when? where? why?* a work of literature exists or has existed and what its relationships are or were to other works of literature and to the whole history of man as a sentient and social being.

In short, the literary historian is an historian among other historians—political, economic, intellectual, cultural, and so on —and his function is to write the history of man as revealed in literature, as the functions of other historians are to write the history of man as revealed in government, commerce, ideas, painting, architecture, or any other kinds of human expression in act or form. For this reason, the literary historian, as such, together with other historians, is involved in the basic problems of historiography, and he may leave to others the problems of literary theory and of methods of critical analysis and evaluation.

These "others" may, of course, be merely other aspects of his own scholarship. As an individual scholar attempting to define and limit his own province and profession, the literary historian may be confused as to the exact lines of demarcation between literature and general culture, between language and literature, between history and criticism, between textual and analytical or evaluative criticism, or even between the role of the scholar and that of the creative artist; but once his primary role as a literary historian is decided upon, he must further decide just where his professional responsibility to his subject begins and ends, what kinds of problems are germane to his role as literary historian, what materials are needed and must be discovered or assembled, and what methods are most likely to produce the information that he has undertaken to acquire. As

he must depend upon other forms of scholarship to support his
inquiries, either in himself or in others to wh)m he may turn,
so other forms of literary scholarship must remain incomplete
unless they depend upon him to supply the historical dimension
of their problems. And there is no act or facet of human experience that does not have a history.

II

There is perhaps less general agreement among historians as
to what their discipline is and how it should be practiced than
among any other group of scholars today, but if we are to be
literary historians, we must at least wet our toes in the sea of
controversy.

Even though historians differ on many questions of theory,
they usually agree that there are two main problems about which
their disagreements may cluster as about the two poles of a
magnet: (1) the first concerns the nature of the materials they
undertake to record and interpret, and (2) the second concerns
their own roles as collectors of factual data and as minds capable of interpreting these data.

These issues may be further narrowed by agreement (1)
that history is not a record of facts as such but of human experience with facts, and therefore it must concern itself with
events and the expression of events in either action or thought;
and (2) that a historian cannot hope to be completely objective,
but that however subjective and prejudiced he may be, his
particular bias—whether a personal one or one shared with a
group—may itself be considered objectively as a factor in the
act of historical writing and therefore be taken into account
in evaluating the result.

But whether we incline from this middle position toward that
of the nineteenth-century positivist view that objectivity is at
least theoretically attainable in historical writing and should
therefore be diligently sought, or toward the contrary modern
relativist view, as expressed by Professor Sir George Clark in
the General Introduction to the revised *Cambridge Modern
History*,[1] that knowledge of the past has come down through

one or more human minds, has been "processed" by them, and therefore there is no "objective" historical truth, we may nevertheless proceed to our special jobs of defining the nature of literary events and the role of the literary interpreter of such events. We may assume that our material is literature and that we as historians are practicing the art of writing as well as discussing it. (By "the art of writing" I mean of course the *whole* creative process which results in a finished work of art and not just the so-called "art" of correct or "good" prose style.)

Literary history is therefore literary in two respects: it deals with the materials of literature and should not attempt to write the history of anything but literature; and it is itself a form of literature and is therefore an art and not a science, however much it may share with science the ideal of discovering and recording truth, and however much it may borrow from science its methods of discovering, selecting, and classifying the data of its researches.

To narrow our field of inquiry thus sharply to two problems is not, of course, to solve either of them, for there are wide differences of opinion as to what literary events are and how they may be related to each other in some sort of historical pattern, and there are also differences of opinion as to what the art of literary history is and how it should be practiced. It is with these two problems, but mainly with the first, that the rest of this essay will attempt to deal.

In order to do research and to write, the literary historian must first set up some sort of working hypothesis as to what a literary event is and how it may be related to other literary events, and he would probably not be too seriously challenged if he merely assumed that the literary event, the unit with which he is to deal, is any piece of formal writing which is generally accepted by the critics as a work of literary art.

The primary task of the historian is then to assemble all the works of literary art, within the limits of his inquiry, which have been identified by literary criticism, and to relate them to each other in at least a time sequence. But here his troubles begin. Is it enough that he treat each work of art as a bead on a string and merely arrange it in its proper order with the others? Does a finished work of art have a final objective reality apart from the artist who created it, the culture which furnished the materials of experience that went into it, the public which received and read it when it appeared, and the readers of other cultures in other places and times? To identify the literary event as the finished work of art is too simple an answer to the problem; for such an answer but opens the Pandora's box of these other questions, all of which are valid and must be taken into account. For a work of art, as an historical event, must have relationships in time and place and person, and its reassuringly static appearance is both misleading and incorrect. Is one work of art related to another merely because they fall into some sort of chronological sequence? Or is such a relationship causal and does one work of art help to create and shape another? Or are the causes quite outside the work of art itself and in the experience to which it gives expression? And is the experience of the reader and critic also involved? Or is the whole idea of relationships illusory except in accidental patterns of kaleidoscopic variation and change?

There are at least four answers to these questions, each of which provides a working philosophy of literary history.

The first of these assumes that literary history is concerned with discovering and defining the works of literary art of the past and with describing each, in chronological sequence, in their contexts of time, place, and authorship, without exploring or attempting to explain the factors which presumably caused them or the influences they may have had on each other or on readers. Such a descriptive and narrative kind of literary history is based on the oldest and simplest concept of time as operating in a straight line, but however inadequate as a final theory, it must remain the starting point for more complex and satisfying hypotheses and methods.

The second theory is concerned not only with discovering and defining the works of literary art of the past but also with explaining the sources and influences of each on preceding and following works of literary art. According to this theory, the only sources and influences of importance to the literary historian are also literary; that is, his field of inquiry is limited to the sources and influences of one work of art upon another. This theory goes beyond the first in that it recognizes the causal factors upon which most historical writing has been based for the past two centuries at least; but it imposes a narrow and perhaps questionable limitation upon the kinds of causes and influences which may be admitted to the historian's inquiry. There is implicit in this theory an assumption that works of literary art occur in causal sequence on a level of their own and without other causal relationships to their creators or their readers. This assumption is, of course, accurate as far as it goes—a work of literature may in itself alone be a source of another work of literature, as has been demonstrated by at least two generations of researchers—but in recent years this method has been questioned as being so limited that its results may well be misleading or false because it fails to recognize other kinds of sources as well. In its extreme form, it reduces the creative artist to little better than a superior kind of plagiarist.

The third theory is concerned not only with discovering and defining the works of literary art of the past and with explaining the sources and influences of each on others, but it is also concerned with explaining the sources of each work of art in the experience of the artist who created it and in the culture of which that artist was a part; and further, with explaining the influences of each work of art on each of its readers or groups of readers and on the cultures of which they are parts. As it is with this theory that the remainder of this essay will be primarily concerned, it need not be further elaborated here. However terrifying it may seem in its apparently limitless range and scope, the literary historian can scarcely avoid its challenge if he is to remain in business.

The fourth and last theory is of comparatively recent development and is closely related to concepts of time which defy historical causation to a greater or less extent. In so far as its proponents retain a basis in chronology, even though they substitute a cyclic for a progressive view of man's past experience, they must be considered as merely extending the causal theory described above by providing one more kind of source for literature; and in so far as they substitute such abstractions as myth, symbol, value, or concept for the more traditional view of literary events, they enlarge and deepen rather than alter the literary historian's understanding of the nature of literature and therefore of the literary events with which he deals. But in its extreme form, the relativism of modern science tends to substitute some form of psychological for chronological time and to merge the past with the present and future as do Eliot, Joyce, and other modern writers. This is probably the point at which historical truth stops and some other more subjective form of truth takes over. However valid such a view may be for a wholly relativistic world and however important it may be for the discipline of critical analysis which is so much in evidence today, it is within the province of the historian only as long as it retains a concern for causal relationships and thereby provides a convenient thread upon which to string the events of literary history; but at the point at which it substitutes a concept of static and configurative time for one of time sequence, it moves over into the province of the literary critic and is no longer of use to the historian except in so far as it helps to define the events with which he is to deal. Mythology itself is, of course, not literature but is rather one of the kinds of material from which literature may be made.

III

If, therefore, the primary task of the literary historian is to record and explain the life histories of literary works, he must make certain assumptions about the kinds of sources with which he is to deal. He may ask the literary critic to identify those writings which are art and to arrange them for him in some kind of hierarchy, the textual critic to provide him with the proper texts, and the historian of language to describe and explain the idiom in which the works are expressed. But he must first decide whether the literary works before him are living organisms or static objects. If he assumes that history is process and not merely sequence, he has no choice but to assume also that each work is a living organism in that it was created by an artist at a given time, in a given place, from the materials of his experience; that it was formed and modified by the conditions under which the artist lived and worked; and that it then had, and perhaps still has, a life of its own apart from that of the artist and in relationship to its hearers and readers.

The concern of the literary historian is with the entire creative process rather than with merely the static form and content of the printed work, even though his studies must begin and end with the literary work itself. Frequently, as we have seen, the relevant factors in the personal biography of the author, the environment in which the literary work appeared, its relationship in form or content to other literary works, or the subsequent history of this work of art become *in themselves* so interesting to the scholar that he forgets the relevance which alone can justify his studies and he becomes a mere antiquarian or a specialist in a discipline other than that of literary history. The failure to relate his findings back to the work under study is as serious as is the equally common failure to relate the work to as many of its creative and conditioning circumstances as possible. Like the player of any game, he must keep his eye on the ball and his mind on the timing and distance of its flight.

Literary historians, therefore, can, and should, develop secondary specializations of their own. One may be an amateur philosopher and psychologist, another a political or religious historian, another a student of the theatre, or printing, or of mass media, a fourth a linguist, another of even so narrow a science as that of handwriting, or watermarks, or bindings, another of the more or less parallel arts of painting, architecture, or music. There is almost no limit to the factors which contribute in one way or another to the history of a literary work, but when these subinterests take over and become primary, the scholar may still be a worthy scholar but he is no longer a literary historian. Literature may be part of the documentary materials of the social or intellectual or cultural historian, but the literary historian should be on his guard against being distracted into any such related fields of study *in themselves* and viewing literature as the cause rather than the result of the historical process. Relationships are always two-way streets, but the true literary historian, however far he may wander, is always on his way, by a circuitous route, back to the literary work as his primary object.

It is sometimes argued also that causal and conditioning factors are of importance only to inferior and subliterary works and that, because great literature is universal, it rises above its circumstances by its unique and inspired powers. Such a view can be justified only as irrational mysticism and is none of the business of the literary historian. To him, the greater the work of literature and the more it achieves universality by seeming to rise above its environment, the more complex and challenging his task. The causal factors have not disappeared by its act of transcendence; they have merely become more complex. The ultimate and highest aim of the literary historian is therefore to help to explain the existence of masterworks. He may leave the lesser works to other historians to be used as documents or he may study them himself as partial or related examples of the process which could produce *Hamlet, Moby Dick, Don Quixote*, or *The Brothers Karamazov*. No less than for the literary critic, the literary masterwork is his ultimate quarry, although he may often content himself with lesser game.

With these precautions, we may turn to those factors which contribute to the existence of literary works and are therefore the legitimate concerns of literary history. The most important of these are *Ideas*. Literature both derives from and contributes to the complex of ideas of the people and time and place of its origin. These ideas too have a history, and some of them are more dominant than others. Usually religious and political ideas have the greatest influences on a writer or on the course of literary history because they are most immediate to daily experience. The writer may draw on or be influenced by or contribute to Calvinism, Catholicism, Rationalism, Progressivism, Communism, or the controlling ideas of Descartes, Luther, Locke, Newton, Darwin, Marx, or Freud as these ideas are parts of his intellectual environment, and, whether or not he is an overt student or advocate of any of these systems, his literary comment upon them may influence the ideas of others. Shakespeare's works as a whole may be taken as a reflection of and comment upon the political thinking of Elizabethan England, Hawthorne's are a part of the history of Calvinism in America, Goethe provides a critique of the German romantic philosophy, and Dos Passos and Koestler offer data on the history and spread of Communism. The examination of these relationships makes the literary historian at least a part-time intellectual historian as well.

A second factor is *Culture,* a convenient word with which to describe the institutions, habits, norms, values, roles, and so on which determine the patterns of life of a people in a time and place. It is expressed in the artifacts and the arts of the culture, including literature, and the literary historian will seek to determine the relationships between the work of art and the culture in which it occurred, even though, in so doing, he may find himself in the role of the economic, social, and cultural historian as well. For example, a close-knit population like that of eighteenth-century coffeehouse London will cultivate the periodical essay and the novel, whereas a rural and sparse population like that of the early American West will depend on the magazine that specializes in short stories and short lyric poems. Similarly, the pace of life of farm and forest produces the poetry of nature and the simple life and the romance of the long ago to help warm the long evenings by the log fire, whereas the urban cultures of today are better expressed in the complex symbolism of modern verse and fiction, with their psychological analyses and their contrapuntal forms.

Closely related to culture is the factor of political and social *Institutions.* Forms of organization of group behavior such as the political party with its elections, conventions, and caucuses; the church with its sacraments and ceremonies, its clubs and its missions; the military establishment; the school, college, or university; the community players, garden, sewing, discussion and other kinds of associations; the learned society; and many other

similar institutions furnish the sources of literature by determining the kinds and shapes of experience in a given time and
place. The literary historian who wishes to place Tolstoi's *War
and Peace* in his history can hardly avoid the study of Russian
military institutions and events; the literary provenience of
Emerson's *Essays* has a causal relationship to the rise of the Unitarian Church in New England; Swift's satires cannot be understood without a study of the political institutions of England and
Ireland in the eighteenth century. The literary historian is inevitably drawn into the history of particular institutions as
well as their accompanying ideas: religious, political, military,
educational, and social.

A fourth factor is *Tradition and Myth*, or the body of beliefs that forms in a people of a given time and place its com-
pensation for reality. Mythology has already been mentioned
above as one of the possible sources of a literary work of art,
and, in so far as it has itself a history, it can provide one of the
most important sources of the history of a literature because,
like literature, it is primarily concerned with the realm of the
imagination rather than with that of knowledge. A complex
construct of the racial or national imagination, these beliefs are
usually expressed in symbols or images and constitute a system
or systems of religion or myth or folk tradition with evolutionary
histories of their own. The Hellenic, Hebraic, and Nordic bodies
of such myth are only the principal ones among many in the
history of man, as Sir James Frazer made clear in his anthro-
pological studies collected in *The Golden Bough*. As nebulous
as this body of experience may sometimes seem, literature draws
upon it constantly to give meaning to the life it is trying to express, and one of the tasks—perhaps the principal task—of the
literary historian is to define and to trace back to their sources
the aspects of such traditions as appear in each literary work and
then to link literary works in causal and sequential relationships in terms of the histories of these systems of belief. In so
doing, he will become, for the time being, a historian of individual and social psychology. He may even take his start from

basic Jungian archetypes, but only as they contribute to historical process.

Biography is the most important source of literary history. It is the life experience of the author or group of authors who produce the literature of a people or age. This experience is usually of two kinds: (1) contact with places and with other people in the normal circumstances of individual, family, communal, or national life; and (2) reading and other means of escaping from the immediate into more vicarious forms of experience. Both kinds are important as sources for the creative process and for the work of art. With advances in the sciences of psychology and sociology in recent years, the study of both of these two kinds of biographical sources has become more complicated and more rewarding, and literary scholarship has tended to adopt many new and experimental methods of exploring the subconscious mind and the group consciousness. The literary historian must rely upon the psychologist and the literary critic to furnish him with the data necessary to historical treatment of these factors, but their causal and sequential relationships remain his concern.

IV

Up to this point it may seem to have been assumed that literary history (as well as history of other kinds) moves in a straight line and a steady pace through chronological time. This is obviously not the case. History is a process that deals with events, as we have seen—it is not the mere record of fact—and process moves in curved lines following the cycles of birth, growth, and decline of organisms, with constant variations in speed, density, quality, and direction. This is not to say that the biological analogy of the life cycle can be strictly applied as a scientific measurement to the histories of such larger units of human experience as cultures, institutions, or nations, which in themselves have no individual biological existence. This is one of the fallacies of the nineteenth-century philosophers of history such as Spencer, Marx, and Spengler, who were immediately influenced by Darwinism and other forms of evolutionary theory, and it led to disastrous racist and national ambitions which were based on the false logic of the inevitability of any single life cycle. But to take the next step and to deny all relationship between the biological and the literary process is to deny the possibility of seeing literature at all in its historical dimension and thereby to reduce the work of art to a static and causeless existence, an equally serious error.

The changing kinds, pace, and fashions in literary history are so obviously related to similar changes in the society of which a literature is the expression that we often find literary historians giving nonliterary names to periods, movements, and coteries with which they deal. Thus we speak of the period of the Enlightenment, the Restoration, the Frontier; we name literary movements after Pericles, Augustus, Louis XIV, and Queen Victoria; we use words like Puritanism, Rationalism, Progressivism almost as though they were adjectives describing kinds of literature; and we move words like idealism, naturalism, and romanticism from philosophy to religion to literature and back again, without taking account of the inevitable shift in meanings that must result from shifts in context or idiom.

However vague and inadequate and confused the terminology of the literary historian may be, the presence of great concentrations of literary production of a single or closely related kind in short periods of time and limited geographical space is perhaps the most obvious single phenomenon with which he has to deal. Matthiessen points out that the five years 1850–1855 in and around Boston, Massachusetts, produced a half dozen or more of the masterworks of American literature of the nineteenth century and that there was a great similarity between most of these works. Here is the peak of a literary movement, romantic in nature, the maturity of some kind of life cycle. The opposite or neoclassical kind of literary production, no less concentrated in time and place, can be discovered in mid-eighteenth-century London. And the historians of literatures other than English and American will have no difficulty in identifying many such concentrations, as well as in isolating

and explaining barren periods between such moments of fulfillment. In attacking the historical problems related to such
hills and valleys of literary achievement, the literary historian
will ask the critic to identify, describe, and evaluate the works
of literature and the authors involved, but the relationships between the works of art, between them and their environments,
and between them and preceding literary and other events are
parts of his special function.

Thus the basic structure of literary history is to be found in
the rise and fall of literary movements, delimited by time into
"periods" which are not sharply marked by specific dates and
may well be coincidental or overlapping, and which are composed of literary works, their authors, and the controlling temper and ideas of that time and place. The literary historian
will trace and attempt to assign causes to the inevitable rise
and decline of such movements. His clues will be mainly
changes in language and literary forms and genres, periods and
movements, and the instruments of literary production and
circulation. Once the movement under observation has been
traced from its first evidences to its moment of greatest concentration and into its decline, a cycle of literary history will
become evident and its deeper causes in the ideas, social conditions, and other factors of the time and place can be investigated.

Among the factors which thus shape literary cycles are:

Language and Form. Although the process of literary creation is much the same always, the idiom of its expression changes
with the fashions of an age or place. Language reflects the kind
and stage of civilization of a people, and its history, as we have
seen, provides a separate discipline closely related to that of literary history. Similarly, the more complex aspects of literary
form, which are but an extension of the symbolic forms of language, are basically problems in aesthetics rather than in history
and are therefore the province of the literary critic or theorist.
But the literary language and forms of a people change with
changing circumstances, and these changes are within the province of the literary historian. Each of the major literary forms
or modes—poetry, fiction, drama, and critical prose—will be

found to have a history of its own which may be limited by other boundaries of time and place or which may transcend them; and secondary literary forms or types like the lyric, the ballad, the epic, the short story, the one-act play, the familiar essay, the feature article, and so on may be studied in terms of its rise and fall or of other historical characteristics. In English literary history, for example, the principal periods for the drama were the Elizabethan and the Restoration, for poetry the beginning of the nineteenth century, and for the novel the mid-eighteenth and the Victorian.

Period and Movement. Like other historical processes, literary history reflects the temper of each age in changes in emphasis on the basic characteristics of human nature. An age and people may be high- or low-pitched emotionally, may be given rather to analysis or to synthesis in thinking, may be ingrown or outgoing, vigorous or passive. Although unsatisfactory and imprecise in definition, the terms "romantic" and "classic" or "neo-classic" are useful in fixing the extremes in the swing of the pendulum of cultural and intellectual temper. The literary historian will therefore look for signs of periods and movements which seem to be dominated by one or another of these controlling characteristics, and then he will attempt to trace their sources, rise, and decline. These usually, but not necessarily, reflect the periods and movements in other aspects of experience like the religious, the political, or the economic, and they often, if not always, run parallel to similar movements in the histories of other arts. The discovery and accurate definition of periods and movements will allow the literary historian to mark out his story in phases and to treat it causally and cyclically rather than in terms of straight chronology, but there is a point at which they may distort historical fact and become elements of his own constructive imagination rather than data in the process of literary history itself.

Instruments and Bibliography. Literature will not be produced unless a people has developed means of training its literary artists and providing the means of communication between them and others and the periods of such technological achievement can be identified and related to other aspects of a civilization. The temper, form, and very occurrence of literary works are determined or influenced far more than is sometimes supposed by such immediate and circumstantial factors as schools, theatres, libraries, newspapers, magazines, publishers, booksellers, lecture halls, mass media, copyright laws, and so on. The study of such factors is sometimes called "the sociology of literature" and is relegated to an inferior status, but no literary history can be written without a thorough examination of all such factors as can be discovered in any literary situation.

The most important aspect of such a study is, of course, that of the book as book, or bibliography. The place, time, and circumstances of the production and appearance of a book and the form which it takes (type, paper, binding, size, number of copies, and so on) are all factors in the history of the work of art which is contained in that book. Bibliography may also be an aspect of biography when the inscribed or marginally annotated book or the presence of a book in an author's library furnishes biographical documentation. For the period prior to the invention of printing, the formal manuscript as produced by the scribe plays the role of the later book. Modern manuscripts provide data on an earlier stage in the creative process.

V

Finally, it is important to distinguish the literary historian as researcher from the literary historian as writer. The literary historian engages in these two forms of activity: historical research and historical criticism. In the first role, his aim is to collect and confirm his data, and he uses many of the methods of the scientist; in the second, his aim is to organize and interpret his data, and he uses many of the methods of the literary artist.

Historical Research is normally analytical and relatively objective. It attempts to discover and establish the truth about past literary events. Like the scientist, the literary research scholar must have a problem and a hypothesis as to its solution before he can direct his investigations. The final proposed literary history toward which his researches are at least theoretically directed is composed of an infinite number of such problems, each of which must be isolated from its context and attacked directly. Many such problems are minute and of relatively little importance except when their solution is put back into context. For example, it may be necessary to establish the date of birth of a minor author or his place of residence at a given time in order to prove the possibility of his part in and influence on the lives of other authors or the development of a chain of events; but the date itself is inconsequential, and the man and his biography may be of little or no concern for the literary critic. In general, the greater the literary work or literary artist under investigation, the more important minor problems in research become.

Wherever possible, the research scholar depends upon primary evidence only and goes back to the document itself: the birth certificate, the court or church record, the original literary manuscript, the corrected proof sheets, the letter to a friend, the newspaper report, the text of the literary work itself as established by the textual critic. Secondary evidence, or truth as reported and commented upon by another, is acceptable only when primary evidence is not available or when the task of retracing the steps in each part of a large undertaking is impractical and the reliability of previous scholars may be safely assumed or can be spot-checked.

Literary evidence is of two kinds: external and internal. External evidence is that derived from sources other than the text of the literary work itself: documents bearing upon the life of the author or the circumstances of his environment, the conditioning circumstances of the work of art itself, or the presence of other works of art in obvious relationship with that under study. Internal evidence is implicit data within the text itself: the use of a dated word, reference to a specific event or association, a characteristic turn of phrase or style of writing, the kind or number of occurrences of certain words or images or literary forms. The careful scholar will try whenever possible to check one kind of evidence against the other. Sometimes it is possible, and may be necessary, to reconstruct at least the psychological aspects of the biography of a writer (e.g., Homer or Shakespeare) from the internal evidence of his writings, and then to reapply the conclusions reached to an interpretation of the works themselves. This form of circular historical scholarship is risky and is greatly reinforced by even a little external evidence at crucial points. On the other hand, the exclusive use of external evidence may be equally misleading. For example, the expressed intentions of the author or the reactions of contemporary critics may lead to conclusions which have little bearing on what the author actually achieved.

Historical Criticism is normally synthetic and subjective to a greater or lesser degree. Once his data are collected and organized around the literary events with which he wishes to deal, the research scholar retires and the historical critic takes over. But in this case, he is not a literary critic: his task is to evaluate and interpret historical rather than literary data, or literary data which has for him historical value. He must accept from the literary critic (who, as has been pointed out above, may even be himself in another role) the aesthetic evaluation of the works under study and then turn to the task of explaining how, why, where, and when these works were conceived, written, published, and read, how the circumstances of their production shaped their meanings and effects, and what their relationships were to other works of art and to the whole stream of historical record. To do so, he must first set up a theory as to what happened and when and why and how it happened, and here it is important that he see his problem in relationship to organic process as well as to chronological time. Was Corneille a part of a reactionary and classical movement in the French drama? Did Melville, a New Yorker of Dutch ancestry, make a contribution to the revolt of Hawthorne and Emerson against the rigors of New England Calvinism? How did political and religious partisanship affect the work of Defoe, Swift, or Fielding? Did the rigidity of the Broadway financial structure stifle originality in modern American drama? Did Dostoevski or Shelley or Villon suffer from specific neuroses? Is it demonstrable that the quest for innocence was the major theme in all of American literature, and if so, was this a result of an inheritance of Christian theology or the circumstances of the American wilderness? Was there a second American "renaissance" in the twentieth century? Were there parallel movements in the literatures of Europe? What of the romantic movement in all the literatures of the Western world?

Once he has satisfied himself with a working hypothesis as to the answer to any one of such problems, the historical critic must then organize his evidence around his thesis and test its validity by the selection, arrangement, and interpretation—but never deliberate distortion—of the historical evidence that has been provided by research.

In this process, the historical critic finally becomes the literary artist himself, and his literary history is a form of literary art and subject to the tests of truth, honesty, and justice to which all art must defer. Different kinds of art permit different degrees of departure from literal truth in the interest of a deeper or broader reading of life than mere facts in themselves can supply. The fantasy or farce is at one end of the spectrum, the critical essay is at the other; and historical criticism is of course a kind of literature which most narrowly restricts and disciplines the imagination. The historical romance must be sharply distinguished in both aim and method from narrative and interpretative historical writing, but they are both kinds of literature if they are well and rightly done. Dangerous as even a partially subjective point of view may seem to the scientific historical scholar, the products of research can have meaning only when they are organized around the insights and aesthetic controls of the artist—in this case, the literary historian.

NOTES

[1](Cambridge University Press, 1957), I, xxiv–xxv.

Index

Is literary history obsolete? Dr. Spiller asks, and challenges those critics and readers who, in their enthusiasm for texture and structure in poetry, fiction, and drama, tend to forget that literature is also the voice of a people, time, and place. In these essays the author argues that only in the dimension of history does a work of art become a living organism with a past, present, and future.

Written between 1929 and 1963, the essays reflect the awakening of the American people to the richness and vitality of their own cultural tradition, and to the need for a new understanding of American literary history. Laying a ground plan for such a reappraisal in the early essays, Dr. Spiller gives new insights into each of the succeeding phases of our national literary growth—from the transplanting of the culture of western Europe to the American wilderness in colonial times. The author then discusses the rise of native romantic and realistic movements, and traces the flowering of America's national literature of international influence in the twentieth century. The final essays probe into the philosophy of literary history itself, and into the present state of American studies both at home and abroad.

As provocative and readable today as when they were first prepared, these essays provide when taken as a whole, both a matured philos ophy of literary history and a running accom